Evolution and Eschatology

Evolution and Eschatology

GENETIC SCIENCE AND THE
GOODNESS OF GOD

Graeme Finlay

CASCADE *Books* • Eugene, Oregon

EVOLUTION AND ESCHATOLOGY
Genetic Science and the Goodness of God

Copyright © 2021 Graeme Finlay. All rights reserved. Except for brief quotations in critical publications or reviews, no part of this book may be reproduced in any manner without prior written permission from the publisher. Write: Permissions, Wipf and Stock Publishers, 199 W. 8th Ave., Suite 3, Eugene, OR 97401.

Cascade Books
An Imprint of Wipf and Stock Publishers
199 W. 8th Ave., Suite 3
Eugene, OR 97401

www.wipfandstock.com

PAPERBACK ISBN: 978-1-6667-0457-0
HARDCOVER ISBN: 978-1-6667-0458-7
EBOOK ISBN: 978-1-6667-0459-4

Cataloguing-in-Publication data:

Names: Finlay, Graeme, 1953–, author.
Title: Evolution and eschatology : genetic science and the goodness of God / Graeme Finlay.
Description: Eugene, OR: Cascade Books, 2021 | Includes bibliographical references and index.
Identifiers: ISBN 978-1-6667-0457-0 (paperback) | ISBN 978-1-6667-0458-7 (hardcover) | ISBN 978-1-6667-0459-4 (ebook)
Subjects: LCSH: Evolution—Religious aspects—Christianity | Evolution (Biology)—Religious aspects—Christianity | Religion and science | Human beings—Origin | Creation | Biological evolution | Eschatology
Classification: BL263 F56 2021 (print) | BL263 (ebook)

Table of Contents

List of Tables and Illustrations vii
Preface ix
Acknowledgments xix

1. Genesis of genes and genre of Genesis 1
2. Evolution of the placenta: Lifeline to humanness 31
3. Developing brains: Genes and personal experience 61
4. Immunity as unity in community: Theology in immunology 91
5. Created histories: Eschatogeny recapitulates phylogeny 116

Appendix 1. A glossary of some biological terms 159
Appendix 2. How to be a historian of DNA 164

Bibliography 169
Index 191

List of Tables and Illustrations

Table 1 Genesis 1 structure
Table 2 Parallels between print- and mind-reading
Table 3 Publications providing genomic coordinates of classes of DNA insertions
Fig 1 Comparison of active and inactive genes
Fig 2 Developmental history: the polyclonal brain
Fig 3 Cancer history: a monoclonal esophageal cancer
Fig 4 DNA sequence used to make the *TP53* messenger RNA molecule
Fig 5 How retroviruses and transposable elements colonize genomes
Fig 6 How transposable elements can copy-and-paste cellular genes
Fig 7 Insertion site of an endogenous retrovirus (ERV-K type) in great ape genomes
Fig 8 Phylogenetic tree constructed from ERV-K inserts in primate genomes
Fig 9 Insertion site of a 5S ribosomal RNA sequence in primate genomes
Fig 10 Insertion site of an *RPS13* ribosomal messenger RNA sequence in primate genomes
Fig 11 Insertion site of an ERV in the genomes of anthropoid primates
Fig 12 Repeated co-option of ERV-derived genes in the biology of the placenta
Fig 13 Central role of the placenta in mediating mutual mother-child influences
Fig 14 Insertion sites of SVA elements that may regulate genes with neural functions
Fig 15 Insertion site of a FLAM element that produced the neuronal *BC200* gene
Fig 16 Effects of childhood neglect on development of brain
Fig 17 ERV that drives *AIM2* gene expression

List of Tables and Illustrations

Fig 18 Insertion site of an ERV activated during septic shock
Fig 19 Antibody gene assembly
Fig 20 Natural selection of antibody-forming cells
Fig 21 Ongoing natural selection: somatic hypermutation of antibody genes leads to antibody affinity maturation
Fig 22 Insertion sites of ERVs with contrasting effects
Fig 23 Insertion site of transposable elements with contrasting effects
Fig 24 Insertion sites of retrocopied *APOBEC3I* (top) and *UTP14C* genes
Fig 25 Phylogenetic trees constructed from insertions of endogenous retroviruses (ERV9 type, upper), transposable elements (Alu elements), and retrocopied genes
Fig 26 Insertion sites that define clonality of cancers in individual patients
Fig 27 Cancer phylogenetic trees constructed from insertions of HTLV-1 retroviral DNA, transposable elements, and retrocopied genes
Fig 28 Jesus the Messiah takes all histories upon himself

Preface

I. Evolution and faith in Jesus

WHEN I ENTERED UNIVERSITY to study biology, I knew little of the science of evolution, except that some people argued about it. I accepted the mainstream science I was taught, evolution included. By doing so, I jettisoned any thought that there might be gaps in scientific knowledge which might be used to argue for belief in God.[1] I did not want props to Christian faith that might prove indefensible. A brief feeling of vulnerability followed. Now my faith had no basis other than God's self-disclosure in Jesus! With that recognition came a great moment of liberation. For that disclosure was the whole point of being a disciple of Jesus! I had discarded a lot of baggage and enjoyed a new freedom. The gospel of Jesus was not only necessary, but sufficient for my faith. And I could follow science wherever the evidence led.

I loved cell biology and worked in a cancer research laboratory. But after a few years, I felt that, just as I had spent years studying biology, I should learn about Christian theology in a systematic way. I sought the advice of a wonderful Christian scholar, Harold Turner (who had described how the roots of science are to be found in the worldview of the apparently insignificant Hebrew tribes).[2] He told me how I could obtain a theology degree by correspondence with the University of South Africa. I especially enjoyed the study, part-time, including what I learned from Professor Adrio Konig, who taught Systematic Theology (see later!).

---

1. I was encouraged by Donald Mackay, who wrote that, "any idea that God's being active in our world means that there must be 'something science can't explain'—about living bodies, or interstellar hydrogen, or whatever—is a complete *non sequitur*," in *Clockwork Image*, 60.

2. Turner, *Roots of Science*, 12, 54-78.

Preface

But I could not escape from the science-theology interface. As I was completing my BTh (in the late 1990s), the human genome was being sequenced. Scientists were determining the order of the three billion letters that make up each set of the human genome (comprising twenty-three chromosomes). Genome science firmly—indeed incontestably—established our evolutionary origins, demonstrating that our closest relatives were chimpanzees, then gorillas, then orangutans. I felt compelled to help Christians see the significance of this revolution. I wrote a book on how mutations have elucidated our evolutionary history.[3] I hoped that everyone would abandon unproductive and harmful controversies and single-mindedly seek out the truthfulness, love, and goodness of God.

Perhaps people who were accustomed to—even addicted to—150 years of controversy were upset by my approach. My defence is that I entered the discussion about evolution and Christian faith *only* because the genetic findings provided *conclusive* evidence of our evolution. (The logic underlying this conviction was inculcated into me through a lifetime's work in cancer research—see later!) I wanted people to know that evolutionary history was not atheistic or dehumanizing. In fact, the historical sciences could be wonderfully integrated with biblical thought. This book represents recent engagements with genome science of humans and other mammals. To engage with as wide a readership as possible, I provide a summary of some important genetic concepts and terms (in what follows and Appendix 1).

---

3. Finlay, *Human Evolution: Genes, Genealogies and Phylogenies.*

PREFACE

II. A crash course in genetics

DNA is the amazing molecule that carries the information needed to assemble our bodies and to maintain life processes. DNA is a linear polymer, consisting of two intertwined strands, but for simplicity I will discuss the information content of only one strand. With a few exceptions (such as mature red blood cells) every cell in our bodies contains two meters of DNA. (That means in one microliter of blood, enough to just cover the dot on an "i", the white cells possess ten kilometers of DNA.) We humans have forty-six chromosomes, each of which contains one DNA molecule. So *each* DNA molecule is about four centimeters long on average (although they vary in length, and like the letters of St Paul, are arranged from the longest to the shortest (apart for the X and Y sex chromosomes).

Straddled along the DNA are chemical units called bases, of which there are four, designated A, C, G, and T. The *order* or *sequence* of these comprises genetic information. One class of genes encodes the information needed to make proteins. The order of the four bases specifies the proportions and order of the twenty amino acids that are linked together to form proteins, and that dictate how the properties of (say) an insulin molecule differ from those of a hair keratin molecule. Another class of genes lacks the information to make proteins. Such genes make nonprotein-coding RNA molecules. The sequence of bases comprising these non-coding RNAs dictates how they will fold into 3-D structures, and how they will interact with other RNA molecules and proteins to mediate a diversity of cell functions.

A gene is said to be active (or *expressed*) when it is copied into RNA molecules. It is inactive (or silenced or *repressed*) when it is not able to produce RNA copies. Genes are turned on and off by proteins called transcription factors that bind to sequence motifs called *enhancers* (which may be far from genes) and *promoters* (which are close to genes, and upon which RNA-making enzymes are assembled). Fig. 1 depicts how genes are arranged on DNA, and how transcription factor-bound enhancers and promoters become linked together into collaborative protein complexes that provide intricate patterns of gene activation. Our bodies contain myriad different cell types, with characteristic shapes and functions. This variety reflects the variety of genes active in each cell type. The suite of genes active in a nerve cell or a liver cell is determined by the set of transcription factors produced in each cell type.

Fig. 1 indicates another fascinating feature of genomes. Our DNA also contains a large number of *repetitive elements* (indicated by the white arrows). These are recognizable lengths of DNA that can be classified into about 1,000 families. They came to populate our genomic DNA by random copy-and-paste (in some cases, cut-and-paste) processes. These strange genome-invaders are *mutagens*—that is, they necessarily change the sequence of DNA when they copy themselves into new sites of the genome. Repetitive elements will be the subject of the genetic aspects of this book.

FIGURE 1

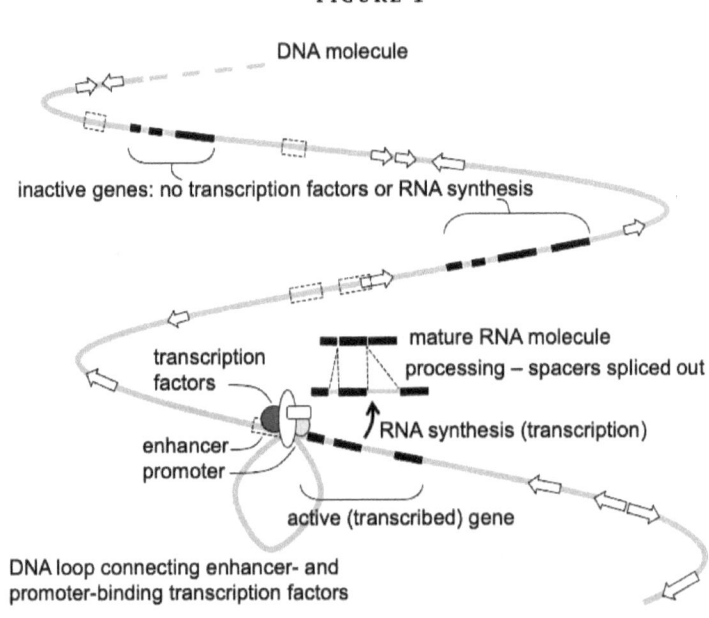

Comparison of active and inactive genes.

The diagram depicts a length of DNA (gray line) with three genes (discontinuous black lines; most genes are interrupted by spacer sequences). The lower gene is *active*: proteins called *transcription factors* are bound to *enhancer* and *promoter* segments, which are brought together to form active complexes that support the copying of gene sequences into RNA molecules. (The stretch of DNA between enhancer and promoter is looped out when the gene-activating complex forms.) The RNA molecules (or *transcripts*) are *processed* in various ways, which include the removal of spacer sequences. The mature RNA molecules may then be used to specify the production of proteins (in which case they will be exported from the nucleus) or perform some nonprotein-coding function. The upper two genes are not active. Transcription factors are not bound to their enhancers and promoters, and they are unable to transcribe RNA copies. In addition to genes, the genomes of all species are littered with large numbers of *repetitive elements*, of which there are a thousand types and over four million individual instances in human DNA (white arrows). Repetitive elements are added to chromosomal DNA randomly, but some of them have acquired genetic functionality. They may provide short lengths of DNA for use as enhancers.

Preface

The study of mutations shows how populations of cells evolve. When a mutation arises in a cell, all the descendants of that cell (that together constitute a *clone*) will be marked by that mutation. In other words, when two or more cells share the same singular mutation, it is accepted that they inherited it from the one ancestral cell in which that mutation arose. That is not controversial. Indeed, during the COVID-19 epidemic, mutations have been used to track the evolution of the SARS-CoV-2 virus through time and place. ("This outbreak originated from someone who travelled from country X, because those viruses share mutations that are different from viruses previously circulating in our city Y.")

During the development of a normal brain, the distribution of mutations in cell populations provides an outline of the progressive origin of clones and subclones of cells. In a particular individual (Fig. 2), brain development was shown to be initiated from multiple cells (identified by the mutations A_1, B_1, C_1, D_1) that were present in the embryo. Each of these cells grew into a clone of descendants. Normal tissues are polyclonal. Later mutations generated subclones (as defined by the mutations B_2, B_3, and B_4, for example).[4]

---

4. Lodato et al., "Somatic Mutation," 94–98.

Preface

FIGURE 2

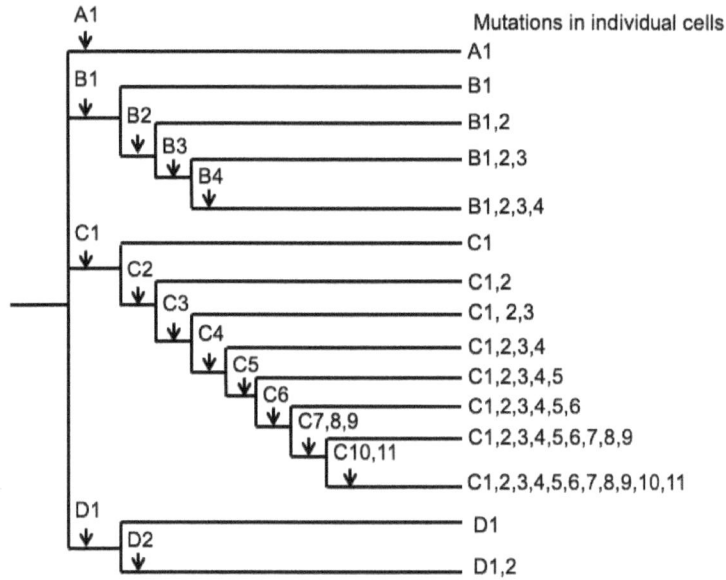

Developmental history: the polyclonal brain.

Lines represent the sequential appearance of clones and subclones of cells, as defined by the mutations they contain. (Lodato et al., "Somatic mutation," 94-98.)

Similarly, during cancer development, the distribution of mutations demonstrates the progressive origin of clones and subclones of cancer cells. An example describing the evolutionary history of an esophageal adenocarcinoma is shown in Fig. 3. These tumors typically develop through stages: chronic inflammation, then Barrett's esophagus (a stress-induced change in cell type), then dysplasia (precancerous change), and finally cancer. All biopsies had a deletion ("del") of the *CDKN2A* gene, indicating that abnormal cells in the various biopsies were descended from the single cell in which that mutation occurred (white boxes on the right, the *presence* of the mutation; "*CDKN2A* del" in a white box on the left, the *time* of the mutation). All dysplastic and cancerous biopsies were characterized by tetraploidy (doubling of chromosome number), and changes to the *TP53* and *MET* genes (lightly shaded boxes). The cancer cells were characterized by

Preface

amplification of the *CCNE1*, *GATA6* and *AKT2* genes ("amp", extra copies of the genes).[5] Mutations define branches of evolutionary trees.

FIGURE 3

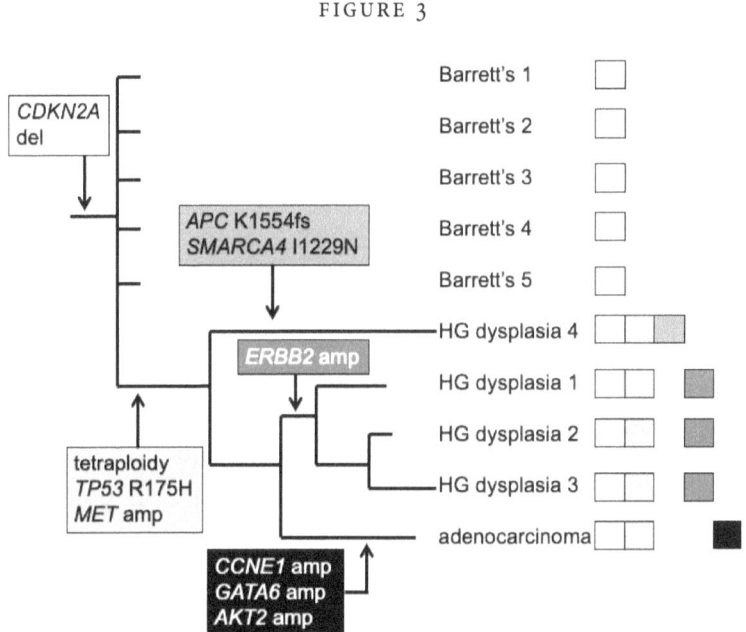

Cancer history: a monoclonal esophageal cancer

The evolutionary tree is based on many mutations (the number being proportional to the length of the branches). Only mutations deemed central to cancer evolution are indicated. (Stachler et al., "Paired exome analysis," 1047-55.)

Exactly the same logic applies to biological evolution—that is, the evolution of species. When two species share the same singular mutation, it must be accepted that they inherited it from the one ancestral (reproductive) cell in which that mutation arose. That cannot be controversial. In this book, I will describe classes of mutations known as *ancient repetitive elements*. These include endogenous retroviruses and transposable elements (or jumping genes). Francis Collins, who led the Human Genome Project (and who was instrumental in establishing Biologos, a scholarly organization seeking to explore science-theology relationships), stated that in many instances, one can identify a degraded ancient repetitive element

---

5. Stachler et al., "Paired Exome Analysis," 1047-55.

Preface

"in parallel positions in the human and mouse genomes.... The conclusion of common ancestry for humans and mice is virtually inescapable."[6]

In chapter 1, I describe instances of ancient repetitive elements shared by different species, and explain how anyone can investigate their evolutionary history for themselves. There are a few basic steps to being your own DNA historian. First, locate a particular repetitive element in human DNA. Second, find the DNA sequence of that repetitive element, together with that of surrounding DNA, using the UCSC Genome Browser. Third, use the relevant part of the human sequence to search the genomes of other species using the NCBI search engine (the BLAST algorithm). The result indicates which species share that particular repetitive element and are therefore co-descendants of the individual in which the mutation arose. That datum of information contributes powerfully to the elucidation our phylogenetic relationships.

People might find the results of such an exploration upsetting. Does a direct genetic connection with (other) apes and monkeys call into question our distinctiveness as humans created by God? We have to reflect on biblical and theological foundations of our faith. If some adjustment of our understanding is needed, it should be liberating—as I found, it may bring us to a new and inspiring vision of the ways of the God revealed in Jesus.

Chapter 2 continues this basic approach, but looks at how ancient repetitive elements have contributed to the evolution of the placenta.[7] Random mutations can contribute to the origins of new complexity and function. The placenta is a biological organ—but its function is affected by the network of social relationships in which the mother lives. Placental function and the well-being of future generations are responsive to personal values and virtues.

Chapter 3 considers how repetitive elements might have been involved in evolution of brain. But DNA alone cannot form human brain: we consider how the human brain develops appropriately only in the presence of environmental signals—especially personal input.[8]

Chapter 4 considers how immune systems arose by natural selection, often involving repetitive elements, over vast tracts of evolutionary time.

---

6. Collins, *Language of God*, 136-37.

7. Chapter 2 is based on the published paper, Finlay, "Amazing Placenta," 306-26; and has been modified with kind permission of the publisher.

8. Chapter 3 is based on the published paper, Finlay, "Interaction," 102-15; and has been modified with kind permission.

Preface

Remarkably, in the lifetime of *each individual*, the system known as adaptive immunity (because it responds actively to environmental cues) arises by a process of natural selection. Natural selection (the random generation of variants followed by the propagation of those that are life-sustaining) is a powerful strategy for generating new complexity. It is arguable that the power of natural selection is compatible with the interpretation of purpose.

Finally, chapter 5 reflects on how mutations can be both constructive and destructive. Mutations can generate life-enhancing functions (over evolutionary time) and also life-destroying cancers (over a human lifespan). We ask where God's activities might lie in this dichotomous behavior. Ultimately, we must consider God's plan for a completed creation.

Many things discussed are speculative. These gray areas exist between several points that I regard as anchors. On the one hand, biological evolution—our descent from progenitors of anthropoid primates, then (further back) of all mammals—is firmly established by the sort of approaches I have described. We and warthogs *do* share common ancestors. On the other hand, the center of my understanding of reality is that the creator God has been made known through Jesus of Nazareth, whose death on a cross is redemptive for me and for all of creation, and whose bodily resurrection is the guarantee that God will transform this groaning creation into one which is imperishable, and which will truly reflect the glory of God. There is a third point which seems to be vital. Biological evolution does not belong to the category of *creation*, but to the category of *history*. Creation includes all histories. We seek to understand the providence of God in biological history in precisely the same way as we seek to understand the providence of God in the history of the Jews, or (for that matter) in the history of the Roman Empire or of the piano.

In between those certainties, I am feeling my way, but hope that my reflections will be useful to others. Many highly erudite writers have already sought to clarify the relation between Christian faith and evolutionary science. An excellent consensus document has been published by Christian scholars,[9] and the following pages insert my lifetime's reflections into this framework.

---

9. Lucas et al., "Bible, Science and Human Origins," 74-99.

Acknowledgements

I HAVE BEEN FORTUNATE to have benefitted from the wisdom of many colleagues. The publication of chapter 2 was made possible by expert input from Dr. Nicola Hoggard-Creegan, who has been a great encouragement through this entire exercise. I also received invaluable advice from Professor Gareth Jones.

Chapter 3 developed approaches initiated elsewhere but was written as a paper in response to encouragement from the late Professor Wilf Malcolm, sometime Vice-Chancellor of Waikato University, and a statesman among Christian scholars. Professor John McClure and Dr. Edward Theakson also provided feedback on this theme.

Dr. Denis Alexander made important suggestions as to the improvement of this manuscript. I am grateful to staff of the Faraday Institute (UK) and Christians in Science (ISCAST, Australia) for help on this long-term journey.

I thank the editors of *Science and Christian Belief* and of *Zygon* for their helpfulness, and their reviewers for suggesting substantial improvements to proffered work. The editors and production staff at Wipf & Stock and been wonderfully patient and obliging.

I have been very fortunate to have worked in the Auckland Cancer Society Research Centre in the University of Auckland. The intellectual atmosphere was always very stimulating. It was here that I read about retrovirally induced tumors, and clonal progression of cancers, and found to my surprise that these oncological phenomena led me into evolutionary genetics. The latter burgeoning research field established as a fact of history that humans evolved from progenitors we share with other species.

I

Genesis of genes and genre of Genesis

Abstract

Controversy over the truth of biological evolution is sustained by the presumption that evolutionary science subverts Christian faith. It may be thought that acceptance of evolutionary theory requires that people dismiss the ancient creation stories in the first chapters of Genesis as so much crude legend. Or that the biological paradigm of evolution is an alternative to the theological idea of creation. Or that knowledge of evolutionary mechanism precludes considerations of cosmic purpose. Or that our (human) biological classification as apes leads to the philosophical doctrine of non-exceptionalism (that we have no status other than apehood). This chapter suggests that the way to resolving conflict is to approach our science and theology *historically*. The amazing information-carrying molecule of DNA, by its very nature, contains within itself a record of its history. The genome is always changing: it perpetually "becomes" (Greek: *ginomai*). If we seek to interpret fully the information in our DNA, we must read it for what it says about its formation in the past. It is irreducibly historical text. Biblical theology is also an empirical science in that it is an interpretation of history. Scripture too is irreducibly historical text. The Genesis stories, the idea of creation, considerations of cosmic purpose, and our status as persons arose in particular historical settings.

Their significance and power are discerned when that history is understood.

Key words and phrases: DNA, mutations, biological evolution, comparative genomics, endogenous retroviruses, transposable elements, interpretation of Genesis, meaning of creation, teleology or purpose, status of humanity

GENETIC INHERITANCE IS THE transmission of information from one generation to the next. Delicate, gossamer-like threads of DNA, sequestered in the nuclei of cells, carry the genetic information that specifies the development of living organisms in all their breathtaking complexity. *Each* somatic cell in our bodies has enough DNA to stretch for two meters if the DNA molecules were arranged end-to-end. Our genome is not only a vast store of information,[1] it is also a micro-ecosystem of intense, incessant, and coordinated molecular activity. Myriad enzymes copy DNA to make more DNA (in preparation for cell division) or to make lengths of RNA from defined segments of DNA (needed for the myriad operations of cells). DNA exists in protein-bound complexes (the whole structure being known as *chromatin*) and enzymes actively pack and unpack this material as the need arises. DNA is always subject to wear and tear, and elaborate enzyme systems maintain the integrity of the genome. And, mysteriously, semi-autonomous gene-like bits of DNA randomly propagate in the genome, with unpredictable and potentially pathogenic consequences for genome function.

DNA embodies information using an alphabet of four chemical letters (called *bases*) known by the symbols A, C, G, and T, which are linked in vast ordered sequences. Our somatic cells contain two sets of genetic material, each of which contains three billion (3,000,000,000) letters. The genome sequencing revolution has used chemical methods to place in order (that is, to *sequence*) the As, Cs, Gs, and Ts that comprise our genome. When cells make a protein, the base sequence of the relevant segment of DNA (known as a *gene*) is copied into messenger RNA molecules, which are transported

1. Normal genetic function depends on appropriate environmental conditions. Genes interact with environment. A second system of information transfer, epigenetic inheritance, consists of environmentally sensitive chemical modifications of DNA and its associated proteins. Epigenetic systems affect every aspect of cell behavior. Epigenetic marks are readily reversible and this instability means that they cannot be used to trace genetic lineages. Epigenetic inheritance will not be highlighted in what follows.

into the cytoplasm where they specify the synthesis of that particular protein. The DNA sequence that is used to make a messenger RNA molecule that leads to production of the TP53 protein (much beloved by cancer cell biologists because it protects cells from genetic damage) is shown in Fig. 4.

FIGURE 4

```
GATGGGATTG GGGTTTTCCC CTCCCATGTG CTCAAGACTG GCGCTAAAAG TTTTGAGCTT CTCAAAAGTC TAGAGCCACC                1
GTCCAGGGAG CAGGTAGCTG CTGGGCTCCG GGGACACTTT GCGTTCGGGC TGGGAGCGTG CTTTCCACGA CGGTGACACG
CTTCCCTGGA TTGGCAGCCA GACTGCCTTC CGGGTCACTG CCATGGAGGA GCCGCAGTCA GATCCTAGCG TCGAGCCCCC           241
TCTGAGTCAG GAAACATTTT CAGACCTATG GAAACTACTT CCTGAAAACA ACGTTCTGTC CCCCTTGCCG TCCCAAGCAA
TGGATGATTT GATGCTGTCC CCGGACGATA TTGAACAATG GTTCACTGAA GACCCAGGTC CAGATGAAGC TCCCAGAATG
CCAGAGGCTG CTCCCCCCGT GGCCCCTGCA CCAGCAGCTC CTACACCGGC GGCCCCTGCA CCAGCCCCCT CCTGGCCCCT           481
GTCATCTTCT GTCCCTTCCC AGAAAACCTA CCAGGGCAGC TACGGTTTCC GTCTGGGCTT CTTGCATTCT GGGACAGCCA
AGTCTGTGAC TTGCACGTAC TCCCCTGCCC TCAACAAGAT GTTTTGCCAA CTGGCCAAGA CCTGCCCTGT GCAGCTGTGG
GTTGATTCCA CACCCCCGCC CGGCACCCGC GTCCGCGCCA TGGCCATCTA CAAGCAGTCA CAGCACATGA CGGAGGTTGT           721
GAGGCGCTGC CCCCACCATG AGCGCTGCTC AGATAGCGAT GGTCTGGCCT GTGTGCCCT  ATGAGCCGCC TGAGGTTGGC
ATTTGCGTGT GGAGTATTTG GATGACAGAA ACACTTTTCG ACATAGTGTG GTGGTGCCCT ATGAGCCGCC TGAGGTTGGC
TCTGACTGTA CCACCATCCA CTACAACTAC ATGTGTAACA GTTCCTGCAT GGGCGGCATG AACCGGAGGC CCATCCTCAC           961
CATCATCACA CTGGAAGACT CCAGTGGTAA TCTACTGGGA CGGAACAGCT TTGAGGTGCG TGTTTGTGCC TGTCCTGGGA
GAGACCGGCG CACAGAGGAA GAGAATCTCC GCAAGAAAGG GGAGCCTCAC CACGAGCTGC CCCAGGGAG  CACTAAGCGA
GCACTGCCCA ACAACACCAG CTCCTCTCCC CAGCCAAAGA AGAAACCACT GGATGGAGAA TATTTCACCC TTCAGATCCG          1201
TGGGCGTGAG CGCTTCGAGA TGTTCCGAGA GCTGAATGAG GCCTTGGAAC TCAAGGATGC CCAGGCTGGG AAGGAGCCAG
GGGGGAGCAG GGCTCACTCC AGCCACCTGA AGTCCAAAAA GGGTCAGTCT ACCTCCCGCC ATAAAAAACT CATGTTCAAG
ACAGAAGGGC CTGACTCAGA CTGACATTCT CCACTTCTTG TTCCCCACTG ACAGCCTCCC ACCCCCATCT CTCCCTCCCC          1441
TGCCATTTTG GGTTTTGGGT CTTTGAACCC TTGCTTGCAA TAGGTGTGCG TCAGAAGCAC CCAGGACTTC CATTTGCTTT
GTCCCGGGGC TCCACTGAAC AAGTTGGCCT GCACTGGTGT TTTGTTGTGG GGAAGAGGAT GGGGAGTAGG ACATACCAGC
TTAGATTTTA AGGTTTTTAC TGTGAGGGAT GTTTGGGAGA TGTAAGAAAT GTTCTTGCAG TTAAGGGTTA GTTTACAATC          1681
AGCCACATTC TAGGTAGGGG CCCACTTCAC CGTACTAACC AGGGAAGCTG TCCCTCACTG TTGAATTTTC TCTAACTTCA
AGGCCCATAT CTGTGAAATG CTGGCATTTG CACCTACCTC ACAGAGTGCA TTGTGAGGGT TAATGAAATA ATGTACATCT
GGCCTTGAAA CCACCTTTTA TTACATGGGG TCTAGAACTT GACCCCCTTG AGGGTGCTTG TTCCCTCTCC CTGTTGGTCG          1921
GTGGGTTGGT AGTTTCTACA GTTGGGCAGC TGGTTAGGTA GAGGGAGTTG TCAAGTCTCT GCTGGCCCAG CCAAACCCTG
TCTGACAACC TCTTGGTGAA CCTTAGTACC TAAAAGGAAA TCTCACCCCA TCCCACACCC TGGAGGATTT CATCTCTTGT
ATATGATGAT CTGGATCCAC CAAGACTTGT TTTATGCTCA GGGTCAATTT CTTTTTTCTT TTTTTTTTTT TTTTTCTTT          2161
TTCTTTGAGA CTGGGTCTCG CTTTGTTGCC CAGGCTGGAG TGGAGTGGCG TGATCTTGGC TTACTGCAGC CTTTGCCTCC
CCGGCTCGAG CAGTCCTGCC TCAGCCTCCG GAGTAGCTGG GACCACAGGT TCATGCCACC ATGGCCAGCC AACTTTTGCA
TGTTTTGTAG AGATGGGGTC TCACAGTGTT GCCCAGGCTG GTCTCAAACT CCTGGGCTCA GGCGATCCAC CTGTCTCAGC          2401
CTCCCAGAGT GCTGGGATTA CAATTGTGAG CCACCACGTC CAGCTGGAAG GGTCAACATC TTTTACATTC TGCAAGCACA
TCTGCATTTT CACCCCACCC TTCCCCTCCT TCTCCCTTTT TATATCCCAT TTTTATATCG ATCTCCTTATT TTACAATAAA
ACTTTGCTGC CACCTGTGTG TCTGAGGGGT G
```

DNA sequence used to make the *TP53* messenger RNA molecule.

The sequence is read from left to right, top to bottom, just like a book in English. The actual *coding sequence* (that specifies production of the TP53 protein) is shaded. It is translated into the linked building blocks of the protein using triplets of bases. (Bases are grouped in tens purely for convenience.) The first triplet is "ATG" (as is typical, specifying the amino acid methionine). The last triplet is "TGA" (one of three *stop* signals). (From https://www.ncbi.nlm.nih.gov/nuccore/NM_000546.5.)

Inevitably, the information content in our cells undergoes unscheduled, accidental changes called *mutations*. Most are innocuous, some are harmful, and rarely, some are beneficial. Some mutations may be tiny, affecting only one or a few bases. Others involve insertions or deletions of tens, hundreds, or thousands of bases. Others may be huge, rearranging segments of DNA that are millions of bases in length, and changing the shapes of chromosomes in ways that are visible microscopically. And some may involve changes in the numbers of whole chromosomes, or even of whole chromosome sets. It is a purpose of this book to indicate how the study of certain types of mutations (focusing on some pretty amazing ones) provides *incontrovertible evidence* for our evolution from primate forebears, and demonstrates how mutations underlie the acquisition of new genetic functionality.

How is it that a cancer cell biologist has presumed to pronounce on biological evolution? Deeply embedded in my thinking after forty years of engagement in cancer research is the fact that cancer cells usually carry mutations, and these act as markers that outline the evolutionary history of the cancer cell population. When a cell acquires a mutation, *all* the descendants of that cell inherit that mutation (so long as it is not obliterated by further mutations). If that mutation is a complex one, uniquely arising, then *only* the founder cell and its descendants will possess it. In other words, shared mutations define lineages of cells. Such mutations characterize populations of cells that are the descendants of *one single ancestor*. This same logic applies to lineages of *species*.

1. The science of comparative genomics

Biology has undergone a revolution since the 1990s. Highly efficient DNA sequencing methods had disclosed the genetic text of more than 300 bird and 200 mammal species by 2017, and a million eukaryotic genome sequences are pending.[2] Publication of new genome sequences is surging with the advent of new technologies. The wealth of information obtained has stimulated the burgeoning of the science of comparative genomics, in which genetic text from multiple species is aligned with a view to understanding their phylogenetic relationships, and the role of genetics in normal development and disease. More recently, the new sequencing methods have been applied to reading the genetic text of individual patient's tumors—50,000 at a recent count. This work has provided new insights into the patterns of tumor evolution.[3]

---

2. Meadows and Lindblad-Toh, "Dissecting Evolution and Disease," 624–36; the evolution of ruminants has been elucidated by whole genome sequencing of forty-four species: see Chen et al., "Large-Scale Ruminant Genome Sequencing," eaav6202; 120 new mammalian genomes were added by Zoonomia Consortium, "Comparative Genomics Multitool," 240–45; powerful analytical algorithms have been developed by Churakov et al., "Multi-Comparative," 1508–16.

3. Nakagawa and Fujita, "Whole Genome Sequencing Analysis," 513–22.

Genesis of genes and genre of Genesis

When the human genome was sequenced it became apparent that every one of us has inherited millions of mutations (novel genetic variants). To be a living organism such as a human is to possess a genome in which is inscribed an encyclopedic record of accumulated mutations. These mutations act as markers that outline the history of human populations—including our pre-human evolutionary history. The use of mutations to map out family trees is, of course, an integral part of the science of genetics. The conclusions arising are not "reductionistic" or "naturalistic" or in any way subversive of Christian belief. They are inherent to the basic science of heredity and, for Christians, provide pointers to understanding ways by which God works in biological history.

The concept of tumor monoclonality is familiar and noncontroversial to everyone who works in the field of cancer biology. This concept arises from the fact that, in most tumors, some mutations are common to *all* the cancer cells, which indicates that *all* those cells are descended from the *one*, truly unique progenitor cell in which each shared mutation was present.[4] A population of cells that are the offspring of one progenitor is called a *clone*.

Interestingly, the same classes of mutations that establish *tumor monoclonality* are identifiable also as features inherent to the human genome, and to the genomes of non-human species. The shared possession of a particular mutation by multiple primate or mammal species demonstrates the reality of *species monophylicity*, which means that all the species that share that mutation are descended from the one progenitor (germ-line) cell in which the mutation occurred.

Complex mutations constitute powerful markers of cell or species relationships. Such mutations include the insertions into genomic DNA of segments of DNA that originate from elsewhere in, or even beyond, the genome. Geneticists have characterized several outstanding classes of such insertions that represent the accumulation within genomes of parasitic units of DNA. In what follows, I will introduce a class of mutations that arise from complex enzyme-mediated cascades of events. Every such inherited mutation arises in a singular occurrence; it is quintessentially

---

4. Leung et al., "Single-Cell DNA Sequencing," 1287–99; Roerink et al., "Intra-Tumour Diversification," 457–62; Bian et al., "Single Cell Multiomics Sequencing," 1060–63; Gerstung et al., "Evolutionary History," 122–28; Dang et al., "Clonal Evolution," eaay9691. The last study shows that subclonal variation develops progressively through cancer evolution; that metastases may be monoclonal or polyclonal; and that metastases may be seeded either from subclones in the primary tumors, or by subclones present only in other metastases.

one-of-a-kind. But the types of mutations discussed below specify the same phylogenetic relationships as other types of mutations that are not discussed further in this book.[5]

Invaders from beyond the genome: viral inserts

Retroviruses are a class of virus that possess RNA as their genetic material (in the virus particle) and copy it into DNA (when they invade cells). They then insert their little piece of DNA (typically about ten thousand bases long) into the chromosomal DNA of infected cells. Retroviruses encode several proteins needed for their infectious life cycle. When a retrovirus invades a cell, the RNA-to-DNA step is performed by an enzyme called a *reverse transcriptase*. Another retroviral enzyme, known as an *integrase* or *endonuclease*, selects a site of the host genome (the *target site*) largely at random, and cuts the host cell DNA at that point. In an elaborate process, the retroviral DNA is spliced into that site in such a way as to become collinear with the cell's DNA.[6] The retroviral DNA becomes a part of the chromosome. The retroviral DNA insert is bracketed between copies of the target site (it lies between *target site duplications*). This may be illustrated in terms of our familiar twenty-six letter alphabet.

Imagine we have a length of cellular (chromosomal) DNA, which we will designate as "...ABCDEFGHIJ..." and an incoming piece of retroviral DNA, designated as "PQRS." (We imply no particular scale here.) The viral enzymes recognize a short sequence, the target site—let's say it is "DE"—at which it cuts the chromosomal DNA, such that the viral DNA "PQRS" is inserted into the cut site. During this process the target site "DE" is duplicated. The mutated chromosomal DNA will then read "...ABC**DE**PQRS-**DE**FGHIJ..." For clarity, the target site is indicated in bold. This concerted process is illustrated diagrammatically in Fig. 5 (left). If two species possess an insert (same type) at the same site of the genome (including the same target site duplications) we can be confident that those species are descended from the same ancestor. This information is shown in later figures which highlight the boundary sequences, in our example "...C**DE**P...S**DE**FG..."

---

5. Kronenberg et al., "High-Resolution Comparative Analysis," eaar6343; Churakov et al., "Multi-Comparative," 1508–16.

6. Engelman and Cherepanov, "Retroviral Intasomes Arising," 23–29.

FIGURE 5

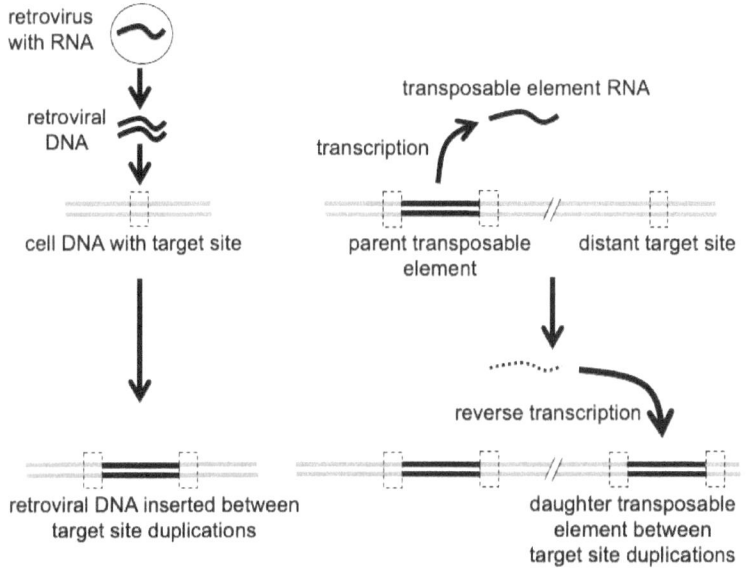

How retroviruses and transposable elements colonize genomes.

Left: an infectious retroviral particle (circle) contains genetic material in the form of single-stranded RNA (black wavy line). During infection, the RNA is converted into double-stranded DNA. Retroviral enzymes select a target site (dashed box) somewhere in the host cell DNA (parallel gray lines). The viral DNA is inserted into the cellular DNA, and is bracketed by a copy of the target site at both ends (target site duplication). The viral DNA is now a part of the genomes of the infected cell and of all its descendants.

Right: transposable elements exist only in the genome. A parent element may be copied into an RNA version. Transposable element-encoded enzymes select a target site at random, and splice a DNA copy into the genome at that point, generating a daughter element, bracketed between the duplicated target site.

If the retroviral DNA invades the chromosomal DNA of *somatic* cells (non-reproductive cells, such as white blood cells), the regulation of cell behavior may be perturbed. The infected cell may become frankly antisocial. Some significant and nasty human diseases develop from retroviral infections. The *human T cell leukemia virus type 1* causes an aggressive type of leukemia. This virus was identified in the early 1980s, and was shown to cause leukemia and other diseases in the southern USA, the Caribbean, parts of Africa, and southern Japan. It has become appreciated relatively recently that it is endemic in indigenous Australian populations, in which the most common manifestation is lung disease.[7] The *human immunodeficiency virus* (HIV) causes the acquired immunodeficiency syndrome (AIDS) by the same mechanism of chromosome insertion. In this case, however, the effect of the virus is to kill cells. The immune system becomes crippled and opportunistic diseases take advantage of the patient's vulnerable state. These secondary diseases proved lethal for patients before the advent of anti-HIV therapies.

If the retroviruses infect *germline* cells (which contribute to the production of reproductive cells; sperm and ova), their inserted piece of DNA may be transmitted to future generations. Retroviral inserts that are inherited—that is, transmitted inter-generationally—are known as *endogenous retroviruses* (ERVs).[8] One of the mind-boggling findings of the genome project is that our DNA contains hundreds of thousands of copies of ERVs and their relatives. These belong to scores of different types and subtypes, and comprise 8 percent of the whole genome.[9] ERVs are a major class of *ancient repetitive elements*. The question must arise: with whom do we share individual inserts? Anyone who possesses a particular ERV that I also possess, received it from an ancestor who is also an ancestor of me. We would be related.

Colonizers within the genome: repetitive or transposable elements

A second fascinating class of mutations involves freewheeling segments of DNA that are indigenous to our genome, and that reproduce semi-autonomously, generating copies that splice themselves, haphazardly, into new sites through the genome. The types of most interest to us reproduce by a copy-and-paste strategy. A DNA original generates an RNA version that translocates to some other region of the genome, where it in turn generates a new DNA copy (Fig. 5, right). These are called *repetitive elements* (because many copies are dispersed around genomes) or *transposable elements* (because they are mobile, dispersing around the genome). Certain classes have

---

7. Einsiedel et al., "Human T-Lymphotropic Virus Type 1 Infection," 787; Einsiedel et al., "Human T-Lymphotropic Virus Type 1c Subtype," e0006281; Einsiedel et al., "Pulmonary Disease," doi: 10.1093/cid/ciaa1401.

8. Johnson, "Origins and Evolutionary Consequences," 355–70.

9. Kojima, "Human Transposable Elements in Repbase," 2.

their own endonuclease enzymes and, like retroviruses, generate target site duplications during the course of their replication cycles.

Our DNA is littered with the remains of millions of these self-propelled transposable elements (unofficially known as *jumping genes*). They comprise the major part of our population of ancient repetitive elements. Geneticists have used computer programmes to scroll through sequenced genomes, identifying, describing, and classifying the complements of transposable elements they possess. Mammalian genomes, such as the human one, possess a zoo of about one thousand different types and subtypes.[10] Indeed, *at least half* of our DNA is of accreted ERV and transposable element provenance.

Most of the transposable elements have accumulated mutations and have lost the ability to reproduce themselves. But some are still competent to replicate, and continue their genome-colonizing pursuits. Many of our cells will have new transposable element inserts that arose only since our conception, or during the development of particular organs (such as brain). A new transposable element enters the human germline approximately once every twenty births.[11] These unpredictable genome-colonizers are secretively, actively, and continuously sculpting our genomes.

As with ERVs, we may confidently use shared transposable element insertion mutations to infer lines of descent from a common ancestor. Research has shown that any *one* such mutation will arise independently in *two* (or more) cells exceedingly rarely—in primate species, approximately one in ten thousand apparently shared transposable elements may have arisen independently in the genomes of humans and one other primate group.[12] Complex mutations such as transposable elements are essentially *homoplasy-free*: in the vast majority of cases, an element present in *multiple organisms* arose in a *unique event*. A particular mutation has occurred *once*, not independently multiple times. This means that when different species share such a mutation, it is only because they have *inherited* it from the one cell in which it arose (as illustrated).[13] In other words, when multiple species share a common mutation, it provides evidence of the most compelling nature that those species have evolved from the one progenitor.

10. Kojima, "Human Transposable Elements in Repbase," 2.
11. Feusier et al., "Pedigree-Based Estimation," 1567–77.
12. Doronina et al., "True Homoplasy," 482–93.
13. Doronina et al., "Speciation Network," 997–1003; Doronina et al., "Beaver's Phylogenetic Lineage," 43562.

The enzymatic machinery of transposable elements can mediate another surprising effect. It can at times associate with RNA molecules copied (or *transcribed*) from cellular genes, and can then copy-and-paste those RNA molecules back into the genome. RNA molecules subject to such duplication events include messenger RNA molecules, that carry the information for assembling new proteins (one such messenger RNA molecule is depicted in Fig. 4), and nonprotein-coding RNA molecules involved in the processing of other RNAs (splicing), and in protein synthesis (ribosomal and transfer RNAs). The unscheduled, stochastic DNA → RNA → DNA events generate retrotransposed gene copies (known as *retrocopies*). These accidental accruals to the genome are considered to be genetic flotsam. However, they may retain or acquire functionality, and are then designated *retrogenes*.[14] This haphazard process is depicted in Fig. 6. Such gene retrocopies are distinguishable from the parent genes because they have been processed, and are bracketed by the telltale target site duplications generated by transposable element-specified endonuclease enzymes.

FIGURE 6

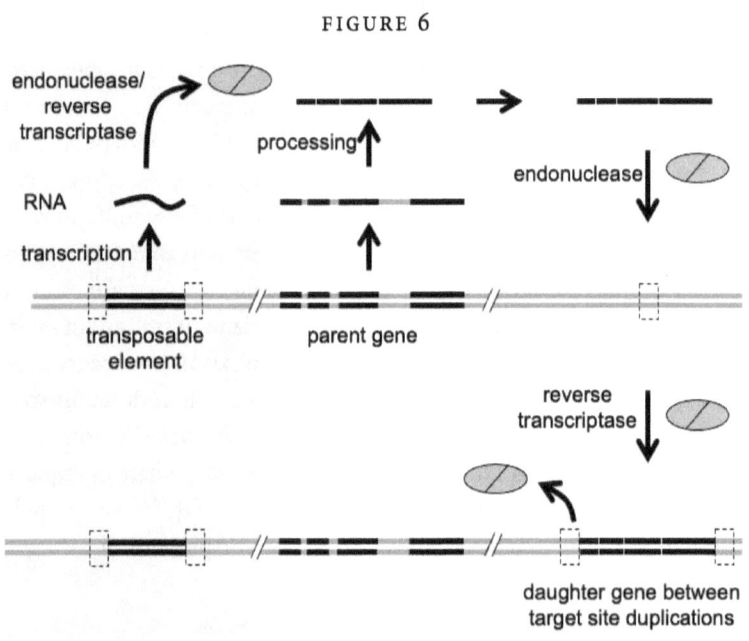

How transposable elements can copy-and-paste cellular genes.

14. Casola and Betran, "Genomic Impact," 1351–73; Cheetham et al., "Overcoming Challenges," 191–201.

The left hand part of the diagram (shaded) depicts the normal transposable element strategy (shown previously, Fig. 5). The central part depicts a cellular gene, composed of four discontinuous segments (black lines), transcribed into RNA, which is processed (spacer segments removed), as is normal. The right hand part shows a stochastic, unscheduled event, in which the *transposable element*-encoded reverse transcriptase/endonuclease enzyme (shaded oval) associates with the *cellular* RNA transcript, and inserts a DNA copy of the latter into a randomly chosen target site (dashed box) in the genome.

We have described how, with the passage of time, DNA accumulates random changes that act incidentally as barcodes to define lines of descent. We now describe how we may construct histories based on the accumulation of these novel features.

2. How to be a historian of DNA

Every feature of our DNA has a history. Each mutation arose at a particular time. Any one ERV or transposable element that has been interpolated into our DNA may be selected for investigation. Each arose through a complex cascade of enzyme-mediated catalytic events. It was transmitted to a particular group of descendants. It may have been modified by subsequent mutations, or at some stage, may have acquired novel functions. We can probe that history. Any one of us may become a DNA sleuth. Our historiographical approach is to compare the sequences of our DNA with equivalent sequences of other species. We can ask whether an ERV or transposable element is shared by different human population groups, or even with other species. All the individuals and species that possess in their genomes the same particular segment of inserted DNA have inherited it from the one ancestor (indeed, from the one ancestral germline cell) in which the mutation uniquely arose. The distributions of such mutations in different individuals, populations, or species indicate the degree of relatedness of those individuals or groups. Identifying such insertions thus enables the construction of family (or more correctly, phylogenetic) trees.

Elsewhere, I have described ways by which our phylogenetic history may be traced backwards in time.[15] In that book, I presented examples of how various classes of mutations served as markers that disclosed our relationships with other mammals. All of the genetic data were obtained from

---

15. Finlay, *Human Evolution*.

published articles. But *we ourselves* may perform this historical research using readily available genome databases. We can check for ourselves the route of our phylogenetic development. Three or four steps are involved in constructing the phylogenetic history of a particular genomic insert. The procedure, starting with a feature of the human genome, is outlined in Appendix 2.

Examples of unique insertion mutations, identified from such database searches, are described below. The insertion site of an ERV of the subclass known as ERV-K is depicted in Fig. 7. Its unique genomic location was first reported in a study of ERV-K inserts in the human genome.[16] Genome searching showed that this very particular ERV is present in the genomes of all the great apes, that is, alongside human, it is present in chimp, bonobo, gorilla, and orang-utan. The presence of this *one* ERV in *multiple* species demonstrates that it arose in a germline cell belonging to an ancestor of the five great ape species. Intriguingly, the target site selected by this ERV is highly unusual: generally, ERVs of this class are bracketed by target site duplications of five or six bases, but in the case of this particular insert the target site is an atypical 111 bases. This bizarre feature increases our confidence that all the species that possess this singular genomic novelty received it by inheritance.

---

16. Kahyo et al., "Insertionally Polymorphic Sites," 487.

FIGURE 7

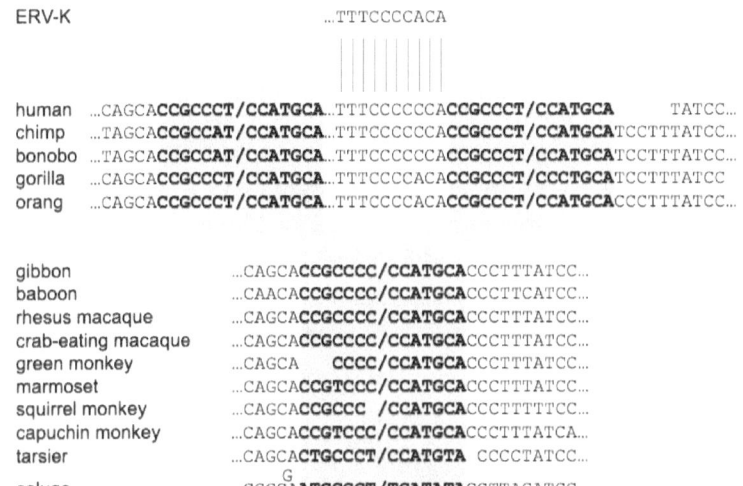

Insertion site of an endogenous retrovirus (ERV-K type) in great ape genomes.

Here and elsewhere, target sites and their duplications are in bold type and shaded. The target site is highly atypical (111 bases rather than the normal five or six), emphasizing the unique nature of this insert and its potency as a phylogenetic marker. The forward slash (/) indicates that internal bases of this singular target site are not shown. Three dots (…) indicates continuity with flanking DNA sequence (on the left and right) and viral sequence that are not shown. Sequences were from an article (Kahyo et al., "Insertionally Polymorphic Sites," 487; human, chimp, orang-utan and rhesus macaque), the NCBI (using BLAST; all other species), and http://www.dfam.org/entry/DF0000540/model (ERV-K "type").

The undisturbed target site is recoverable from the gibbon (a lesser ape), and representatives of Old World monkeys (baboon, macaques, green monkey) and New World monkeys (marmoset, squirrel monkey, capuchin monkey). The usefulness of this sort of mutation is that the *direction* of the genetic change is obvious. (We cannot with certainly identify the precursor and the derived sequences with all classes of mutations.) In the case of ERVs and transposable elements, the precursor state is pre-infection (no insert); the derived state is post-infection (interpolation of the viral insert). Monkeys and lesser apes possess the precursor state; great apes possess the derived state, and are a monophyletic group.

Extensive computational studies have shown that the distribution of multiple endogenous retroviruses of this subclass (ERV-K) discloses the phylogenetic relationships of the higher primates (Fig. 8).[17] The box marked "5," for example indicates that humans, chimps, and gorillas (but not orang-utans or macaques) possess this set of five ERVs. Each of these five ERVs thus entered the primate germ-line in an ancestor of humans, chimps and gorillas (also known as the African great apes). These species comprise a monophyletic group. A set of eight ERVs is also present in the genomes of the four great apes species, and establishes that these four species are also monophyletic. And a different set of eight ERVs establishes that the apes and Old World monkeys (exemplified by the macaque) are also monophyletic. Congruent primate family trees are obtained with other classes of ERV.[18]

FIGURE 8

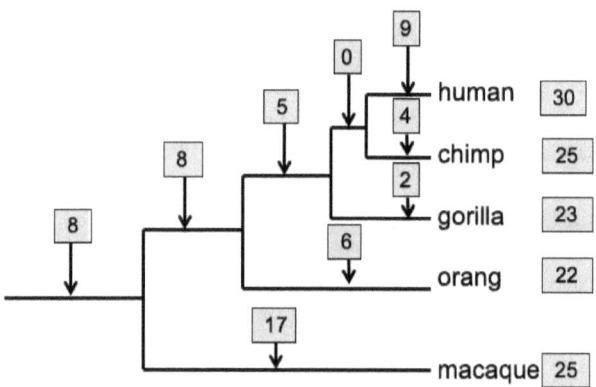

Phylogenetic tree constructed from ERV-K inserts in primate genomes.

Numbered boxes on the *right* indicate the number of ERVs shown to be present in the genomes of the different species; numbers *above the branches* of the phylogenetic tree indicate the times in primate history at when ERVs were added to genomes. (From Gemmell et al., "Phylogenetic Analysis," e1004964.)

We move on to examples of markers provided by transposable elements, active within, and covertly remodelling, mammalian genomes.

17. Gemmell et al., "Phylogenetic Analysis," e1004964.
18. Grandi et al., "Contribution of Type W," 67.

We have noted that enzymes derived from transposable elements can haphazardly associate with bystander, gene-derived, RNA molecules, and copy-and-paste them back into the genome (Fig. 6). Our genome is littered with thousands of such retrocopies. Ribosomes are the protein-making factories of cells. They are huge complexes made of RNA molecules and proteins. One of the former is the so-called 5S ribosomal RNA molecule. Through history, the enzymes made by transposable elements have repeatedly reverse-transcribed ribosomal RNA molecules and spliced the DNA copies back into the genome. An instance of this is depicted in Fig. 9.[19] The inserted sequence and its target site duplications are shared by all simian primates (monkeys and apes). This uniquely generated sequence feature appeared in a germline cell from which all anthropoid (simian) primate species are descended. The precursor sequence, becoming more variable with the passage of time, is visible in prosimians and in even in non-primates such as the colugo and Chinese tree shrew (the mammals most closely related to primates).

FIGURE 9

5S rRNA	GTCTACGGCCA...TCTCGTCTGA T...
human	...AAG**TACCCAGTGAG**GTCTACAGCCA...TCTCATCTAAA **TACCCAGTGGA**CT...
chimp	...AAG**TACCCAGTGAG**GTCTACATCCA...TCTCATCTAAA **TACCCAGTGGA**CT...
bonobo	...AAG**TACCCAGTGAG**GTCTACATCCA...TCTCATCTAAA **TACCCAGTGGA**CT...
gorilla	...AAG**TACCCAGTGAG**GTCTACAGCCA...TCTCATCTAAA **TACCCAGTGGA**CT...
orangutan	...AAG**TACCCAGTGGG**GTCTACAGCCA...TCTCGTCTAAA **TACTCAGTGGA**CT...
gibbon	...AAG**TACCCAGTGGG**GTCTACAGCCA...TCTCGTCTAAA **TACCCAGTGGA**CT...
baboon	...AAG**TACCCAGTGGG**GTTTATAGCCC...TCTCGTCTTAAT**TACCCAATGGA**CT...
drill	...AAG**TACCCAGTGGG**GTCTATAGCCC...TCTCGTCTTAAT**TACCCAATGGA**CT...
macaque	...AAG**TACCCAGTGGG**GTCTATAGCCC...TCTCGTCTTAAT**TACCCAATGGA**CT...
green monkey	...AAG**TACCCAGTGGG**GTGTATAGCCC...TCTCGTCTTAAT**TACCCAATGGA**CT...
sooty mangabey	...AAG**TACCCAGTGGG**GTCTATAGCCC...TCTCGTCTTAAT**TACCCAATGGA**CT...
marmoset	...AAG**TAGCAAGTGGG**ATCTATAGCCA...TCTTGTCTAG **TTAGCGAGTGGA**CT...
night monkey	...AAG**TAGCGAGTGGG**ATCTATAGCCA...TCTTCTCTA ...
squirrel monkey	...AAG**TATTGAATGGG**ATCTATAGCCA...TCTTGTCTAA **TTAGCGAGTGGA**CT...
capuchin	...AAG**CAGCGAGTGGG**ATCTATAGCCA...TCTTGTCTAA **TTAGCGAGTGG** ...
tarsier	...TAT**TACGCAGTAGA**CA...
mouse lemur	...TAT**TACCCGGTGGA**CA...
colugo	...TAT**TACGCAGTAGA**CA...
Chinese tree shrew	...TAT**TGACCAGTGGA**CG...

Insertion site of a 5S ribosomal RNA sequence in primate genomes.

19. Noll et al., "Ancient Traces," 889–900.

Enzymes produced by transposable elements mediated the insertion events. The 5S ribosomal RNA retrocopy (starting "GTCTAC..." in human DNA), is found in all simian primates. Prosimians and non-primates (colugo, Chinese tree shrew) retain the uninterrupted site. The genome coordinates of the human 5S ribosomal RNA insert (hg19; chr1:15976865–15976906) were from Noll et al "Ancient Traces," 889; sequences were from the UCSD Genome Browser (human), the NCBI (using BLAST; all other species) and https://www.ncbi.nlm.nih.gov/nuccore/NR_023369.1 (5S ribosomal RNA).

RNA molecules derived from genes encoding ribosomal proteins also have been retrocopied into the genome we have inherited. The progenitor *RPS13* gene was reverse transcribed to generate the particular copy depicted in Fig. 10.[20] This event occurred in a reproductive cell from which Old World primates are descended. Does this inserted sequence have any function other than acting as a signpost for people who study evolution? Who knows—no function has been ascribed to it. It may be a mere relic of past random events.

FIGURE 10

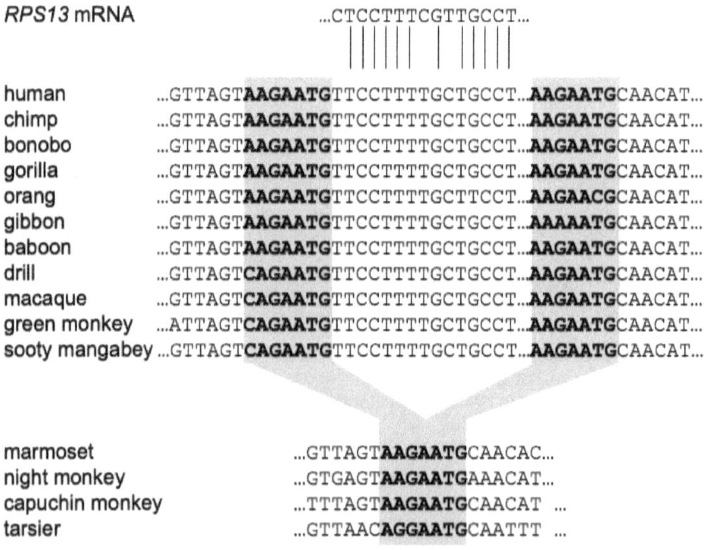

```
RPS13 mRNA                    ...CTCCTTTCGTTGCCT...
                                 |||||| |||||||

human          ...GTTAGTAAGAATGTTCCTTTTGCTGCCT...AAGAATGCAACAT...
chimp          ...GTTAGTAAGAATGTTCCTTTTGCTGCCT...AAGAATGCAACAT...
bonobo         ...GTTAGTAAGAATGTTCCTTTTGCTGCCT...AAGAATGCAACAT...
gorilla        ...GTTAGTAAGAATGTTCCTTTTGCTGCCT...AAGAATGCAACAT...
orang          ...GTTAGTAAGAATGTTCCTTTTGCTTCCT...AAGAACGCAACAT...
gibbon         ...GTTAGTAAGAATGTTCCTTTTGCTGCCT...AAAAATGCAACAT...
baboon         ...GTTAGTAAGAATGTTCCTTTTGCTGCCT...AAGAATGCAACAT...
drill          ...GTTAGTCAGAATGTTCCTTTTGCTGCCT...AAGAATGCAACAT...
macaque        ...GTTAGTCAGAATGTTCCTTTTGCTGCCT...AAGAATGCAACAT...
green monkey   ...ATTAGTCAGAATGTTCCTTTTGCTGCCT...AAGAATGCAACAT...
sooty mangabey ...GTTAGTCAGAATGTTCCTTTTGCTGCCT...AAGAATGCAACAT...


marmoset         ...GTTAGTAAGAATGCAACAC...
night monkey     ...GTGAGTAAGAATGAAACAT...
capuchin monkey  ...TTTAGTAAGAATGCAACAT ...
tarsier          ...GTTAACAGGAATGCAATTT ...
```

Insertion site of an RPS13 ribosomal messenger RNA sequence in primate genomes.

20. Navarro and Galante, "Genome-Wide Landscape," 2265–75.

The *RPS13* sequence (starting "TTCCTTTT...") lies between the duplicated target site "AAGAATG" (or similar) in Old World monkeys and apes. New World monkeys and tarsiers retain the undisturbed progenitor sequence. The genome coordinates of the human *RPS13* insert were from Navarro and Galante, "Genome-Wide Landscape," 2265–75. Sequences were from the UCSD Genome Browser (human), the NCBI (using BLAST; all other species), and https://www.ncbi.nlm.nih.gov/nuccore/NM_001017.2 (*RPS13* messenger RNA).

Such analyses demonstrate that we are the end result of an unbroken genetic history. The DNA we have inherited possesses large numbers of identifiable markers that arose through known molecular reactions before there were humans. In myriad cases, they arose before apes or even anthropoid primates roamed the savannahs and jungles. Human history is shared with those of other species—our history extends back to the same forebears as do the histories of other species. The remarkable nature of the data allows us to come to this conclusion with confidence. Computational analysis has shown that the genomes of humans and chimpanzees share more than *four million* orthologous insertions (that is, insertions inherited from shared ancestors).[21] The selected examples above are typical of a vast population of genomic markers.

It may be concluded that comparative genomics provides compelling evidence for large-sale phylogenetic development. The data it generates supersede old arguments such as "no one has even seen a monkey change into an ape." Mechanistic questions may remain unsolved, but the fact that all living primate species (including humans) share distant common ancestors cannot be doubted.

3. Interpreting historical science

The comparative genetics approach to phylogenetic history generates findings that may be disquieting for some people. Conflict over biological evolution is of long standing. Perhaps some people expect it to rumble on in perpetuity; they may even have become addicted to it. People may be threatened by the use of biological terminology. We have concluded that we are anthropoid (simian) and, more narrowly, hominoid primates. That is, in the great scheme of biology, we are classified with the monkeys and apes. In fact, we humans constitute one of the African great ape species, along with

---

21. Ward et al., "Silencing of Transposable Elements," e33084; Tang et al., "Mobile Elements Contribute to the Uniqueness," 521–33.

chimps, bonobos, and gorillas. Not only did we evolve from apes, we *are* (in biological parlance) apes. How does this biology fit in with the special status that the Bible ascribes to us?

As we approach the Bible, including the early chapters of Genesis, we must continue to think *historically*. Genesis was composed in a particular historical and cultural context. It is so easy to imagine that the Hebrew authors were preoccupied with the same issues that obsess us, and that we should read Genesis just as we read *National Geographic*. But the questions we ask are not the same as those that concerned the ancients. Here is a warning from the Old Testament scholar Gordon Wenham: "Though historical and scientific questions may be uppermost in our minds as we approach the text [of Genesis], it is doubtful whether they were in the writer's mind, and we should therefore be cautious about looking for answers to questions he was not concerned with."[22] And Christians who are senior scientists have likewise warned that we must eschew the error of projecting "back onto an ancient author a way of thinking that that author did not have and could not have had."[23] The fully fledged scientific enterprise is, after all, only four hundred years old. Modern thought-patterns are late arrivals. We need the humility to recognize that "words and concepts do not always travel neatly between languages or between historical periods."[24] It seems that the ancient Israelites were obsessed about the nature of their liberating God; we are obsessed rather with the technological wizardry that substitutes for reflection about the real issues of personal being. Our historical context may dictate the way we approach the early chapters of Genesis. We have much to learn from the priorities of the ancient Israelites.

Genesis in history

The debate often degenerates into whether people should take the Bible "literally." This terminology is based upon an unsustainable over-simplification. The Bible indubitably contains historical writings that tell us about concrete happenings in the past. A careful, critical read (as is required in all approaches to historical records) discloses the broad lines of the history of ancient Israel over many centuries. Other types of literature in the Bible include law, poetry, philosophy (the love of wisdom), romance, moral and

22. Gordon Wenham, *Genesis 1–15*, liii; also xlv, 40.
23. Briggs et al., *It Keeps Me Seeking*, 306.
24. Briggs et al., *It Keeps Me Seeking*, 348.

theological critique, biography, and personal correspondence. We cannot apply the concept of "literal" readings to the Bible as a whole when it includes texts of such diverse genres (unless we define "literal" as the Reformers did: i.e., as "the sense originally intended").[25] We must fit the approach we use to the type of text before us.

When it comes to reading the Bible, including the creation stories of Genesis, a key consideration is genre: what *type* of literature are they? Again, to quote the three professors: "Each part of the Bible must be read with respect for the genre of literature that it represents and the intention of its author in writing it."[26] Many people see the biblical creation stories as *either* factually precise science *or* crude tribal legend, and they decide to be Christians or atheists on the basis of this stark dichotomy. But both alternatives are simplistic and are entirely untenable! Our approach *must* be to identify the genre to which the Genesis creation stories belong. We may start by asking whether there are literary parallels to the early chapters of Genesis, located in the comparable historical and cultural context in which Genesis was composed, which would inform our interpretative approach.

Fortunately, there are plenty of texts from the ancient Near East that enable us to ascribe a particular genre to the earliest chapters of Genesis. It is fascinating that, at about the time Darwin published his *Origins of Species* (1859), breath-taking strides were being made in deciphering cuneiform writing (1857 locates a major event), in discovering great libraries of tablets from the ancient Near East, and in publishing the creation stories they told.[27] And—surprise!—this ancient literature was found to provide a rich background to Genesis, elucidating the purposes for which the early chapters of Genesis were written.

The Mesopotamians, such as the people of Sumer, Babylon, and Assyria, had creation stories that described their gods and established their place in the world. The gods who comprised the crowded pantheons of Mesopotamian religion were like human despots writ large. They were conniving, competing, and violent. The stories that described these gods could be classified as *cosmogonies* ("how did the world become like it is?"), although some of them might better be considered as *theogonies* ("how did the *gods* come to be the way they are?"). These stories were narrated in cultures that were stable over some two thousand years, and they often possessed similar narrative motifs.

25. Wright, "Scripture," 54–55, 99.
26. Briggs et al., *It Keeps Me Seeking*, 307.
27. Wagner and Briggs, *Penultimate Curiosity*, chs. 38–44.

Some of the ancient cuneiform texts could be aligned with the early chapters of Genesis to discover their similarities (elements that are *conserved*, as a geneticist might say) and differences (*mutations* representing the rejection of old ideas, or the acquisition of new perspectives). The strategy of inter-textual comparison is analogous to aligning genetic text derived from multiple species (as we have done, Figs. 7, 9, and 10) to reconstruct biological histories. "When a story is retold, the point and meaning of the retelling can sometimes be found in the changes that are made from the original. It was reasonable to hope that by putting ancient versions of these stories alongside each other it might be possible to gain some sense of the original intention of the Genesis writer (or writers) and some insight into what these narratives might have meant in their original context."[28]

The authors of the early chapters of Genesis adopted narrative motifs that prevailed throughout the ancient Near East, but adapted them to proclaim a revolutionary new worldview. The Genesis creation stories, audaciously and with cutting satire, subverted pagan religion and replaced it with a breathtaking new understanding of the relationship between Israel's holy God, humanity, and the world. As Gordon Wenham says, "Genesis is a major *theological* reinterpretation of traditional origin stories."[29]

Biblical scholar Daniel Harlow[30] describes the creation stories of *Enki and Ninhursag* and the *Adapa*, *Atrahasis*, and *Gilgamesh* epics (among others), and how many of their motifs were appropriated and radically reinterpreted in the biblical parallels. The early chapters of Genesis constitute an "inspired retelling of ancient Near Eastern traditions about cosmic, world, and human origins" that make "pointed theological assertions." Genesis subverts the ancient Near Eastern polytheistic stories by both "adaptation and critique." The current scholarly consensus is that the creation stories of Genesis were artfully composed, sophisticated narratives, which served polemical purposes. They comprise a worldview declaration in creative narrative form, intended to subvert and supplant prevailing pagan creation stories.[31]

---

28. Wagner and Briggs, *Penultimate Curiosity*, 342.

29. Wenham, *Pentateuch*, 15.

30. Harlow, "After Adam," 179–95.

31. Gordon Wenham, *Genesis 1–15*, xlv-l, 36–40; Waltke and Fredericks, *Genesis: A Commentary*, 74–78; Walton, *Lost World*, 66–69, 104; see Ernest Lucas, "Interpreting Genesis in the Twenty-First Century," in Alexander, *Has Science Killed God?* 67–79.

Wenham provides a concise summary of the contrasting worldviews on offer. "Thus as Genesis retells familiar oriental stories about the origins of the world, it dramatically transforms them theologically. Polytheism is replaced by monotheism, divine weakness by almighty power. Human beings are no longer seen as a sideline but central to the divine purpose. God looks after man by supplying him with food, not the other way round. Finally, the God of Genesis is very concerned about human sin . . . ."[32]

Hebraist Robert Gordon has stated that to judge the truth claims of Genesis "by the criterion of scientific awareness is a category error."[33] These narratives do not set out to teach science (although they presupposed cosmological understandings prevalent in the world of their composition)[34] but to introduce people to a God of authority, wisdom, faithfulness, and sheer goodness. This God was totally different from the fractious gods who were worshipped by Israel's mighty neighbors. The Genesis creation stories cannot be classified as either inspired science or crude legend. They are *neither* divinely inspired data prosaically describing exact earth or biological history, *nor* crude legends describing a primitive and wholly discredited "science." Both poles of this dichotomy are false, despite the number and vehemence of their supporters. It is an abuse of the Genesis creation stories to adduce them as ammunition in controversies over scientific theories or paradigms. Anyone who wants to learn from them should recognize that they are far more important than that. In the words of the Harvard astronomer and historian of science Owen Gingerich, they are "Truthful drama, but not actual history."[35] I am convinced that ancient Israel's discovery of the God of wisdom, faithfulness, goodness, and covenant is one of the two greatest ever revolutions in human thought. The supreme application of Genesis for us today is that these texts introduce us to the peerless God of creation and redemption. The creation stories of Genesis possess the power to quicken and uplift individual people, societies, and humanity; and this power is unleashed when they are read as literary creations with a theological message, not as a scientific ball-by-ball commentary about ancient events.

---

32. Wenham, *Exploring the Old Testament*, 16.

33. See Robert P. Gordon, "The Week that Made the World: Reflections on the First Pages of the Bible," in McConville and Moller, *Reading the Law*, 229.

34. Lamoureux, *I Love Jesus*, 43–70.

35. Gingerich, *God's Planet*, 91.

The internal evidence of the text of Genesis 1 demonstrates its theological intentions. Old Testament scholars interpret the text as a symmetrically crafted, topical arrangement of God's creative acts. On days one to three, God establishes the ordered spaces of his world. On days four to six, God populates those spaces with their respective creatures, so that days one and four, two and five, and three and six are paired (Table 1). So close is this symmetry that days three and six both involve a double action, and a repeated statement that God saw creation as being (very) good. No chronology is implied.[36]

Table 1. Genesis 1 structure	
days 1–3	**days 4–6**
tohu (without form)	*bohu* (empty)
God confers form, provides habitats	God populates the forms, provides inhabitants
day 1: light and darkness separated	day 4: lights in the day and night sky
day 2: upper and lower waters separated	day 5: creatures in the waters and sky
day 3: sea and land separated; vegetation	day 6: terrestrial animals and humans, the image of God
day 7: rest	

The writer's purpose was to proclaim a new and liberating vision of reality. Humans have worshiped as divine every habitat and every inhabitant of those habitats. But Genesis 1 presents the radically new perspective that everything is in fact the creation of the One who is divine. Every potential god is in fact a creature of the God made known to Israel. Genesis 1 is an audacious polemic subverting all pantheistic, polytheistic, or dualistic religion. God's world is ordered. It is good. It has been emptied of gods, spirits, occult influences, and magical powers. An implication of this revolution is that physical and biological reality becomes wholly open to our investigation. Science becomes possible! And day seven celebrates the Sabbath day of rest, the first-ever weekend day off work. Good news for us all.

We conclude. The earliest chapters of Genesis comprise a stupendously powerful statement of faith in Israel's creating and liberating God. They are a foundation of everything that Christians, such as I am, hold dear. But they do not provide data on phylogenetics, and cannot be undermined by the science of human evolution. Which brings us to a second oft-repeated dichotomy.

36. Konig, *New and Greater Things*, 12; Wenham, *Pentateuch*, 19.

Creation and evolution

Does the genetic history outlined above provide an alternative to the biblical concept of *creation*? Whenever the stark "evolution-creation" dichotomy is held as a presumption, a first requirement for obtaining resolution is that people attend closely to the meanings of the words. The biblical concept of creation pertains to the divine gift of *existence* or *being*. St. Paul wrote that God's "command brings into being what did not exist," and that "all things were created by him and all things exist through him and for him."[37] Regardless of whether people believe in the biblical concept of creation, all must accept that, by definition, it refers to the *giving of being*, which includes time and therefore encompasses all histories. As David Hart says, God is that unconditioned reality "upon which all else depends; otherwise nothing could exist at all."[38] Every photon and electron, every instant of time, and the wholly consistent and wonderfully fruitful ways in which they behave, owe their being, continuously, to God. In Colin Gunton's terms, "everything that is not God has its being only by virtue of the past creation of God, his present conservation, and the directedness toward perfection that they together involve."[39] The ways by which the created components of reality alter their relationships through created time constitute their *histories*.

Biblical creation, then, is not restricted to any particular point (or points) in time. "Creation does not refer to an initiating event, but to the giving of all spacetime."[40] Creation is "a continuing act of God's will which maintains the cosmos moment by moment." In other words, God's "role is to sustain the world in being."[41] Creation does not refer to a *temporal* beginning, but to *ontological* origin—the idea that physical reality at every instant is given being by God.[42]

In Christian thought, the three-in-one (triune) God acts in all aspects of creation. As Colin Gunton states, this God, revealed through Jesus the Messiah, is the one through whom creation "comes to be, by whom it is held

---

37. Rom 4:17; 11:36; see also Acts 17:28; 1 Cor 11:12; Rev 4:11.

38. Hart, *Experience of God*, 26, 28, 105–6.

39. Gunton, *Christ and Creation*, 90; Gunton's "past creation," "present conservation," and "directedness toward perfection" reflect the same divine creative action, which is to confer upon everything "its being."

40. Steane, *Faithful to Science*, 46.

41. Polkinghorne, *One World*, 66.

42. Polkinghorne, *Science and Creation*, 54; *Reason and Reality*, 80; Hart, *Experience of God*, 102, 106–7, 304.

in being, and to whom it is directed."[43] Biblical creation looks to the future as much as it looks to the past. It is irreducibly teleological (purpose-laden).

On this definition, cosmic, planetary (or terrestrial), and biological evolution are *histories* that describe change *within* an ordered creation. Again, regardless of whether we accept *creation* as a foundational bedrock of our wordviews (a metaphysical decision either way), it is incumbent on all to stress that the concepts of *creation* and *evolution* denote different things: they cannot be seen as mutually exclusive or incompatible, and they cannot justify conflict in the science class (or indeed in the theology class). Christians are free to accept *both* creation *and* evolution without any fear of inconsistency. Creation is divine activity and includes evolution; and evolution is simply history, change with time.

It is likely that the theistic concept of creation, with its inherent understanding of a Creator who is rational, faithful, and good, underlies the scientific assumption that nature is intelligible, consistent, and lawful and worthy of study.[44] Polkinghorne has listed four ways by which the biblical concept of creation has promoted the development of science. First, God is rational and consistent, and so people can expect the world to be orderly. Second, God creates freely, and so people have to observe and experiment (not merely reason from first principles as the Greeks did) to find out what the world is like. Third, because it is God who creates, the world is worthy of study. And fourth, God is separate from the creation, so we can investigate it without being impious.[45] The Oxford historian of science Allan Chapman has stated that science stems from monotheism.[46] To Owen Gingerich, "the Judeo-Christian philosophical framework has proved to be a particularly fertile ground for the rise of modern science."[47] Science could not arise, nor can it be sustained, in a metaphysical vacuum.[48] And science is only one of the benefits to be gained from encountering the God who alone is Creator.

The sentiment that Darwinian evolution is atheistic, or a facilitator of atheism, has been articulated repeatedly by the science writer Richard Dawkins, who reiterated it at a public event at which I was present (May

---

43. Gunton, *Christ and Creation*, 76.

44. Jaki, *Science and Creation*; Kaiser, *Creation and the History of Science*; Turner, *Roots of Science*; Worthing, *Unlikely Allies*.

45. Polkinghorne, *Quarks Chaos and Christianity*, 18.

46. Chapman, *Slaying the Dragons*, 13, 17–18, 239–40.

47. Gingerich, *God's Universe*, 6.

48. Trigg, *Beyond Matter*.

2018, Auckland). But it is a fundamental tenet of the scientific method that science does not address metaphysical questions, although science itself requires supportive tacit metaphysical presuppositions (which are derived from the biblical portrayal of God). Such claims as are made by Dawkins, that transgress the science/metaphysics boundary, are bound to confuse students in biology classes, and generate hostility to science among those who have theistic beliefs.

Evolution and God, evolution and purpose, evolution and the meaning of evolution are paired concepts that belong to different ways of thinking. As Briggs, Halvorson, and Steane say, "The fact that evolution is a natural process does not tell you whether it signifies anything as a whole, because the issue of its overall signification is at another level, in a different category." These authors insist that "the argument from physical process to absence of message [overarching significance or purpose] is not an argument; it is illogical."[49] If Dawkins somehow adduces biological evolution as a foundation on which to rest his atheism, it is an ill-considered footing indeed: not merely shaky, but wildly inappropriate. One feels sympathy for an educated man whose defining atheistic philosophy of life is based on a transparent *non-sequitur*.

Disbelief or belief in a personal God is not arbitrated by the natural sciences, including those that are historical (cosmic, terrestrial, or biological evolution), but arises from the totality of a person's experience. Indeed, historians of science offer the precise counterclaim to that made by Dawkins and his ilk: the biblical worldview emphasized that God acts in history, and thus presupposed the reality of historical change. In recognizing the arrow of time, the Bible differed from the classical Greek worldview, which saw the heavens as unchanging, and time as cyclic.[50]

Purpose

We have all probably heard it stated somewhere that "Darwinian evolution has made it impossible to think teleologically." That is, some writers think that evolutionary science precludes the idea that natural history is the bearer of *purpose*. Any such claims are faith-based statements and are questionable. The decisive split between science and teleology (or considerations of purpose) occurred centuries before Darwin. The pioneering philosopher

---

49. Briggs et al., *It Keeps Me Seeking*, 8–9.
50. Jaki, *Science and Creation*, ch. 6; Judge, "Religion of the Secularists," 307–19.

of science (and deeply Anglican churchman) Francis Bacon (1605), in rejecting the organismic universe of Aristotle and Ptolemy, stipulated that teleology had no role in science.[51] Those who participated in the scientific revolution of the 1600s turned away from the final causes (pertaining to teleology) that were central to the Aristotelian worldview, and concentrated on efficient causes, the *how* of the phenomena.[52] The question of teleology cannot arise in science *qua* science.

As *scientists*, we may neither deny nor affirm purpose to biological process. Those who insist that science legitimates *exclusion* of the possibility of purpose open the door to those who argue that science *demonstrates or requires* the possibility of purpose (as is argued by Intelligent Design theorists). However, as *persons*, we almost inevitably *interpret* evolutionary biology to either deny or affirm that it is purposive. Either response is a metaphysical interpretation of biological history, and requires that dialogue partners deport themselves with humility, and that they also show respect for those who see things differently.

It is incorrect to argue that to ask about *purpose* is an illegitimate question. This is true for scientists *doing science*, but not for persons interpreting the entirety of their experience of the world, including those aspects of the world that have been disclosed by the advances of science. Some people believe that the great epic from sterile matter and energy, to living organisms, to multi-cellularity, nerve nets and brains, self-consciousness, culture, and the pursuit of virtue is a cosmic sideshow that is ultimately inconsequential. They are welcome to their metaphysical belief. Owen Gingerich has written: "For me, part of the coherency of the universe is that it is purposeful—though probably it takes the eyes of faith to accept that idea."[53] He posits that "the Book of Nature, in all its astonishing detail . . . suggests a God of purpose."[54] Gingerich concludes, "rather than believe that the universe is simply meaningless, a macabre joke, I would prefer to accept a universe created with purpose and intention by a loving God."[55]

Science is an onlooker when people raise issues pertaining to cosmic or biological purpose. As Briggs, Halvorson, and Steane state, "the analysis and description of a process cannot, logically, even address the issue of the overall meaning and purpose of that process, nor can it address what made

---

51. Harrison, *Bible, Protestantism and the Rise of Natural Science*, 182–83.
52. Gingerich, *God's Universe*, 12.
53. Gingerich, *God's Universe*, 77.
54. Gingerich, *God's Universe*, 79.
55. Gingerich, *God's Universe*, 96.

it possible for that process to happen in the first place."[56] Christians have data from another (personal) source that motivates their conviction that the great cosmic and biological evolutionary story is eminently compatible with God's purposes that the history of creation will find its ultimate meaning in Jesus the Messiah.[57]

The status of humanity

Among materialistic biologists, there is a widespread metaphysical assumption that, because we are evolved primates, we have no special status relative to other species. This may be called the *doctrine of non-exceptionalism*. It is a doctrine that makes the colossal mistake of viewing us *only* as biological organisms. Nathaniel Comfort a (non-Christian) historian of science, rejects the rationalist Enlightenment view by which "we have tended to define human identity and worth in terms of the values of science itself, as if it alone could tell us who we are." Comfort sees that sort of reductionism as being "odd and blinkered"; it is "no longer tenable"; and is the problematic child of scientism (the religious doctrine that "science and technology are the only reliable sources of self-knowledge").[58]

We are also *persons*—a category of being that is invisible to science but that makes us exceptional indeed. A biblical worldview sees us also as spiritual beings and objects of divine grace. This does not imply that we are despotic lords over creation, or that non-human organisms exist only for our exploitation. The abuse of non-human creatures for our own gratification is an anthropocentric perspective that issues rather from the Enlightenment, and that underlies the catastrophic ecocide overwhelming our planet.[59] Rather, we are a species that is called to serve God, to care for his creation, to submit to a moral law that is not of our making, and to give expression to a theocentric perspective on reality that leads us to learn and practice humility and obedience.

If we call someone an "ape," it is taken as a term of abuse. But we should eschew emotive reactions as we reflect on the findings from science. The sequence alignments we have presented demonstrate our biological continuity with apes, monkeys, prosimians, and (were we to use more

56. Briggs et al., *It Keeps Me Seeking*, 186.
57. Rom 8:18–25; Eph 1:3–14; Col 1:15–20.
58. Comfort, "How Science Has Shifted," 167–70.
59. See for example Crist, "Reimagining the Human," 1242.

ancient transposable elements) with rats, pigs, and sloths. What then of our status as creatures who bear God's image; as objects of divine grace; as co-heirs with Jesus the Messiah?

Our approach must be to recognize that there are different ways of looking at complex entities such as we are. As Polkinghorne says, "Reality is a multi-layered unity. I can perceive another person as an aggregation of atoms, an open biochemical system in interaction with the environment, a specimen of [H]omo sapiens, an object of beauty, someone whose needs deserve my respect and compassion, a brother for whom Christ died."[60]

It is ridiculous, entirely fallacious, to be fixated on only one of those levels of complexity, to the exclusion of all others. Polkinghorne has memorably reminded us that the world of science sees us as highly complicated meta-stable reproducing systems—but there are no *people* in it.[61] Science is blind to concepts such as personhood, responsibility, and beauty. Three distinguished professors conclude that "evolutionary biology does not diminish at all the validity of moral philosophy, nor the notion that humans are responsible agents called to a high purpose."[62]

Recognition of our biological nature cannot demean us as persons. The recognition that we sense a Handel oratorio as sound waves that travel through the atmosphere cannot lead us to reject it as an experience of music. The fact that a painting is light-absorbing chemical pigments on canvas cannot diminish it as a work of art. Our biological embodiment is the means of our capacity to worship. Humanity's "evolved capacity to respond to his Creator is the highest and most striking illustration of that potentiality with which the physical world has been endowed."[63]

The question might be asked (with some heat): "Are you saying that I am just a glorified ape?" My answer would be proffered (with a sense of awe): "That's correct! I cannot envisage any description as being more liberating or uplifting." For in *biological* terms, I am indeed an ape. Just think how similar my DNA sequence is to that of Clint the chimp (Figs. 7, 9, 10). But in *theological* terms, I am glorified ("if we share Christ's suffering, we will also share his glory"),[64] loved and reconciled by God, commissioned to serve in the self-denying way of Jesus, endowed with God's Spirit, a servant

---

60. Polkinghorne, *One World*, 97.
61. Polkinghorne, *The Way the World Is*, 16; *One World*, 60; *Science and Creation*, 20.
62. Briggs et al., *It Keeps Me Seeking*, 356.
63. Polkinghorne, *One World*, 70.
64. Rom 5:2; 8:17–18, 30; 1 Thess 2:14; Col 1:27; 1 Pet 5:1, 10.

of the new covenant,[65] a participant in the new creation.[66] If there is scandal in being a glorified ape, it is the scandal of God's grace. As Tom Wright says, the Christian hope is "of God's promised new heavens and new earth and of our promised resurrection to share in that new and gloriously embodied reality."[67]

The Bible sees all human beings as made in the image of God—in brilliant contradistinction to the ancient Mesopotamians and Egyptians who saw only the king as bearing the image of the gods.[68] Our biblically defined status as creatures that bear God's image and likeness refers to our functional role, our commission, as God's representatives in creation.[69] Such a role speaks of our calling and responsibility, our value to God, and the absolute equality we share as human beings. As apes that bear God's image, our unique and eternal dignity is guaranteed. Here is the objective basis of human rights, of the requirement that all people should be free, of the assessment that slavery and the exploitation of others are absolute evils, of the true humanism. It has been said that "there would be no human rights without the highly audacious Christian hypothesis of man as a creature in God's likeness and therefore inviolable."[70]

Science can be exploited for monstrous purposes when our status as the image of God is ignored. This biblical evaluation of humanity stands in opposition to social Darwinism, the disastrous early twentieth-century extrapolation of evolutionary science into evolutionistic ideology. "Social Darwinism inappropriately applies evolutionary concepts to groups of individuals in a social context. It takes Darwin's theory and turns it into a moral mandate for society, as if survival of the fittest is the morally appropriate mechanism for social development and not merely a description of how species evolve over time."[71] Such ideas were pioneered by Francis Galton, Darwin's brilliant cousin, and they presaged the development of eugenic theory in all its horror. David Bentley Hart says, with bitter irony, that eugenics, the development of weapons of mass destruction, the

---

65. 2 Cor 3:6.

66. 2 Cor 5:17.

67. Wright, *Surprised by Hope*, 197.

68. Alexander, *Genes, Determinism and God*, 282–83; also, *Are We Slaves to Our Genes?*

69. Alexander, *Genes, Determinism and God*, 285.

70. B. Levy in Hobson, *God Created Humanism*, 143 and also 40, 130; Spencer, *Evolution of the West*, 74–77.

71. Giberson and Collins, *Language of Science and Faith*, 24.

experimentation on human beings—"all of this required the scientific mind to move outside or 'beyond' Christian superstitions regarding the soul and the image of God within it."[72]

Ultimately, the image of God idea gives us unassailable dignity because, as brain scientist Malcolm Jeeves says, we cannot "interpret and understand the imago dei without reference to the Lord Jesus Christ."[73] The first Christians described Jesus as the exact image or likeness of God.[74] Our statements about humanity cannot be articulated "apart from the discovery that in Jesus Christ we see who we are and we also see God for us." Our identity can be defined only eschatologically[75]—in the light of God's final purposes for Jesus and for a redeemed humanity.

In summary, then. This chapter has provided genomic comparisons that demonstrate, beyond doubt, the fact of our phylogenetic relatedness to other primate species. We have also provided instructions by which anyone can use publicly accessible databases to generate similar data for themselves (Appendix 2). We can all be historians of DNA. But if this conclusion comes as a shock, we must remember that the scientific story provides a desperately *partial* account of humanity. The evolutionary data are eminently compatible with other ways of knowing. Phylogenetic history cannot be held to controvert the teaching of Genesis, or to deny the concept of creation, or to belittle the idea that history carries purpose, or to question the dignity and calling of humans as the *imago Dei*. Indeed, because the pioneers of science believed they possessed the image of God, and therefore something of God's rationality, they believed also that they would be able to understand something of God's world,[76] which includes (as it has transpired) phylogenetic history.

---

72. Hart, *Atheist Delusions*, 232.

73. See Malcolm Jeeves, "The Emergence of Human Distinctiveness: The Story from Neuropsychology and Evolutionary Psychology," in Jeeves, *Rethinking Human Nature*, 204.

74. 2 Cor 4:4; Heb 1:3; Col 1:15.

75. Patrick Miller quoted in Jeeves, *Rethinking Human Nature*, 205.

76. See Roger Trigg, "Does Science Need God?" in Alexander, *Has Science Killed God?* 22.

2

Evolution of the placenta
Lifeline to humanness

Abstract

The placenta arose recently on evolutionary timescales. In fact, placental development is so recent that genetic changes responsible for many steps in its formation are clearly identifiable in the genome. Genetic changes underlying placental evolution can be placed in temporal sequence by the science of comparative genomics. Innovations in placental biology have been brought about (in part) by retroviruses and transposable elements that have provided both new structural genes and short blocks of DNA that contribute to the regulation of existing genes. We conclude that stochastic genetic events contribute to new functionality. Theological questions arise from these findings. Tentative responses are discussed. First, the finding that random mutations can be constructive leads to the conclusion that chance events are part of the strategy by which the divine purpose for humanity is attained. Second, placental function critically underlies human brain development, and suboptimal placental function contributes to enduring mental health deficits. Many people enter life with handicaps arising from contingent events *in utero*, mandating understanding and compassion. Third, the advent of the placenta ensures that fetuses have an extended time of development in the mother's body, giving rise to the phenomenon of *prenatal parenting*, with implications for maximization of the quality of commitment of parents to each other, and to the baby.

Key words

placenta, evolution, mutations, purpose, providence, neurodevelopment, prenatal parenting

PEOPLE MAY RAISE VARIOUS objections to theological interpretations of evolution. Most mutations are disruptive, and it is hard to see how they might contribute to new functionality. Phylogenetic novelty arises from mutations; and the randomness of the genetic processes involved does not seem (at first sight) to be compatible with divine intentionality. These issues relate to divine providence (the action of God in his world). In this chapter, such concerns will be addressed using genetic data relevant to the origins of the placenta. We will also consider our status as vulnerable biological creatures bearing God's image. Finally, placental contributions to the uniquely developed human social brain call for ethical reflection.

The placenta and the mammary gland are required to sustain human life.[1] The mammalian placenta manifests a diversity of morphologies, depending on taxonomic grouping,[2] but despite this variety, performs multiple essential functions to support fetal development *in utero*. The placenta provides oxygen and nutrition to the fetus, and removes wastes. It offers protection from pathogens, toxins (by excluding or metabolizing them), and maternal immunity directed against *paternal* antigens. It secretes hormones. And in humans, it sequesters the fetus within the body of the mother, providing the capacity for early neural development, learning, and bonding or relationship.[3]

The history of the placenta is recent in evolutionary terms. Indeed, the placenta and mammary gland, alone of all the organs in our bodies, have evolved from some progenitor tissue to their current complexity during

---

1. Guernsey et al., "Molecular Conservation," 27450.

2. Chavatte-Palmer and Tarrade, "Placentation," 67–74.

3. Soares et al., "Hemochorial Placentation," 196–211; Aplin et al., "Tracking Placental Development," 479–94.

mammalian history. Such relative recentness gives us the confidence to expect that discrete genetic events contributing towards placental evolution will be discernible in mammalian genomes. Genetic novelties may be identified by aligning and comparing the genomes of multiple species (as described in chapter 1). The application of comparative genomics has shown that most of the genes involved in placental function are ancient; that is, they existed long before the placenta appeared, but they were *repurposed* for new roles that supported the formation and function of the developing placenta. Such repurposing involved altered gene regulation.[4] Comparative genetics strategies indicate that, repeatedly, such altered, placental-specific regulation has arisen from random additions to the genome. In particular, parasitic units of genetic material, replicating semi-autonomously within host cell genomes, and that are often disruptive, have made enormous contributions to the evolution of placental form and function.

1. Retroviral contributions to placental evolution

First, we consider some recent developments of old stories featuring ERVs and their actions in the placenta. The genes present in ERVs usually decay with time. But contrary to expectation, a few ERV genes have retained their integrity over large expanses of primate history; and several of these strikingly durable viral genes have been assimilated into the functioning of the placenta. Retroviruses possess *envelope* (*env*) genes, the products of which enable virus particles to stick to cells during the infection process. In the case of the unique ERV-WE1 insert, which lies on chromosome 7, the (viral) *env* gene retains the capacity to direct the production of a functional protein. The *env* gene has been domesticated to specify a protein that serves human reproduction. The modified env protein is expressed on the surfaces of cells called cytotrophoblasts, and enables these cells to stick together and fuse into a continuous layer called a syncytium. This layer, called the syncytiotrophoblast in placental tissue, forms the critically important interface between fetal and maternal placental tissues. The re-purposed env protein has been re-named syncytin-1.

The ERV-WE1 insertion event occurred in an ancestor of Old World monkeys and apes, but the ERV decayed in the former group (such that only fragments remain), and was preserved and its *env* gene retained functionality in the latter. New World monkeys retain the undisturbed target

---

4. Hao et al., "Baby Genomics," 35–47.

site. I have related this story, together with gene sequence comparisons, elsewhere.[5]

But can a gene of viral provenance really acquire a brand new role in the context of primate gestation? Two very recent technologies—unimaginable when I started out in research—have provided strong evidence for this scenario. First, it has recently become possible to determine the total complement of active genes in *individual cells*. This is done by characterizing all the gene outputs (in the form of RNA molecules) present in isolated cells. This technique is called *single cell RNAseq*. At the time when the blastocyst implants into the uterine wall, about ten days after conception, invasive syncytiotrophoblast cells are present. They express the *syncytin-1* gene (as well as the *syncytin-2* gene, see below).[6] In addition, RNAseq has been used to analyze gene activity in each of 21,000 cells recovered from human first-trimester placentas. Many cell types were identified, each characterized by the set of RNA molecules it contains, and the *syncytin-1* and *syncytin-2* genes were active, but *only* in trophoblastic cells, and especially in syncytiotrophoblast tissue.[7]

Second, minute placentas can now be cultivated in dishes. The artificial placental tissues form structures very like real human placentas. They also behave like real placentas—they form finger-like projections that have the capacity to invade adjacent tissues. And again, the erstwhile viral *envelope* (now the *syncytin-1*) gene is active in these cultured placental tissues, and specifically in the trophoblastic component.[8]

Do these virus-derived genes really provide absolutely essential functions in the placenta? The answer is *yes*. Certain viral infections—Zika, rubella, Herpes Simplex—can damage the placenta, and cause fetal injury or death. Virus infections induce cells to make proteins called type 1 interferons. These have protective, anti-viral roles: they *interfere* with viral replication. Interferons in turn activate proteins called *interferon-induced transmembrane proteins*, and these act by preventing the viral membrane from fusing with cell membranes. The effect is to block the process of infection. So far, so good. But the interferon-induced transmembrane proteins can also alter the structure of trophoblastic membranes, so as to prevent

---

5. Finlay, *Human Evolution*, 48–51; see Finlay, "Amazing Placenta," 306–26, for the ERV-WE1 insertion site in an increased number of species; see Bonnaud et al., "Natural History," 57, for original identification of the insertion site.

6. West et al., "Dynamics of Trophoblast Differentiation," 22635–42.

7. Suryawanshi et al., "Single-Cell Survey," eaau4788.

8. Turco et al., "Trophoblast Organoids," 263–67.

syncytin-1 (and syncytin-2, see below) on placental cells from working. Consequently, cytotrophoblastic cells do not fuse. The syncytiotrophoblast does not form properly. Pathologies arise. The fetus may die. Such pathological effects may reflect both direct viral toxicities, and the *anti-virus responses that block the activity of syncytins, the erstwhile viral proteins*. We conclude that syncytin-mediated cell fusion is an essential process, and we interfere with it to our peril—even under the emergency conditions of viral attack.[9]

Another question naturally arises. Can a randomly inserted viral gene be incorporated into networks of regulatory pathways so as to conform to the demands of a complex, dynamically changing organ? The regulation of the *syncytin-1* gene is effected by DNA sequence motifs present in a more ancient ERV into which the ERV-WE1 viral genome inserted itself.[10] So the answer to our question is, yes—a randomly inserted viral *env* gene can come under new physiologically appropriate controlling influences that emanate from a fortuitously located set of regulatory motifs.

But there is more to be said about syncytin-1 regulation. Another protein called suppressyn balances the activity of the syncytin-1 protein, and inhibits the cell fusion process that produces syncytiotrophoblast tissue. Suppressyn is produced in trophoblastic cells in a way that is complementary to that of the syncytin-1 protein.[11] Remarkably, suppressyn is itself a domesticated *env*-derived product of a third ERV. The ERV, to which the *suppressyn* gene belongs, is located on chromosome 21 and entered the primate germline in an ancestor of Old World monkeys and apes.[12] These findings demonstrate both that an essential gene (*syncytin-1*) has arisen in primates from the haphazard insertion of an ERV, and that regulatory DNA sequences and protein networks (involving suppressyn) arose from interactions with other ERV-derived sequences that were added to primate genomes by the same stochastic processes.

The retroviral provenance of the syncytin-1 fusion-generating protein is not an isolated story. Another ERV-derived *env* gene has remained intact over vast periods of time, and now specifies a protein with cell-fusing functionality necessary for syncytiotrophoblast development.[13] The

---

9. Buchrieser et al., "IFITM Proteins," 176–80; Zani et al., "Interferon-Induced Transmembrane Proteins," 19844–51.
10. Prudhomme et al., "Retroviral Promoter," 12157–68.
11. Sugimoto et al., "Suppressyn Localization," 19502.
12. Sugimoto et al., "Novel Human Endogenous Retroviral," 1462.
13. Lu et al., "Fine-Tuned and Cell-Cycle-Restricted," 1150–59.

unique ERVFRD-1 sequence was spliced into the genome of an anthropoid primate (simian) ancestor, and the insertion site is depicted in Fig. 11. The undisturbed, progenitor site is retained in prosimians (lemur and galago). This *env* gene has been transmogrified to encode what is now known as the syncytin-2 protein, which, like syncytin-1, induces cell fusion to sustain human development.

But syncytin-2 seems to perform an additional role. Retroviral env proteins possess a domain that dampens down immune defences—an aspect of the cunning viral survival strategy of evading immune attack. Syncytin-2 retains this ability to suppress immune reactivity. Cytotrophoblast cells release tiny membrane particles bearing syncytin-2, and these suppress the production of signalling molecules (such as interferon-γ) that induce immune reactions that suppress viral infections. Syncytin-2 helps form an immune suppressive environment and so may contribute to the marvel of immunological tolerance by which the mother's immune system does not destroy the fetus (which expresses paternal proteins).[14]

FIGURE 11

```
ERVFRD-1/MER50              TGTTACAGTA...ACCGGTAACA
                            |||||  ||||    |||||||
human           ...TTAAGCTGGTTCTGTTAGAGTA...    GGTAACAGTTCCACCATT...
chimp           ...TTAAGCTGGTTCTGTTAGAGTA...    GGTAACAGTTCCACCATT...
bonobo          ...TTAAGCTGGTTCTGTTAGAGTA...    GGTAACAGTTCCACCATT...
gorilla         ...TTAAGCTGGTTCTGTTAGAGTA...    GGTAACAGTTCCACCATT...
orang           ...TTAAGCTGGTTCTGTTAGAGCA...    GGTAACAGTTCCACCATT...
gibbon          ...TTAAGCTGGTTCTGTTAGAGTA...    GGTAAAAGTTCCACCATT...
baboon          ...TTAAGCTGGTTCTGTTAGAGTA...    GGTAACAGTTCCACCATT...
drill           ...TTAAGCTGGTTCTGTTAGAGTA...    GGTAACAGTTCCACCATT...
macaque         ...TTAAGCTGGTTCTGTTAGAGTA...    GGTAACAGTTCCACCATT...
green monkey    ...TTAAGCTGGCTCTGTTAGAGTA...    GGTAACAGTTCCACCATT...
sooty mangabey  ...TTAAGCTGGTTCTGTTAGAGTA...    GGTAACAGTTCCACCATT...
snub-nosed m    ...TTAAGCTGGTTCTGTTAGAGTA...    GATAACAGTTCCACAATT...
marmoset        ...TTAAGCTGGTTCTGTTAGAGTA...    GGTAACAGT   CAGCATT...
night monkey    ...TTAAGCTGGTTCTGTTAGAGTA...    GGTAACAGTTCCAGCATT...
squirrel monkey ...TTAAGCTGGTTCTGTTAGAGTA...    GGTAACAGTTCCAGCATT...
capuchin        ...TTAAGCTGGTTCTGTTAGAGTA...    GGTAACAGTTCCAGCATT...

grey mouse lemur               ...TTGAGATGACTTCAGCACC...
galago                         ...TTGAGACAACTTTGGCACC...
MER57E1 type sequence          ...CTGAGGCGGCTCCAGCGCC...
```

Insertion site of an ERV in the genomes of anthropoid primates.

14. Lokossou et al., "Endogenous Retrovirus-Encoded Syncytin-2," 185–98.

The unique ERV (FRD subclass) present at this insertion site contains an *envelope* gene that now functions in placental development as the *syncytin-2* gene. The human sequence (as ERVFRD-1) was obtained using the UCSC genome browser, other primate sequences from the NCBI, and the ERV subclass sequence (MER50) from Dfam. This ERV inserted into an older ERV (MER57E1), the type sequence of which was obtained from RepeatMasker.

Molecular approaches are elucidating the complex regulatory mechanisms by which placentas form in the early embryo. Mouse and human placental initiation are most studied, and show similar but by no means identical regulation—and in each species, ERVs feature in the regulatory networks that lead to formation of the placenta.[15] The incorporation of randomly acquired ERV sequences into regulatory networks is a recurring theme. The *INSL4* gene specifies an insulin-related protein that may control life-and-death decisions in cells of the placenta. The gene is regulated by DNA sequence motifs located within a nearby ERV that was spliced into the primate germline in an Old World monkey-ape ancestor, and thus dates from the same epoch as the ERVs that provided the antecedents of the *syncytin-1* and *suppressyn* genes.[16]

Placental syncytiotrophoblast tissue of anthropoid primates (but not of other species) produces corticotropin-releasing hormone (CRH) in late pregnancy. Placental CRH delays parturition. Regulation of the *CRH* gene is controlled by sequences within an adjacent ERV that was spliced into the primate germline in an ancestor of anthropoid primates.[17] A related ERV sequence, also dating from an anthropoid ancestor may also partake in placenta-specific regulation of an immunological signalling molecule (the IL-2 receptor β).[18]

2. Transposable element contributions to placental evolution

Transposable elements in various stages of decay litter mammalian genomes. In remote mammal history, two transposable elements of the

---

15. Hemberger et al., "Mechanisms of Early Placental Development," 27–43.

16. Macaulay et al., "Genes of Life and Death," 1700091; Macaulay et al., "Hypomethylation," 722–35.

17. Dunn-Fletcher et al., "Anthropoid Primate-Specific," e2006337.

18. Cohen et al., "Placenta-Specific Expression," 35543–52.

sushi-ichi type (studied and named by Japanese workers) each contributed a gene that, appropriately modified, was recruited into protein networks sustaining placental development. These genes are now known as *PEG10* and *PEG11*. The transposable element carrying the *PEG10* precursor sequence was spliced into the mammalian germline in an ancestor of marsupials and eutherian mammals. The PEG10 protein functions during the invasion of placental trophoblastic cells into the uterus,[19] and supports the development of trophoblastic stem cells into differentiated cells including syncytiotrophoblasts.[20] The element carrying the *PEG11* precursor sequence was spliced into the genome of an ancestor of eutherian mammals. The PEG11 protein contributes to placental blood vessel development.[21] In both cases, most of the transposable element sequences, as well as the target sites, have degenerated beyond recognition into the genomic background. The insertion events happened in deep time, and only functional sequences have survived.

Glycoprotein hormone-alpha (GPHα) is a subunit of the hormone chorionic gonadotropin, and it is secreted by the syncytiotrophoblast layer. GPHα exists in two forms. The larger form possesses novel placenta-specific functions. It has an extended protein sequence that is encoded by a stretch of DNA donated by a transposable element (specifically of the Alu-J subtype) that was inserted into the genome of an ancestor of anthropoid primates.[22]

Other transposable elements have provided "start" sites of genes that are active in the placenta, and so affect the way in which those genes are regulated. A family of transposable elements called L1PA2 elements includes multiple instances involved in the activation of genes that specify nonprotein-coding RNAs.[23] An Alu-Y element drives placenta-specific expression of the growth-promoting *KCNH5* gene.[24]

Finally, there is the wonder of the decidua, the maternal (endometrial) part of the placenta. Gene regulatory networks have been reorganized to orchestrate the remodelling of this remarkable tissue that receives placental tissues from the fetus, and that underlies the provision of nourishment and

---

19. Chen et al., "Silencing of Paternally Expressed Gene 10," e0144845.
20. Abed et al., "Gag Protein PEG10," e0214110.
21. Kitazawa et al., "Severe Damage," 174–88.
22. Chen et al., "Exonization and Functionalization," 3216–31.
23. Chishima et al., "Identification of Transposable Elements," 23.
24. Macaulay et al., "Retrotransposon Hypomethylation," e95840.

the induction of immune tolerance.[25] The hormone progesterone regulates decidualization, and in decidual cells many binding sites for the progesterone receptor are located within transposable elements.[26] A binding site for three gene-regulatory proteins occurs repeatedly and *exclusively* in Alu elements.[27] Randomly accrued parasitic strips of DNA have been co-opted repeatedly to re-wire placental regulatory circuits. And time and again, such transposable elements entered the primate genome in ancestors we share with other species of primate.

3. Extending the story: embryo and mammary gland

Two amazing organs define us as mammals. Both of them have arisen recently on evolutionary timescales. They are the *placenta*, composed of both fetal and maternal (decidual) components, and the *mammary gland*, the source of nutrition for the young. Remarkably, early embryos, prior to implantation into the uterine wall and the development of the placenta, are also characterized by frequent activation of ERVs.[28] The regulation of gene activity in embryos is mediated by sequences found in ERVs and transposable elements.[29] It seems that relatively young (hominoid-specific) ERVs and transposable elements have been enlisted (or *exapted*) for new roles in the regulation of genome activity at the commencement of ontogenetic development—that is, development of the individual organism. ERVs and transposable elements have contributed to the early events that specify our human body plan as being human, rather than a body plan characteristic of a gorilla or a gibbon.

Mammary gland development and function have been orchestrated by thousands of ERVs and transposable elements. These possess sequence motifs with the capacity to bind proteins that regulate genes active in forming the mammary gland and in producing its life-giving secretions (milk). Many of these are ancient elements that colonized genomes, acquired regulatory activity, and contributed to the rewiring of genetic activities, in ancestors of eutherian mammals. For example, candidate regulatory function

---

25. Vento-Tormo et al., "Single Cell Reconstruction," 347–53; Ander et al., "Immune Responses," eaat6114.
26. Lynch et al., "Ancient Transposable Elements," 551–61.
27. Vrljicak et al., "Analysis of Chromatin Accessibility," 2467–77.
28. Gemmell et al., "Exaptation of HERV-H," 1339.
29. Pontis et al., "Hominoid-Specific Transposable Elements," 724–35.

is found in an ancient MIR element associated with the gene that specifies *bone morphogenetic protein-4*, a master controller of cell development. This element entered the mammalian genome in an ancestor of eutherian and metatherian (marsupial) species.[30] We and the opossums are descended from the same ancestor.

Neonates obtain milk by suckling, an action that requires a closed secondary palate (a structure that separates the mouth from the nasal cavity). This morphological feature is specific to mammals. Formation of the palate is controlled by the *WNT5a* gene, itself activated by regulatory sequences embedded in ancient transposable elements that entered the genome in an ancestor of all extant mammals.[31] The mammary gland (providing milk) and the secondary palate (enabling suckling) may have co-evolved during the same epoch of evolutionary history.

Evidence is growing for the hypothesis that ERVs and transposable elements make major contributions to evolutionary developments. Particular classes of such elements characterize particular taxa of living organisms, and a proportion of these may contribute to the characteristic form and function of those organisms. These genome-colonizing elements may affect the regulation of developmental genes and accelerate the development of functional complexity.[32] According to Gould's and Eldridge's theory of *punctuated equilibrium*, species may remain unchanged for extended periods of time, but these spans of evolutionary stasis may be interrupted by bursts of rapid evolutionary change. Evolution often proceeds stepwise. ERVs and transposable elements may undergo bursts of activity, windows of time during which they colonize genomes at relatively more rapid rates. At such times, they may provide abundant new genetic material that becomes domesticated or exapted to provide new regulatory functions. This activity may change the activity of genes that orchestrate developmental processes (*DevReg* genes). These genome-colonizing ancient repetitive elements may provide a likely mechanism of punctuated equilibrium.[33]

---

30. Nishihara, "Retrotransposons Spread Potential *Cis*-Regulatory Elements," 11551–62.

31. Nishihara et al., "Coordinately Co-Opted Multiple Transposable Elements," e1006380.

32. Nishihara, "Transposable Elements as Genetic Accelerators," 269–81.

33. Casanova and Konkel, "Developmental Gene Hypothesis," e1900173.

4. Providence: chance and purpose in history

Scientific findings are fascinating—and to open and curious minds, they provoke theological questions. The study of comparative genomics has demonstrated that random mutations, arising from ERV and transposable element activities, have generated new genetic information and novel functionality. Chance events have contributed to the formation of new organs—the placenta and mammary gland—and to the ascent of *Homo sapiens*. Nevertheless, the fact of randomness, and the postulate that evolutionary change is the bearer of God's purposes, seem to sit uneasily with each other.

Reality is permeated with randomness and unpredictability. We have demonstrated the generative role of chance (genetic mutations) in impersonal *biological history* (above). But chance events also occur in personal *human history*, in which people's choices and actions are often unpredictable, arbitrary, and irrational. (*Molecular* processes in brains underlie the operation of *minds*, so the characteristics of biological and human histories cannot be entirely dissimilar. Both run on the same laws of physics and chemistry, although physics is ultimately transcended by the emergent reality of mind.)

It is axiomatic for biblical faith that God acts in human history[34]—in all its randomness and messiness. Strictly analogously, we should expect that God acts in the randomness of biological history. Happenstance in biological evolution does not introduce new types of questions to people who recognize God's action in human history. We will explore happenstance and God's purposes below.

History is a biblical concept

The ideas of *creation*[35] and of the linear passage of *history*[36] have biblical origins. A compelling court history of King David of Israel was written five hundred years before Herodotus was born.[37] We owe the concepts of *creation* and *history* to the Jews. The insight that the *created* world has an

---

34. For example, Wright, *New Testament and the People of God*, 298–99; also 9–10, 302, 426.

35. Jaki, *Science and Creation*, 146–60.

36. Konig, *New and Greater Things*, 167–68, 171; Judge, "Religion of the Secularists," 307–19.

37. Knight, *I AM: This Is My Name*, 42.

unfolding *history* combines deeply theological themes. The biblical emphasis on history encouraged the pioneer scientists to recognize the reality, and seek understanding, of physical and biological history. During the development of geological science, "one major source—even arguably *the* major source—for this new vision of nature as historical was the strong sense of history embodied in the Judeo-Christian scriptures."[38] Biological evolution (along with cosmology, geology, and archaeology) is a historical science, and belongs to the category of history. Attention to God's action in biblical history should inform our understanding of God's action in biological history. As has been demonstrated above, the text inscribed in mammalian DNA molecules provides data-rich documentation of the (historical) processes of change, diversification, innovation, and development that occurred during the evolution of the placenta.

Histories are part of creation

We readily discourse on God's creative work in terms of the physical cosmos, living organisms, and humanity.[39] The biblical concept of *creation* refers to the giving of existence to all of physical reality—to the entirety of our space-time continuum. (And if there are other space-time continuums or antecedent quantum vacuums, they too are created; see chapter 1.) But the Bible describes additional creations—of each individual, of Israel, of the church, and of the new creation at the eschaton—using words related to the Hebrew root *bara*, and the Greek root *ktizo*. The multiplicity of creations does not imply that God's creative acts are sporadic. Rather, it indicates a continuous relationship, a *creatio continua*, between God and his ever-dependent world.[40] Significantly, all of these creations have time dimensions, *histories* (allowing of course that they are all part of one great overarching history).

---

38. Rudwick, *Earth's Deep History*, 4; the author describes histories such as those of nature itself (3, 139, 299), the planets (289–91) and earth (180–81, 220–21); of life (281, 296), molluscs (136), quadrupeds (137, 147), and humanity (155, 180, 188, 203, 206, 263).

39. Gen 1:1, 21, 27. If in fact creation refers to the giving of *function* or *order* (Walton, *Lost World*, 23–37), the logic is the same. Creation is all God's work.

40. Polkinghorne, *Science and Christian Belief*, 75–76; *Reason and Reality*, 102.

God is the Creator of biological organisms, of humanity, and of each individual.[41] But biology and humanity have histories (their evolutionary or phylogenetic development, as exemplified by the ancient DNA modification indicated in Fig. 11). Each of us is a created being with a history. The history of living organisms is a dimension of their created existence. Any process of which we can conceive represents change-with-time, history, within God's created order.

God is the Creator of Israel and of the church.[42] Each of these creations has a history. These histories contain meanderings, dead ends, disasters—as well as times of newness and reformation, and coruscations of glory. Konig has stated that Israel saw God as the Creator of her history. He writes of "the Creator God who holds the entire life of his people in his hands, who indeed creates their history."[43] God is the one who fashions history, determines its course, and sustains it by his love.[44] The prophetic book of Isaiah provides an expression of this pervasive idea: Israel's God calls "forth the generations from the beginning."[45] The concept of *generations* denotes the passage of time. An alternative translation of this statement is that God determines "the course of history" (GNT). The study of biological (including, specifically, human) evolution describes the history of living organisms in the same way as the Hebrew Scriptures record the history of Israel. Biblically, they are created histories.

We look forward to a new creation,[46] of which Jesus' resurrection is the prototypical instance, perceived by his first followers as a decisive act of the Creator God.[47] The giving-of-being to the current creation has been understood traditionally as *creatio ex nihilo*. The giving-of-being to the new creation is *creatio ex vetere*, a transformation from the old,[48] the new

---

41. God as Creator of organisms (Gen 1:21; Ps 104:30), humanity (Gen 1:27; Deut 4:32), individuals (Ps 139:13; Gal 6:15; 2 Cor 5:17; Eph 2:10; 4:24; Col 3:10).

42. God as Creator of Israel (Deut 32:6; Ps 149:2; Isa 41:20; 43:1, 7, 15; 45:8; Jer 31:22), the church (Eph 2:15); the reality of "God's creation of Israel" is expressed by Gordon, "The Week that Made the World: Reflections on the First Pages of the Bible," in McConville and Moller, *Reading the Law*, 229.

43. Konig, *Here Am I*, 4; also 6, 37, 88.

44. Konig, *Here Am I*, 30, 26, 37–38.

45. Isa 41:4, NIV.

46. Isa 65:17–18; 2 Pet 3:13; Rev 21:1.

47. Wright, *Resurrection of the Son of God*, 122, 124, 541, 548, 730; Polkinghorne, *The Way the World Is*, 91: Resurrection is "God's real re-creative act of a whole man."

48. Polkinghorne, *Reason and Reality*, 103; *Science and Christian Belief*, 167–69.

generated from the womb of the old,⁴⁹ but it is creation nevertheless. It was inaugurated in the career of Israel's Messiah, and will be consummated in a future time. So even new creation includes within its scope a historical dimension. The church has understood that new creation is *already* and *not yet*—inauguration and consummation separated by the passage of time.⁵⁰

The study of our phylogenetic history has been clouded by controversy. It has been all too easy to conceive of God as the Fabricator of objects rather than the Sustainer of history. If Christians had perceived divine purpose and action in the complexities and messiness of biological history in precisely the same way as they have perceived divine purpose and action in the complexities and messiness of human (particularly, biblical) history, then the discovery of phylogenetic history would have caused no problems. As Peter Harrison has stated, "if the history of nature were understood to be more akin to human history at the time Darwin published the *Origin*, no one would have expected to see conspicuous instances of purpose at every moment."⁵¹ The succession of species in natural history and of kingdoms in human history are equally the locus of God's hidden activity.

We cannot entertain a "creation versus history" dichotomy. The widespread "creation versus evolution" antithesis is an egregious category error. It seems to follow that interpretive principles that apply to human history (such as those that we use when reading biblical history) can be applied to make sense of biological history. Small wonder that Polkinghorne identified the theological endeavor most akin to the historical sciences (cosmology, evolution) as being New Testament studies.⁵²

Created histories are not perfect at their inception

It is often assumed that God's creation was perfect at the beginning of its history (that is, at $t = 0$), and that creation thereafter unravelled when sickness, suffering, wickedness, and death arrived on the scene. But we find that God's created histories did not start in idyllic innocence. God created Israel *ex vetere* from a ragbag of slaves, steeped in polytheism and Baal worship,

---

49. Wright, *Surprised by Scripture*, 106; also 99, 203, 205.

50. For example, Polkinghorne, *Science and Christian Belief*, 158, 160; Wright, *How God Became King*, 162; *Surprised by Scripture* 35.

51. See Peter Harrison, "Evolution, Providence, and the Problem of Chance," in Giberson, *Abraham's Dice*, 265, 274–80.

52. Polkinghorne, *The Way the World Is*, x; *Reason and Reality*, 15.

often unfaithful, rebellious, and self-absorbed. Miriam, Moses, and Aaron, the chosen agents of liberation, were portrayed with brutal honesty as flawed people. The church was created *ex vetere* from communities of Jews and gentiles, often mutually suspicious or violently hostile. The founding apostles, such as Peter and John, were frustratingly earthy men. The person who has aligned him- or herself with Jesus is a new creation.[53] But we dare not suggest that this miracle of creation instantaneously transforms that person into a paragon of perfection. When joined to the Messiah, people are suspended in the space of *already* (new) but *not yet* (perfect). As Luther said, *simul iustus et peccator*—we are at the same time both righteous and sinners. We change only by that painfully slow historical process known as sanctification.

From these biblical precedents, we would not expect biological history to have issued from a primeval phase of idyllic sweetness. DNA has always been subject to random derangements. Creatures have always sickened and died. The lion has never lain down with the lamb. Perfection of the physical creation or of persons will be achieved as a reality only in the consummation of the new creation. The completion of all phases of history awaits the full outworking of God's cosmic act of redemption, achieved by Israel's Messiah, Jesus (see chapter 5).

The study of mammalian genomes shows that genetic mechanisms as they operate *now* (in all their randomness and potential for pathogenic disruption) are the same as those that operated before eutherian mammals appeared on earth. The accumulation of ERVs and transposable elements in the genome we have inherited has proceeded uninterruptedly for scores of millions of years (at least). Such an extended and continuous history shows that the physical or biological creation was never "perfect," free of mutational disruption, deformity, decay, disease, death, or—in the case of humanity—territoriality, greed, or violence. Retroviruses have always been invaders with the potential of introducing useful raw material into genomes, and also of disrupting life processes. And even those ERV genes that have been domesticated to specify the body-plan of mammalian species can malfunction to cause suffering. Creations with histories (and can we envisage any other sort of creations?) develop through travail.

---

53. 2 Cor 5:17.

EVOLUTION AND ESCHATOLOGY

The chaos of history leads to God's order

Christians must acknowledge the chaos of history even as they look forward to the goal of history. The biblical text, with disturbing—indeed shocking—honesty, describes the carnage and suffering of human affairs over some two thousand years. Genesis opens with a picture of *tehom*, the darkness that enveloped the raging deep, which George Knight has described as indicating "chaos, nonbeing, unreality, negation."[54] God was said to create light over against this chaos. God creates in the presence of chaos, "by actually employing chaos as the necessary instrument to gain his ends."[55] Other manifestations of *tehom*, chaos, were the scorching, desiccating wilderness, where Moses encountered "the God who brings forth good by means of chaos,"[56] the horror of the Babylonian exile,[57] and Jesus' abandonment in darkness on the cross.[58] Truly, God works in history by *using chaos*—a feature of God's own created world—to produce good and the vibrancy of life.[59]

The ancient Jewish wisdom literature developed the chaos-to-order insight. The Book of Job describes the anguished questioning of a man whose life had been devastated by random occurrences (lightning strikes, storms, bandits). Eventually God answered by referring Job to the magnificence of cosmic, meteorological, and biological phenomena. Was God's answer a cop-out? Not according to physicist Tom McLeish, for whom the take-home message of Job is that randomness at the microscopic level (to which humans are exposed and vulnerable) issues into order, stability, and beauty at the macrocopic level. Here is a basis for a theology of evolution.[60]

Similarly, thinking scientifically, randomness at the micro level can result in order and predictability at the macro level. It takes a physicist to describe that. McLeish has described how all the beauty and order of our planet and of life "becomes both possible and predictable because of the chaotic world underneath them."[61] The turbulence-to-order theme is inher-

---

54. Knight, *I AM: This Is My Name*, 20.
55. Knight, *I AM: This Is My Name*, 22.
56. Knight, *I AM: This Is My Name*, 27–28.
57. Knight, *I AM: This Is My Name*, 5, 9–10.
58. Knight, *I AM: This Is My Name*, 65–66.
59. Konig, *New and Greater Things*, 60–62, 135–36.
60. McLeish, "Evolution as an Unwrapping," 43–64.
61. McLeish, *Faith and Wisdom in Science*, 99–101.

ent to the nature of reality: "the underlying chaos of the molecular world turns out to be an essential, if unseen, supporting structure for all sorts of ordered phenomena."[62] It is striking that "the beautiful structures of the natural world" are "built upon a microscopic world of disorder which is the substrate of life itself."[63]

Hutchings and McLeish state that "God has made a world in which uncertainty and chance—from our point of view—operate at a local level in order to produce a functioning, habitable world overall."[64] There is a structure, a coherence, to the randomness that underlies our being: "countless biological processes depend on the wild frenzy of particle collisions. As the particles wheel around crazily, they are effectively "exploring" every possible shape or material combination. Those that are even slightly more likely will end up as heavily favoured."[65] The outcome of this molecular mayhem is the breath-taking order, complexity, and integration of life—even new organs such as the placenta and mammary gland.

The biologist Rick Colling has described God as "the Random Designer." Colling cites the marvel of our life-sustaining adaptive immune system, in which cells called T and B lymphocytes acquire the capacity to produce an uncountably vast number of protective proteins. During the development of each lymphocyte, a small set of genes undergoes random rearrangements, generating innumerable protective proteins. Many of these rearrangements are of no use, and the cells are culled. Chance genetic events, in the context of lawful selection, lie at the base of the stupendously intricate functions of the immune system.[66] Colling wrote, "random design may be the only way to truly maximise biological productivity and ensure ultimate success. It guarantees that virtually every possible solution will be generated and also checked."[67] We will return to this theme when reflecting on the immune system (chapter 4).

We are justified in applying the chaos-to-order theme to the genetic history we have illustrated in the development of the placenta. The unruly, disruptive ERVs and transposable elements are part of this underworld of chaos that underlies life-enhancing complexification, the gradual

---

62. McLeish, *Faith and Wisdom in Science*, 187.
63. McLeish, *Faith and Wisdom in Science*, 190.
64. Hutchings and McLeish, *Let There be Science*, 123–24.
65. Hutchings and McLeish, *Let There be Science*, 124–25.
66. Colling, *Random Designer*, 70–72, 178–81.
67. Colling, *Random Designer*, 68.

development of the life-sustaining placenta, and the elaboration of minds. We may worry that this mechanism seems all too heartless. But Holmes Rolston reminds us that this pervasive genetic randomness has contributed to the advent on earth of creatures that show the personal capacity of care.[68]

Chaotic history is directed

God achieves his ends in history despite and indeed *through* the randomness that characterizes the behavior of his creatures. When the Hebrews escaped from Egypt, their exodus wanderings were the resultant of divine constancy and human inconstancy. Konig has expressed it thus: "Israel's history is the result of what both God and Israel do. The particular course of the journey through the wilderness is determined by the interplay between God and the people: God who leads and cares for them, the people who complain and rebel."[69] Konig describes this partnership of polarities as "covenant history . . . in which God quite deliberately allows his covenant partner scope to influence its course. . . . In the progress of history God truly allows his covenant partner to move."[70] We conclude that history is the product of what both God *and Israel* do, such that the reality of creaturely freedom can frustrate, but not ultimately thwart, and indeed is able to collaborate with, God's purposes.

We may see the combination of randomness and inevitability in the career of Jesus. It was the chanciness of history when Judas the betrayer, Caiaphas, and Pilate conspired to condemn and kill Jesus. (There were other groups that also wanted to rid themselves of him.) But it was written into the deepest moral structure of the universe that when God-as-a-human-person, the embodiment of pure Beauty, Truth, and Justice, confronted the

---

68. See Holmes Rolston, "Care on Earth: Generating Informed Concern," in Davies and Gregersen, *Information and the Nature of Reality*, 205-45.

69. Konig, *New and Greater Things*, 173. Moreover, "it is precisely because the people really share in the formation of this history that it can ultimately miscarry in the sense that it results in God's final judgement on that particular generation." Konig states elsewhere (in *Here Am I*, 128-29) that "history was formed by a faithful God and an unfaithful nation." Indeed, the history of Israel "is genuine *history* (and not some kind of puppet-show), in which two covenant partners each have their own responsibility, allocated to them respectively by God alone, but not executed by God alone."

70. Konig, *New and Greater Things*, 173.

corrupt powers of this world, he *must* die. Jesus recognized the inevitability of his death. Jesus said that he *must* suffer and for that matter, rise again.[71]

The character of human history allows us to make sense of biological history. Just as the interplay of happenstance and order are seen in Israel's history, between a people who showed constant inconstancy and a dependable God, so also cosmic and biological history proceed by the productive interplay of creaturely randomness and divinely upheld consistency.[72] Chance molecular events and human volition are so constrained by (respectively) divinely ordained physical law and moral law, that histories move directionally (but often confusingly, from our perspective) to their divinely purposed consummation.

We can see this directionality in the phenomenon of evolutionary convergence. Insertion of each retrovirus is a stochastic event; but different retroviruses have contributed *repeatedly* to formation of placental function in mammals (Fig. 12).[73] Retroviruses have contributed to placentation also in live-bearing lizards, and transposable elements are singularly active in placental tissue of live-bearing fish.[74] Indeed, regulatory networks based on transposable elements may underlie development of two embryo-sustaining organs: the placenta in animals and the endosperm in flowering plants.[75]

---

71. He "must suffer" (Mark 8:21 and parallels) and "rise again" (Luke 24:7, 26, 44–46; Acts 2:24).

72. Polkinghorne has emphasized the productive operation of chance events in the context of lawful order. See *The Way the World Is*, 8, 11–12; *One Word*, 50–56, 68–69; *Science and Creation*, 47–50; *Quarks, Chaos and Christianity*, 39–42.

73. Denner, "Expression and Function," 31–43; Imakawa et al., "Phylogeny of Placental Evolution," 89–109; Funk et al., "Capture," e01811–18.

74. Cornelis et al., "Endogenous Retroviral Envelope Syncytin," E10991–11000; Jue et al., "Tissue-Specific Transcriptome for *Poeciliopsis*," 2181–92.

75. Qiu and Kohler, "Mobility Connects," 1005–17.

Figure 12

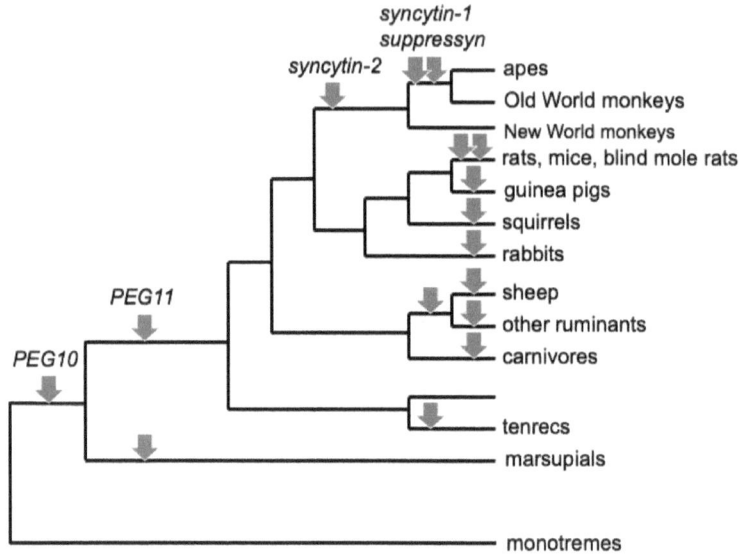

Repeated co-option of ERV-derived genes in the biology of the placenta.

The dendrogram depicts a partial mammalian phylogenetic tree showing those branches on which ERV genes have been domesticated (or *exapted*) to serve functions in placentation.

Each arrow indicates the addition of an ERV (or transposable element, in the cases of *PEG10* and *PEG11*) to the respective genome, and its recruitment to provide a protein that functions in the placenta.

Theologically, chance serves God's purposes. As physicist Paul Ewart states, there "is purpose to chance, . . . random events provide a robust method to explore the range of possibilities allowed by physical laws."[76] To Andrew Steane, "Random seeking has led to non-random finding." In evolutionary problem-solving, "the randomness serves chiefly as a mechanism to discover the niches that are made available by the environment."[77] It is widely recognized that chance genetic events may have consequences that are *directed* or *constrained* along certain trajectories. A comment in the

---

76. Ewart. "Necessity of Chance," 111–31.
77. Steane, *Faithful to Science*, 6571, 149.

journal *Science* has expressed the chance-consistency synergy thus: evolution rolls the dice, but physics makes the rules.[78]

Both polarities (chance–order) of our world are necessary: "If our world was entirely random or entirely predictable, life as we know it would not be possible."[79] In summary, we may accept that evolutionary histories (such as that of the placenta) are deeply contingent (as illustrated by the randomly chosen insertion sites, Fig. 11), but their routes are constrained by a deeply embedded order. We may with justification perceive that history is directed.

Histories must be interpreted

Histories—whether human or biological—are complicated and do not lend themselves to knock-down interpretations. However, interpret them we must. We may decide history is an unstructured mess, mere brute fact that allows no more questions. Or we may see patterns, significant events and achievements that act as *hermeneutic keys* that make sense of the whole. The mid-twentieth-century historian Herbert Butterfield said: "we decide on our total attitude to the whole of human history when we make our decision about our religion—and it is the combination of the history with a religion, or something equivalent to a religion, which generates power and fills the story with significance."[80] Butterfield allowed that people could find this in a Christian interpretation of history, or indeed in any number of other interpretations.

It is striking that biblical faith is an interpretation of history.[81] Perspectives arising from a prior deeply considered faith engender the capacity to perceive order in a succession of events. The prophets of Israel made sense

---

78. Camargo, "Physics Makes the Rules," 236.

79. Hutchings and McLeish, *Let There Be Science*, 125.

80. Butterfield, *Christianity and History*, 37; and for emphasis: "Our final interpretation of history is the most sovereign decision we can take, and it is clear that every one of us, standing alone in the universe, has to take it for himself. It is our decision about religion, about our total attitude to things, and about the way we will appropriate life" (p. 39). Our interpretation is formed by our total picture of reality: "I do not think that any man can ever arrive at his interpretation of the human drama by merely casting his eye over the course of the centuries in the way that a student of history might do. I am unable to see how a man can find the hand of God in secular history, unless he has first found that he has an assurance of it in his personal experience" (p. 140).

81. Finlay, *Gospel According to Dawkins*, 28–30.

of their history. Many "religious" movements emerged during the so-called Axial period of 550–450 BC. However, the ancient Jewish faith resurged with particular vigor at this time. It was unique in that it "was a corporate interpretation of historical fact. This interpretation, of all religions of the world, is alone based on fact."[82] That fact, counter-intuitively, was the destruction of Jerusalem in 587 BC, and the end of a thousand years of religious history. Both Judaism and, later, Christianity perceived that a new start came from this moment of disaster. "This new understanding of historical event required a person's total response to what God *had already done* in history, a response of obedience, gratitude and joy."[83]

Christian faith interprets history in the light of the advent of Jesus of Nazareth. Konig states, "No other religion is so out-and-out historical as Christianity, grafted on to the stem of Israel's faith. The view of history as a succession of cohesive events directed towards a goal in the future—it was not without reason that this originated in Israel. . . . Nowhere else but in Christianity is the truth (and therefore the meaning of history) defined in a historical person."[84] That meaning-conferring person is Jesus of Nazareth, whom the Bible describes as the *Eschatos*, the end and goal of history.[85] The history of Jesus yields on close examination a compelling hermeneutic key for interpreting *all* of history, including biological history.

Faith sustains a natural, fruitful, and inspiring engagement between Christian theology and the historical sciences. The evolution of the placenta is a component of our history for which numerous formative events are clearly inscribed in our DNA. The placenta has enabled the rise of big-brained, intensely social, culture-transmitting, morally aware, and worshipping primates. Placental history may be subsumed into the all-encompassing history of God's purposes underlying the *missio Dei*, which is to populate God's world with creatures that bear the *imago Dei*, and ultimately, to bring all creation to perfection.

---

82. Knight, *I AM: This Is My Name*, 4; Knight continues: "This interpretation is so strange, so utterly different from the thoughts of any other human being at any time in history, that the reader is compelled to ask whether it does not actually come from the mind of God."

83. Knight, *I AM: This Is My Name*, 6.

84. Konig, *New and Greater Things*, 171; biblically, "history's meaning lies irrevocably *within* history."

85. Konig, *Eclipse of Christ*, 56, 81–82, 85–86, 96.

5. Human vulnerability: the imago Dei embodied

The syncytin proteins, either individually or together, are expressed abnormally in various placental pathologies.[86] These include abnormalities associated with Down's syndrome, preeclampsia (high blood pressure), fetal intrauterine growth restriction (IUGR), the maternal *haemolysis, elevated liver enzymes, low platelets* (HELLP) syndrome, gestational diabetes, and tumors of trophoblastic tissue. Such correlations indicate (at the least) that the retrovirally-derived syncytin proteins are fully assimilated into essential functional networks. Aberrant expression may even cause pathologies. For example, a *syncytin-2* gene variant may predispose to the development of preeclampsia.[87] Total integration of syncytins into molecular pathways entails the risk that aberrant activity of these proteins will lead to disease or at least contribute to disease progression.

As a species, we pride ourselves with having big brains capable of performing very elaborate operations. As far as we know, our brains constitute the most complexly arranged accumulation of matter in the universe. But this complexity comes at a cost. It is highly vulnerable to disruption. During fetal history, the development of brains is sensitive to myriad chemical and physiological inputs—as well as the mothers' states of mind. Evidence is growing that placental malfunction can predispose the brain to psychopathologies that are not manifest until childhood or even adulthood.[88] This means that our vaunted brains are critically dependent on the humble placenta.

Expressed positively, optimal placental function is essential for the development of the unique capacities of human brain and mind. Placentation serves mentalization. Expressed negatively, placental abnormalities have enduring disruptive effects on mental health, affecting cognition, behavior, and mood.[89] Fetal development through preeclamptic pregnancies has been linked to long-term neurobiological sequelae including altered brain vascular diameters[90] and abnormal white matter connections between distant

---

86. Bolze et al., "Contributions of Syncytin," 111–62.

87. Hua et al., "A Tag SNP in Syncytin-2," 265–70.

88. Monk et al., "Prenatal Developmental Origins," 317–44; Kratimenos and Penn, "Placental Programming," 157–64.

89. Figueiro-Filho et al., "Neurological Function," 1–6; Shallie and Naicker, "Placenta as a Window," 41–49.

90. Ratsep et al., "Brain Structural and Vascular Anatomy," 939–45.

brain centres, as defined both structurally[91] and functionally.[92] Experiments have suggested that oxygen deprivation, such as might be experienced with placental insufficiency, leads to altered secretions from placental tissue, and changes to fetal brain biochemistry and structure.[93]

The risk of developing autism spectrum disorder (ASD) may be associated with atypical features of placental morphology (decreased eccentricity of shape, increased maximum thickness and variability). Perhaps these gross changes reflect a reduced capacity to adapt to stresses in the placental environment.[94] The risk of developing ASD is affected by diverse complications of pregnancy[95] and more specifically, by placental pathologies such as acute inflammation, chronic vasculitis, and inadequate perfusion.[96] Placental inflammation in the context of preterm birth may predispose children to ASD, ADHD, and other neurodevelopmental abnormalities.[97]

The connection between environment, placenta, and later manifestation of ASD may be mediated by epigenetic changes that dysregulate genes in the placenta. Some four hundred sites where placental DNA shows altered tagging with methyl groups have been linked to later development of ASD.[98] The risk of developing schizophrenia is affected by genes that are active in the context of prenatal complications affecting placental function.[99]

Our mental capacities may be limited by the contingencies of a less-than-ideal placenta, or of abnormal expression of domesticated genes that once served a viral pathogenic programme. Individuals may be predisposed to enduring struggles with mental health challenges as a result of maternal hypertension or placental dysfunction. The dependence of human brain and mind on (what might be considered) disposable, single-use plumbing emphasizes our rootedness as physical creatures with a contingent evolutionary history. It is easy to forget that we are anchored in biology. It is hubris that distances us from our biological antecedents. Intrinsic to the

---

91. Figueiro-Filho, "Diffusion Tensor Imaging," 801–6.
92. Mak et al., "Resting-State Functional Connectivity," 23–28.
93. Phillips et al., "Treating the Placenta," 9079.
94. Park et al., "Placental Gross Shape," e0191276.
95. Chien et al., "Prenatal and Perinatal Risk Factors," 783–91.
96. Straughen et al., "Association between Placental Histopathology," 183–88.
97. Raghavan et al., "Preterm Birth Subtypes," 17–25.
98. Zhu et al., "Placental DNA Methylation," 2659–74.
99. Ursini et al., "Convergence of Placenta Biology," 792–801.

human condition is the understanding that we are physically vulnerable anthropoid primates.

It is instructive that to the Maori people of New Zealand/Aotearoa, the word for placenta, *whenua*, is also the word for *land*. The Maori bury the placenta, a practice that "reinforces the relationship between the newborn child and the land of their birth."[100] Such earthy vulnerability emphasizes the polarities inherent in our humanness. We must hold our earthiness in mind, despite the distractions and mirages of our technological age. In biblical terms, we are Adam from *adamah*; the earthling from the earth; humans from humus; "we share common ground with the Earth because we are *common ground*."[101] God "knows our frame; he remembers that we are dust."[102]

We are, however, much more than the product of a genetic history modulated by environment. The declaration of God's knowledge of us, as we are formed *in utero*,[103] in all our bewildering variety, requires a response that recognizes both the contingencies of our development and the Creator's supervening care and concern.

The church should be a community where people find acceptance despite weaknesses of cognition and temperament. Many congenital limitations that affect mind are not irreversible, but are ameliorable by loving nurture.[104] When Jesus said, "Do not judge others,"[105] he surely was not proscribing the responsibility to assess moral behavior for its rightness or wrongness; rather he may have been charging his followers to accept the personality quirks—moodiness, anxiety, social remoteness, cognitive dullness—that (for all we know) had their roots in suboptimal intrauterine environments. We are called to bear one another's burdens.[106]

The Christian gospel indicates that creatures characterized by such weakness are loved, called, and destined for transformation and glory. It puts our hominoid physicality into a lustrous perspective. To elaborate on St Paul: just as we wear the likeness of the man made of earth (Adam)—a selfish, territorial, and aggressive hominoid primate, conditioned *inter*

---

100. https://teara.govt.nz/en/papatuanuku-the-land/page-4.
101. Carol Newsome in Richard Bauckham, *Bible and Ecology*, 21.
102. Ps 103:14.
103. Ps 139:13–15.
104. Glover and Capron, "Prenatal Parenting," 66–70.
105. Matt 7:1; Luke 6:37.
106. Gal 6:2.

alia by its intra-uterine environment—so we will wear the likeness of the man from heaven (Christ).[107] We have reflected on our status as glorified apes, and the scandal of grace that allows us to affirm gladly both of the terms that constitute such an apparent paradox (chapter 1). We recognize now that at least some of our diverse susceptibilities may be seen in terms of prenatal development. The incarnation assures us that the Creator has shared in that earthy weakness, has affirmed the value and belovedness of each person, and calls his followers to accept and care for those who have been handicapped by the vagaries of their biology.

6. Human relationality: the ethics of prenatal parenting

Placentation allows mother and fetus to influence each other over an extended timeframe. Bonding between mothers (and fathers) and children starts to develop *in utero*. The strength of both maternal and paternal bonding with their baby *prenatally* anticipates the strength of that bonding *postnatally*.[108] The placenta also plays a central role in mutual maternal-to-fetal and fetal-to-maternal programming. That is, the placenta influences physiology and mental states that flow in both directions.

The advent of the placenta has provided the conditions enabling *prenatal parenting*. Parents "can alter the development of their child, even before birth. . . . The mother's emotional state during pregnancy can have a direct influence on fetal development by fetal programming."[109] The significance of such influence is that the uterine environment during sensitive periods of fetal life alters development with potentially long-term consequences. In particular, neural abnormalities may arise, and these may be poorly reversible.

Maternal stress, anxiety, and depression during pregnancy may have harmful effects on fetal development. The child's growth may be retarded, and he or she may be born earlier than is typical. However, the most widely recognized effects are on the neural system, leading to deficits in emotional state (depression, anxiety), behavior (ADHD, conduct), and cognitive development. The mothers with the 15 percent highest levels of stress have children with double the risk of mental illness relative to all other mothers. These effects may be mediated by hormones (such as cortisol) and signalling

---

107. 1 Cor 15:49.
108. Glover and Capron, "Prenatal Parenting," 66–70.
109. Glover and Capron, "Prenatal Parenting," 66–70.

molecules that control inflammation (called *cytokines*). These signals modify placental biochemistry and the regulation of genes expressed in the placenta. Such genes include *HSD11B1* and *HSD11B2* (responsible for the metabolism of cortisol) and *NR3C1* (that encodes the cortisol receptor).[110] There are, however, differences between populations that may reflect the effects of social environment or of ethnicity.[111]

Fathers have an important role in supporting pregnant mothers, and in protecting them from stress that can adversely affect fetal neurological development. Paternal depression during pregnancy places stress on mothers and has been associated with preterm birth.[112] A significant contribution to maternal stress comes from strained relationships with partners. Pregnant women who reported divorce or separation, serious arguments with partners, or partner emotional abuse, produced children with reduced cognitive ability or heightened fear responses (at fourteen to nineteen months). Paternal hostility accounts for an estimated three quarters of the maternal stress-related effects on infant cognitive and fearfulness scores.[113] In addition, stressful life-events during early pregnancy (in which, again, partner hostility features) have been associated with depressive symptoms or major depression in the offspring at eighteen to nineteen years of age.[114] Hypothesized mechanisms linking parental stress, placental dysfunction, and fetal neurological defects implicate fetal programming mediated by stress hormones (such as cortisol) or inflammation.[115]

Conversely, the fetus conditions the mother. The placenta produces hormones that programme the behavior of the mother. The *PHLDA2* gene is active in trophoblastic cells of the placenta. It is subject to precise regulation and may influence patterns of maternal care. In mice, the activity of the *PHLDA2* gene affects the relative effort spent on nest-binding on the one hand, and on direct attention to the pups (licking, grooming) on the

---

110. Janssen et al., "Role for the Placenta," doi: 10.1111/jne.12373; Glover et al., "Prenatal Maternal Stress," 843–54. In term placentas, high expression of *HSD11B1* is associated with reduced anger, fear, and frustration in young children; high expression of an opposing component of the stress hormone axis, *NCOR2*, has the opposite effect. See Finik et al., "Placental Gene Expression," 783–95.

111. Capron et al., "Maternal Prenatal Stress," 166–72.

112. Glover and Capron, "Prenatal Parenting," 66–70.

113. Bergman et al., "Maternal Stress during Pregnancy," 1454–63.

114. Kingsbury et al., "Stressful Life Events," 709–16.

115. Shallie and Naicker, "Placenta as a Window," 41–49; Dowell et al., "Cellular Stress Mechanisms," 134368.

other. In humans, the paternally derived *PHLDA2* gene copy is silenced. It has been hypothesized that the activity of this gene must be minutely controlled to sustain optimal maternal behaviors. The appropriate window of *PHLDA2* activity promotes placental lactogen production, which signals to increase maternal behavior.[116]

Interactions are summarized in Fig. 13. The biological environment, including diet, is important for placental growth and function, and for fetal growth.[117] We might say that "we are what we (or our parents) eat." In addition, there is a seamless interaction between parental love, placental optimality, and fetal mental development. Our status as being placental mammals, rather than (say) being toads, suggests also that "we are how our parents loved."

FIGURE 13

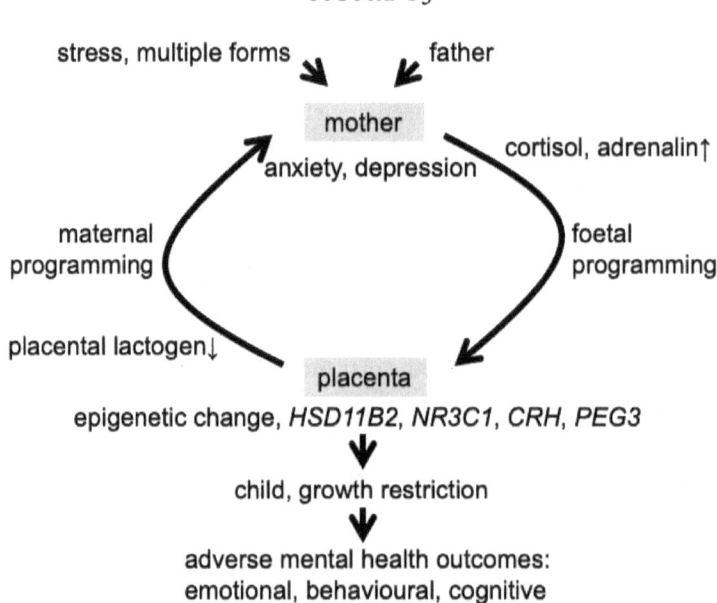

Central role of the placenta in mediating mutual mother-child influences.

But the toad model of human reproductive activity is widespread. A pervasive presupposition in our world is that people should be able to enjoy

116. Creeth et al., "Maternal Care," e2006599.
117. Timmermans et al., "The Mediterranean Diet," 1399–1409.

their own sex lives in any way they choose, so long as it damages nobody else. Promulgation of a mechanical understanding of sex is inherently self-contradictory, oxymoronic. Engagement in sexual activity cannot be dissociated from the calling-to-be of a third party, a new person, who can be profoundly damaged in the absence of an optimal environment of care. The absence of a profound and sacrificial commitment to the well-being of that child is inimical to his or her development through the potential hazards of a nine-month gestation (and beyond, into adulthood). A *laissez-faire* approach to sexual activity carries an increased probability of long-term neural damage to each conceptus, even if that damage does not manifest itself until late adolescence as neuropathology. Worldwide, up to 20 percent of children and adolescents struggle with mental illness.[118] Being a eutherian mammal with potential for highly honed sociality connects the quality of parental love to the efficiency of placental function and the vibrancy of mental health of succeeding generations.

For placental, big-brained, and social creatures, such as humans are, reproduction should occur only in the context of the utmost parental commitment to each other and to the fetus. This commitment of love should continue postnatally, of course. A distinctive ethic that recognizes the demands and opportunities arising from placental biology is to be found in the household codes of the first Christians.[119] Such codes had the *form* of those emanating from Greek philosophers (Aristotle, Xenophon, and Plutarch produced household codes).[120] The Christians adhered to basic norms and forms because they were suspected of sedition and had to demonstrate that they were not anarchists. However, Christian codes had *content* that enjoined radically new, indeed unprecedented commitment to family relationships.

The Greek philosophers addressed elite students only; the Christians sought to encourage and reform their communities at grass-roots level.[121] The Greeks addressed only the males in charge of households. Women, slaves, and children were regarded as property. The Christians addressed husbands and wives (as well as masters and slaves, parents and children) equally as free agents, and this address was articulated in public discourse.[122]

118. Glover et al., "Prenatal Maternal Stress," 843–54.
119. Eph 5:21—6:9; Col 3:18—4:1; 1 Pet 2:17—3:7.
120. Hurtado, *Destroyer of the Gods*, 177.
121. Hurtado, *Destroyer of the Gods*, 170–72.
122. Hurtado, *Destroyer of the Gods*, 177–80; Wright, *Paul and the Faithfulness of God*, 1108, 1375–76.

Contra Greek mores, a revolutionary equality of husbands and wives was promulgated: marital faithfulness applied as much to men as to women.[123] Submission was to be mutual.[124] The Christian codes were modelled on the nature of Christ, and in particular, husbands were enjoined to love their wives as Christ loved the church.[125] Others-directed sacrificial love is the basis for optimizing the flourishing of a society in which the vitality of every generation is placenta-dependent.

---

123. Hurtado, *Destroyer of the Gods*, 166–67.
124. Eph 5:21.
125. Eph 5:25–33.

3

Developing brains
Genes and personal experience

Abstract

Humans have complex brains. These have evolved over a vast phylogenetic history. Scientists are discovering genetic innovations that may have led to the development of novel functionality in neural cells and that may have contributed to brain development over evolutionary time. The science of comparative genomics reveals *when* during evolution each such formative genomic event occurred, and the *mechanism* by which it arose. Evidence is growing that endogenous retroviruses and transposable elements have contributed to the evolution of genetic networks underlying brain functions. However, genetic systems are necessary but not sufficient to account for our mental capacities. For example, our ability to interact as persons (to possess *theory of mind*) is not genetically encoded, but is learned. During infancy and childhood, brains follow normal developmental trajectories only in the context of attentive, loving care-giving. Human brain development and function require personal input. We share in the fullness of being human by interpersonal relationship, and a Christian interpretation of this fact is that human flourishing requires that people know, and are known by, God.

Evolution and Eschatology

Key words

evolution, ERV, transposable element, brain, theory of mind, neglect, species expectant experience, knowing God

POPULAR UNDERSTANDINGS OF SCIENCE have attributed to genes an almost unlimited capacity to determine the development of brain and mind. But our personal histories are the outcome of a complex interplay of genetics and environment.[1] It is so easy to forget about the role of our environment—especially our social environment—in the formation of brain and mind. This chapter will address four issues. We will consider (1) illustrative data describing genetic change during evolution that may have contributed to the development of the human brain; (2) recent studies investigating the role of language; (3) the importance of nurture (as revealed by studies of neglected children) in the formation of each individual's social brain; and (4) implications for a biblical view of humanity as a social being destined for fellowship with God.

Our genes underlie everything that we may achieve with respect to our mental and personal capacities. After all, we have a human genome and not that of a papaya or a wombat. In addition, some very small mutations can have devastating impacts on brain and mind. Apart from the placenta and mammary gland that have developed in their entirety during mammalian evolution (previous chapter), the brain has grown faster than has any other organ.[2] Human brain tissue shows distinctive features, relative to those of other primates, and such features can be observed early in fetal development and in cultured organoids. Human brain tissue manifests increased cellularity, deeper cerebral folds, more pronounced long-distance connections, lengthened mitoses in progenitor cells, and delayed development.[3] Human and chimp brain organoids differ in the way they express a group of genes (some one hundred are expressed differently in the

---

1. Excellent discussions of the interaction of genes with environment are found in Alexander, *Genes, Determinism and God*; and for an updated and less technical account, *Are We Slaves to Our Genes?*

2. See Holmes Rolston, "Care on Earth: Generating Informed Concern," in Davies and Gregersen, *Information and the Nature of Reality*, 227.

3. Gibbons, "New Tools," 705–6; Bermudez-Mora et al., "Differences and Similarities," e18683.

Developing brains

two species), and in the way by which specific (regulatory) regions of the genome are conformed for action.[4]

Our behavior is intimately connected with our biochemistry. The hormone oxytocin communicates between brain cells and sustains social behavior, such as bonding with mates and parenting—and thus provides the conditions that underlie acts of kindness.[5] However, parenting styles and personal histories also affect the way the oxytocin system operates.[6] Genes and experience interact to form us as personal beings.

Our brains have formed over a vast history of evolutionary development. Recent evidence for this established paradigm has accrued from multi-species genome comparisons, an approach that has flourished from about the turn of the century. Molecular geneticists are identifying many genetic changes that have occurred during evolution and that are associated with brain development.[7] I will provide illustrative examples of when and how candidate genetic innovations arose through our evolutionary history. The most recent events described occurred in the lineage specific to humans; the earliest, in an ancestor of all mammals. We must integrate this evolutionary history into our reflections on our status as biological creatures—anthropoid primates—beloved of, and called by, God.

The science of comparative genomics is discovering pointers as to how the human brain has formed over millions of years. Since the time of our last common ancestor with chimpanzees, numerous new genes, including many with putative functions in the brain, have arisen through gene duplication events.[8] Genes that are active in brain cells appeared also in much more distant ancestors. An insertion (of unknown provenance) gave rise to a gene specifying a regulatory RNA (*MIR320B1*). The insertion event occurred in an ancestor that we share with all anthropoid (simian) primates.[9]

Gene activity can also be modified by deletions of segments of DNA. Some seventeen thousand insertions and deletions exist in ape genomes relative to Old World monkey genomes. Sixteen of these affect coding regions of genes acting in brain function; and twenty affect regulatory (enhancer) sequences of genes associated with brain function. For example,

---

4. Kanton et al., "Organoid Single-Cell Genomic Atlas," 418–22.

5. Preston, "Rewarding Nature," 1353.

6. Rilling and Young, "Biology of Mammalian Parenting," 771–76; Baker et al., "Early Rearing History," 11769–74.

7. Mitchell and Silver, "Enhancing our Brains," 23–32.

8. Dennis et al. "Evolution and Population Diversity," 69.

9. McCreight et al., "Evolution of microRNA in primates," e0176596.

the *NEDD9* gene underwent increased activity in cerebellum as a result of a large deletion (1,128 bases), affecting regulatory sequences, that occurred in an ape ancestor. *NEDD9* has been implicated in dendritic spine maintenance, cognitive ability, and hindbrain development.[10]

1. Endogenous retroviruses and the evolution of the brain

We have discussed the capacity of retroviruses to colonize host genomes, and for endogenized retroviral genomes (ERVs) to accumulate to large numbers in them. Retroviral DNA possesses gene-regulating motifs, components of the molecular circuitry that drive the retroviral life cycle. Those motifs may be retained in ERVs over vast expanses of time. They have the potential to perturb the activities of nearby genes. ERVs can rewire genetic networks—for better or worse. Abnormal production of ERV-encoded proteins may contribute to neurological diseases.[11]

Post-mortem studies on brain tissue of Alzheimer's patients revealed that some ERVs, members of the small family ERV-Fc1, are active in the presence of neurofibrillary tangles (markers of pathology). Perhaps the neurofibrillary tangles somehow turn on ERV transcription (that is, they stimulate RNA production from the ERVs), contributing to inflammation and neurodegeneration.[12] A genetic variant close to another member of the ERV-Fc1 family is associated with an autoimmune neurological disease, multiple sclerosis. The effect of this variant is not known, but its correlation with disease development is suggestive. This ERV dates from an ancestor of the African apes.[13] A member of the ERV-W family is located adjacent to the *GABBR1* gene that encodes a receptor for a neurotransmitter (γ-aminobutyric acid, GABA). This ERV has been hypothesized to be of relevance to genetic events underlying the development of schizophrenia, and dates from an ancestor of all ape species.[14]

A class of ERV-like inserts, known as MER41 elements, is non-randomly associated with genes that function in the development of cognition. Many MER41 elements contribute to gene regulation in the brain and their sequences are conserved more than those of other classes of ERV. MER41

---

10. He et al., "Long-Read Assembly," 4233.

11. Gruchot et al., "Neural Cell Responses," 655; Lapp and Hunter, "Early Life Exposures," 100174.

12. Guo et al., "Tau Activates Transposable Elements," 2874–80.

13. De la Hera et al., "Human Endogenous Retrovirus HERV-Fc1," e90182.

14. Hegyi, "GABBR1 has a HERV-W LTR," 5.

elements possess binding sites for numerous transcription factors. The era of MER41 element colonization was earlier than that of the preceding examples. One instance appeared in an ancestor of all extant anthropoid (monkey and ape) species.[15]

ERVs also contribute to brain function by suppressing genes. ERVs themselves are silenced by so-called zinc finger proteins (KZFPs—part of the cellular anti-virus arsenal). But when zinc finger proteins dock on to ERVs, nearby genes are also silenced. This is mediated by an ERV-KZFP-TRIM28 silencing complex. This mechanism contributes to neuronal differentiation.[16]

2. Transposable elements and brain evolution

Transposable elements may also possess regulatory potential—either as an integral property of their characteristic sequence, or as a consequence of mutations that arise after they have inserted into host genomes. Transposable elements have the potential to exert diverse effects on brain cell activity. Epigenetic changes deregulating transposable elements may occur in some cases of autism-spectrum disorder and schizophrenia. Links between transposable element activity and psychiatric disease will be an active area of research in the future.[17]

In neural progenitor cells, multiple members of a phylogenetically young subset of LINE-1 elements can be reactivated as a result of epigenetic change. The hypothesis arising is that this class of transposable elements includes sequences that have reorganized regulatory networks that control the activities of neural genes. One example of such a young LINE-1 arose in an ancestor of the African great apes.[18]

Another class of young transposable elements may have reconfigured gene-regulating networks in brain cells during hominid (great ape) history. This rewiring may be achieved by the proliferation of hominid-specific SVA elements, of which 2,700 copies are dispersed around the human genome.[19] Many SVA elements are located near (or in) genes with neural functions. For example, SVA elements, found only in humans, may modulate the activity

---

15. Nataf et al., "Promoter Regions of Intellectual Disability," 321.
16. Turelli et al., "Primate-Restricted KRAB," eaba3200.
17. Lapp and Hunter, "Early Life Exposures," 100174.
18. Jonsson et al., "Activation of Neuronal Genes," 3182.
19. Levy et al., "Integrating Networks and Comparative Genomics," e1701256.

of the *PARK7* gene[20] and the *FUS* gene[21] (Fig. 14, top two alignments). Variants of these genes are associated with neurodegeneration. *PARK7*, for example, gets its name from Parkinson's disease. Other SVA elements are situated near genes encoding neuropeptides,[22] a γ-aminobutyric acid receptor and a potassium ion channel (Fig. 14, bottom two assignments).[23] These latter inserts entered the primate germline in an ancestor of the African great apes. Future research should clarify the roles of SVA elements during brain morphogenesis.

FIGURE 14

```
SVA element                        CTCTCCCTCT...
                                   ||||||||||
human       ...TCTCACTTCAAGAAATAAGATCCTCTCCCTCT...AAGAAATAAGATGCTGGCTGG...


chimp                ...TCTCACTTCAAGAAATAAGACGCTGGCTGG...
bonobo               ...TCTCACTTCAAGAAATAAGATGCTGGCTGG...
gorilla              ...TCTCACTTCAAGAAATAAGATGCTGGCTGG...
orang                ...TCTCACTTCAAGAAATAAGATGCTGGCTGG...
gibbon               ...TCTCACTTCAAGAAATAAGATACTGGCTGG...
baboon               ...TCTCACTTCAAGAAATAAGATGCTCGCTGG...
drill                ...TCTCACTTCAAGAAATAAGATGCTCGCTGG...
macaque              ...TCTCACTTCAAGAAATAAGATGCTCGCTGG...
green monkey         ...TCTCACTTCAAGAAATAAGATGCTCGCTGG...
snub-nosed monkey    ...TCTCACTTCAAGAAATAAGATGCTCGCTGG...


SVA element                        CTCTCCCTCT...
                                   ||||||||||
human       ...TCAAGCTAAAACAAGAGATGTCGCTCTCCCTCT...AAGAGATGTCCACAAAATTTTG...


chimp                ...TCAAGCTAAAACAAGAGATGTCCACAAAATTTTG...
bonobo               ...TCAAGCTAAAACAAGAGATGTCCACAAAATTTTG...
gorilla              ...TCAAGCTAAAACAAGAGATGTCCACAAAATTTTG...
orangutan            ...TCAAGCTAAAACAAGAGATGTCCACAAAGTTTTG...
gibbon               ...TCAAGCTAAAACAAGAGATGTCCACAAAGTTTTG...
baboon               ...TCAAGCTGAAATAAGAGATGTCCACAAAGTTTTG...
macaque              ...TCAAGCTGAAATAAGAGATGTCCACAAAGTTTTG...
green monkey         ...TCAAGCTGAAATAAGAGATGTCCACAAAGTTTTA...
snub-nosed monkey    ...TCAAGCTGAAATAAGAGATGTCCACAAAGTTTTG
```

20. Savage et al., "Characterisation of the Potential," 101.
21. Savage et al., "Evaluation of a SVA Retrotransposon," e90833.
22. Gianfrancesco et al., "SVA Retrotransposons," 3.
23. Vasieva et al., "Primate Specific Retrotransposons," https://arxiv.org/pdf/1602.07642.

SVA element   CTCTCCCTCT...
                                     |||||||||
human   ...AAGAT**AAAGTTTAGAAACAGA**GCTCTCCCTCT...**AAAGTTTAGAAACAGA**ACCAAA...
chimp   ...AAGAT**AAAGTTTAGAAACCGA**GCTCTCCCTCT...**AAAGTTTAGAAACAGA**ACCAAA...
bonobo   ...AAGAT**AAAGTTTAGAAACAGA**GCTCTCCCTCT...**AAAGTTTAGAAACAGA**ACCAAA...
gorilla   ...AAGAT**AAAGTTTAGAAACAGA**GCTCTCCCTCT...**AAAGTTTAGAAACAGA**ACCAAA...

orang   ...AAGAT**AAAGTTTAGAAACAGA**ACCAAA...
gibbon   ...AAAAT**AAAGTTTAGAAACAGA**ACCAAA...
baboon   ...AAAAT**AAAGTTTAGAAACAGA**ACCAGA...
macaque   ...AAAAT**AAAGTTTAGAAACAGA**ACCAGA...
green monkey   ...AAAAT**AAAGTTTAGAAACAGA**ACCAGA...
marmoset   ...AAAAT**AAAGTTTAGAAGTAGA**ACCAAA...
night monkey   ...AAAAT**AAAGTTTAGAAGCAGA**ACCAAA...
squirrel monkey   ...AAAAT**AATGTTTAGAAGCAAA**ACCAAA...

SVA element (internal)   ...TGCCCGGCCA...
                                     | |||||||
human   ...CCTTTAAA**AATTAAATGAGG**TACCCGGCCG...**AATTAAATGAGG**CAACGCAGGC...
chimp   ...CCTTTAAA**AATTAAATGAGG**TACATGGCCG...**AATT**   **AGG**CAATGCAGGC...
bonobo   ...CCTTTAAA**AATTAAATGAGG**TACATGGCCG...**AATTA**   **AGG**CAATGCAGGC...
gorilla   ...CCTTTAAA**AATTAAATGAGG**TACCCGGCCA...**AATTAAATGAGG**CAGCGCAGGC...

orangutan   ...CCTTTAAA**AATTAAATGAGG**CAACACAGGC...
gibbon   ...CCTTTAAA**AATTAAATGAGG**CAACGCAGGC...
baboon   ...CCTT AAA**AATTAAATGAGG**CAACACAGGC...
macaque   ...CCTT AAA**AATTAAACGAGG**CAACACAGGC...
green monkey   ...CCTT AAA**CATTAAATGAGG**CAACACAGGC...
marmoset   ...CCTT AAA**AATTAAATGAGA**CAACACAGGC...
night monkey   ...CCTT AAA**AATTAAATGAGA**CAACACAGGC...

Insertion sites of SVA elements that may regulate genes with neural functions.

Top to bottom: SVA elements located near the genes encoding *PARK7*, *FUS*, *GABBR2* and *KCNJ6*. Sequences were from the UCSC browser (human), the NCBI (BLAST search; all other species) and https://www.dfam.org/family/DF0001070/model (SVA).

Transposable elements of greater antiquity have altered the activity of genes in brain cells. Corticotropin-releasing hormone responds to stress, and its receptors (CRHRs) show increased activity in people suffering from major depression or anxiety disorders. One of these receptors includes a variant (CRHR2γ) expressed only in Old World primates. This variant was generated following the insertion of a FLAM transposable element in a simian primate ancestor.[24]

The insertion of another ancient FLAM element gave birth to a gene specifying a long non-coding RNA (now called *BC200*; Fig. 15). The FLAM insertion occurred in a simian ancestor. The target site duplications have become altered with the passage of time, but can be reconstructed as "AATTTGA". The *BC200* RNA appears to control protein production in dendrites of neurons.[25]

FIGURE 15

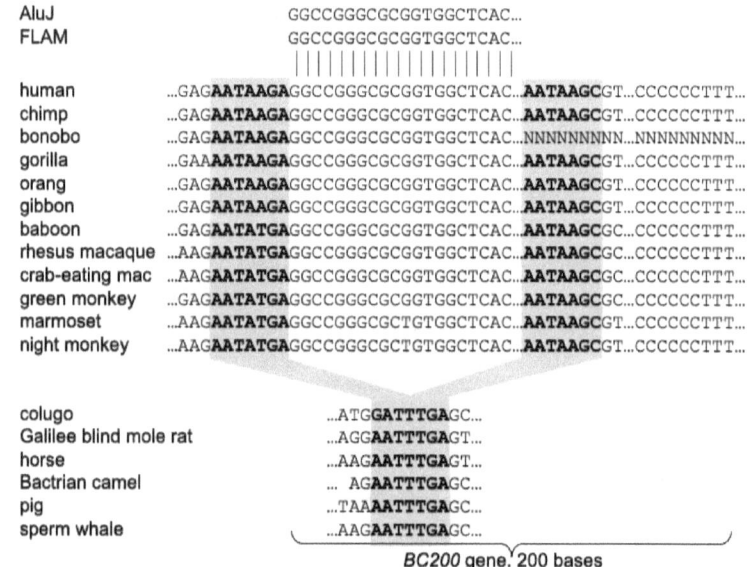

Insertion site of a FLAM element that produced the neuronal BC200 gene.

The insertion event occurred in an ancestor of simian primates (monkeys and apes).

N, sequence gap. Human sequences are from articles (Jang et al. "Regulation of BC200," 393–405; Booy et al., "Comprehensive Analysis," 11575–91) and all other sequences from the NCBI database (BLAST).

Transposable element insertions in more even remote ancestors have generated brain-forming genes. An element of the *sushi-ichi* type

---

24. De Groef et al., "Evolutionary Origin," 318–23.

25. Jang et al. "Regulation of BC200," 393–405; Booy et al., "Comprehensive Analysis," 11575–91.

appeared in an ancestor of all eutherian mammals. Sequences belonging to this jumping gene were incorporated into a gene, now called *SIRH11*, active in brain cells.[26] AmnSINE1 elements proliferated in genomes early in mammalian history. Their sequence content has degenerated beyond recognition, apart from particular sequences that have been retained because they have assumed roles in gene regulation. Many AmnSINE1 elements are shared by all mammals (101 instances, each of which entered the germ-line in a cell ancestral to all extant mammals), by marsupials and eutherians (195 instances), and by eutherians (311 instances).[27] Sequences derived from some of these now orchestrate development of the mammalian brain. Sequences from an AmnSINE1 element are present in an enhancer element that drives brain development in mammals—from platypuses to humans—by turning on the *FGF8* gene.[28] Sequences from another such element—present in marsupials and placental mammals—contribute to a similar outcome by controlling the *SATB2* gene.[29]

These examples provide compelling evidence of human descent from ancestors shared by all humans, by other primate species, and even by all other existing mammals. They illustrate how myriad tiny incremental steps have provided genetic specifications underlying the unimaginable complexity of the human brain. They emphasize our embeddedness in the materiality of biological history—although that materiality is transformed, transcended, and given lasting meaning by relationship with personal agents. It is the thesis of this chapter that genes underlying sociality are themselves regulated by environmental inputs that emanate from communicating, caring, and moral beings.

3. Genes do not explain everything about brain function

A philosophical perspective that could be called *geneticism* posits that genes direct all our behaviors and values. But according to such logic, genes must be responsible for our belief that genes underlie all our behaviors and attitudes. Such reductionistic proposals collapse into incoherence. The idea of the omnipotent gene has been promulgated by the media, and in

26. Irie et al., "LTR Retrotransposon-Derived Gene," 26.

27. Hirakawa et al., "Characterisation and Evolutionary Landscape," 100–110.

28. Sasaki et al., "Possible Involvement of SINEs," 4220–25; Nakanishi et al. "A SINE-Derived Element," e43785.

29. Tashiro et al., "A Mammalian Conserved Element," e28497.

high school and undergraduate education.[30] Perhaps the myth of genetic determinism endures because of its connections with the promise of a technologically attainable utopia: "Genomic science, moving within a space of neoliberal markets, makes the rhetoric of hype and hope indispensable precisely because credible promises generate cycles of investment and value. The determinist gene (or the determinist genome) is part of this social machinery of expectations and profits."[31] The *selfish* gene may in fact be the *neo-liberal* gene, or the *social control* gene. Or even the *money-for-genetics research* gene.

Researchers have sought to ascertain how human and chimp brains differ in gene activity, by characterizing the sets of RNA molecules (the transcriptomes) generated in cells from the two species.[32] Undoubtedly interesting findings will be obtained. But these approaches are inherently ambiguous because they compare systems that differ by two independent variables. Firstly, what is the difference in brain gene activity resulting from *genetics*? To address this question, we would need to study brain transcriptomes of chimps and chimp-reared humans. Secondly, what is the difference in gene activity resulting from *social* and *cultural* environments? To address this, we would have to compare brain transcriptomes of humans who have been denied all social contact with those of humans who have been raised in richly interactive societies. But we cannot banish infants to the wild, only to biopsy their brains. Such experiments are forbidden.

An attempt to perform the "forbidden experiment" was attributed to the Holy Roman Emperor Frederick of Hohenstaufen II (1194–1250). He sought to raise children under conditions of socioemotional (but not physical) deprivation, in order to find out what language they would speak. To quote his chronicler, Friar Salimbene, Frederick ordered "foster-mothers and nurses to suckle and bathe and wash the children, but in no wise to prattle or speak with them; for he would have learnt whether they would speak the Hebrew language (which had been the first), or Greek, or Latin, or Arabic, or perchance the tongue of their parents of whom they had been born." But his experiment produced an unanticipated result. It appears that children raised in the absence of verbal communication failed to flourish and soon died. Salimbene continues: "But he laboured in vain,

---

30. Carver., "Young Adults' Belief," e0169808.
31. Esposito, "Expectation and Futurity," 1–9.
32. Sousa et al. "Evolution of the Human Nervous System," 226–47.

for the children could not live without clappings of the hands, and gestures, and gladness of countenance, and blandishments."[33]

The effects of social interaction on brain development can be studied in less radically intrusive ways. In general, adverse early life experiences, from low socioeconomic status to lack of emotional nurture, affect almost 50 percent of children in the USA, and are associated with major changes in brain function through life. These effects are especially damaging when they occur at sensitive or critical periods of neural development (that is, in neonates and infants). It has been suggested that inconsistent or erratic signals from parents disrupt the development of connections (synapses) between nerve cells. Aberrant development of brain circuitry may contribute to memory loss in children, cognitive decline in middle age, and dementia in old age.[34]

Questions may be asked concerning the effects of reduced socioemotional input on children. For example, how does *deafness* affect the development of children's neural circuitry, and their understanding of other people's mental states, including their feelings, intentions, and beliefs? How does *childhood neglect* affect neural and mental development? Our take-home message in the section following is that good genes are *necessary* for neural and mental functioning, but they are *not sufficient*. The development of human brains requires exposure to personal, indeed spiritual qualities such as love, compassion, and joy.

Language and theory of mind

The highly developed human ability to interpret other people's mind states is known as *theory of mind* (ToM),[35] and its development during childhood is called *mentalization*. Preschool children with specific language impairment struggle with ToM. They show deficits in *cognitive* ToM: the ability to share a focus of intention with another, and to perceive that someone else may understand a situation incorrectly and act consistently on that misunderstanding. They also show deficits in *affective* ToM: the ability to interpret facial expressions and emotions. A hypothesis that naturally arises

---

33. Masson, *Frederick II of Hohenstaufen*, 230.

34. Short and Baram, "Early-Life Adversity," 657–69.

35 Not to be confused with what philosophers mean by a "theory of mind," which is a philosophical account of the nature of mind.

from this association is that *language facilitates the development of ToM*.[36] In support of this suggestion, teacher-led conversations with primary school children about mental states facilitated the development of the children's ToM.[37] We are not born with a genetically specified ToM. The capacity for ToM is *learned*, and *communication* with people who possess ToM is the medium by which it is transmitted across generations.

If exposure to mental-state language is required for the development of ToM, then deafness (in the absence of compensating modes of communication) would lead to defective ToM acquisition. Dutch children with moderate hearing loss showed delayed development of ToM relative to children with normal hearing. The hearing-impaired children showed normal understanding of other people's intentions, but delayed understanding of others' desires and beliefs—presumably because they were exposed to less social communication (or *mental-state talk*).[38] Japanese children with hearing loss also showed delays in the development of ToM. The deficit was related to vocabulary and appreciation of sentence structure (syntax), not to the children's age or non-verbal intelligence. The development of ToM requires that infants engage in conversation that conveys information about other people's thoughts and feelings.[39] In deaf adults who communicate only through a sign language developed in their localized community, ToM remains underdeveloped, even though memory and comprehension are normal, and visual capacities are heightened. A lifetime of social interaction cannot generate ToM in the absence of "participation in a shared linguistic community" and exposure to "mental-state verbs."[40]

Scholars have argued persuasively that the capacity for ToM (or *mind reading*) is learned to the same extent as the capacity to read print. According to Heyes and Frith, "Most, possibly all, human neurocognitive skills are shaped by culture and many are culturally inherited but the parallels between mind reading and print reading are extraordinary." Some of these parallels are indicated, Table 2.) The authors continue: "If a group of human infants managed to survive on a desert island, in a cruel Lord of the Flies-like experiment, they would be no more likely to develop a theory

---

36. Vissers Koolen, "Theory of Mind Deficits," 1734.
37. Bianco and Lecce, "Translating Child Development," 592–605.
38. Netten et al., "Can You Hear what I think?" 588–97.
39. Fujino et al., "Theory of Mind," 77–83.
40. Gagne and Coppola, "Visible Social Interactions," 837.

of mind and become explicit mind readers than to develop a writing system and become literate print readers."[41]

Table 2. Parallels between print- and mind-reading (from Heyes and Frith, 2014)

feature	print reading	mind-reading
brain areas	occipito-temporal	medial prefrontal
developmental disorders	dyslexia	autism spectrum
capacity develops to	late adolescence	late adolescence
cognitive effort needed	executive processes	executive processes
individual variation	environmental > genetic	environmental > genetic
teaching is needed to relate	print to referents and pronunciation	mental states, situations and behavior

It is easy to assume in our technologically driven society that the fullness of humanness is genetically specified. Rather, it is acquired in proportion to the quality of our nurture as social beings. Severe hearing deficiency during infancy leads to compromised incidental learning, difficulties in expressing and regulating emotions, problems in socialization, and internalizing (depression, anxiety) and externalizing (disruptiveness, aggression) behavior. In children with normal hearing and in hearing-impaired children provided with cochlear implants, language proficiency is related to psychosocial development.[42] We possess complex neural pathways for vocal learning and spoken language, perhaps duplicated during evolution from prior pathways dedicated to motor learning.[43] But when infants are exposed to language, they do not learn that language; rather, language forms their social brains.[44]

Neglect and the social brain

The neglect of young children—the absence of input from devoted parents or other caregivers—is a widespread phenomenon with haunting echoes of Frederick's "forbidden experiment." A child's genetic potential to form brain is sensitive to the quality of attentive nurturing he or she receives. Multiple interacting processes—stress and endocrine responses, inflammation and

---

41. Heyes and Frith. "Cultural Evolution," 1243091-96.
42. Netten et al., "Terrible Twos," 495-502.
43. Jarvis, "Evolution of Vocal Learning," 50-54.
44. Halpern. "How Children Learn," 1173-81.

epigenetic change—provide connections between early life stress (including neglect), the development of brain structure, and mental wellbeing.[45]

Childhood abuse, including emotional and physical neglect, influences the development of personality traits (such as fearfulness) that lead to major depression, both in the general population,[46] and in people with schizophrenia.[47] Functional magnetic resonance imaging (MRI) of the brains of depressed or schizophrenic adults engaged in ToM reasoning indicates that, in each case, childhood maltreatment, including neglect, correlates with altered brain activity. In depressed people, the amygdala (a region involved in processing emotions and anxiety) is activated. Perhaps hurtful memories are used as lenses by which depressed people interpret ongoing social interactions.[48] In schizophrenic people, the dorsomedial prefrontal cortex (PFC) (a region associated with the interpretation of other's intentions) is activated. This may indicate difficulties in inferring others' mind-states.[49]

Optimal emotional development requires the formation of connections between the medial PFC and the amygdala. Parental nurture contributes to regulation of infant emotions and responses to stress (a phenomenon known as *parental buffering*). Such nurture may facilitate the development of medial PFC-mediated control of the amygdala during a critical period of neuroplasticity. Once formed, the neural circuits remain stable. Parental separation or neglect may lead to accelerated formation of adult-like medial PFC-amygdala circuitry (possibly with loss of plasticity), internalizing symptoms (withdrawal), deficits in emotion regulation, and potentially, mental health disease (*psychopathologies*).[50]

Childhood abuse, including neglect, is a risk factor for self-inflicted injury[51] and for suicidal behavior.[52] It promotes externalizing behaviors that are related to lower age of initiation of alcohol and cannabis consumption.[53]

---

45. Gonzalez-Mariscal and Melo, "Bidirectional Effects," 97–116; Nemeroff, "Paradise Lost," 892–909.
46. Dannehl et al., "Childhood Adversity," 247–54; Otsuka et al. "Interpersonal Sensitivity," 2559–68.
47. Okubo et al., "Mediator Effect of Personality," 126–31.
48. Hentze et al., "Functional Correlates," 1–11.
49. Quide et al., "Childhood Trauma-Related Alterations," 162–68.
50. Gee, "Sensitive Periods," 87–110.
51. Kavurma et al., "Do Serum BDNF Levels," 130–35.
52. Liu et al., "Associations Between Suicidal Behaviour," 147–55.
53. Proctor et al., "Child Maltreatment," 64–69; Scheidell et al., "Childhood Traumatic

Adverse childhood experiences, especially neglect, have been associated with poor adjustment to high school learning environments,[54] with elevated high school dropout rates[55] and, by affecting *executive functions* (the capacity to focus one's thoughts and to plan for the future), with difficulties in adapting to university life.[56]

Memories of childhood abuse (including physical and emotional neglect) during pregnancy are associated with depression,[57] and with subtle changes in thyroid function (as measured by altered levels of thyroid-stimulating hormone).[58] Compromised thyroid hormone function may affect neural development in the fetus. Indeed, childhood emotional neglect has been associated with increased rates of stillbirth.[59] Childhood maltreatment, most commonly neglect, tends to be transmitted across generations.[60] Mothers who were neglected as children tend to be less attentive to their own infants. Functional MRI shows that such mothers showed heightened responses to their children's cry in the cingulate and insular cortices—areas responsible for empathy and emotion processing. The exaggerated neural activity may represent an aversive response; but regardless of the mechanism, it is clear that early neglect is encoded in long-term neural activity.[61]

Neglect changes brain *structure*. A study using structural MRI showed that childhood neglect leads to reduced right and left caudate volumes (in females, not males). These regions of the subcortex are associated with regulation of cognitive and emotional processes.[62] People who were maltreated as children and who suffer from bipolar disorder possessed decreased volumes of gray matter (cell bodies) in the PFC. Neglect in particular was associated with reduced volumes of gray matter in thalamic regions (which relay information regarding potential threats between the PFC and amygdala), thus perturbing PFC-thalamus-amygdala circuitry.[63] Abuse, including neglect, is a risk factor for eating disorders. Women with eating

---

Experiences," 44–56.

54. Oh and Song, "Mediating Effect of Emotional/Behavioural Problems," 393–402.
55. Morrow and Villodas, "Direct and Indirect Pathways," 327–41.
56. Welsh et al., "History of Childhood Maltreatment," 1091.
57. Inanici et al., "The Relationship between Subjective Experience," 76–80.
58. Moog et al., "Childhood Maltreatment Is Associated," 190–6.
59. Freedman et al., "Maternal Exposure," 459–65.
60. Plant et al., "Association between Maternal Childhood Trauma," 144–50.
61. Wright et al., "Mothers Who Were Neglected," 158–66.
62. Frodl et al., "Childhood Adversity Impacts," 58–65.
63. Duarte et al., "Gray Matter Brain Volumes," 74–80.

disorders who were neglected as children possessed reduced gray matter volumes and white matter (cell connections) integrity in particular areas relative to those who were not maltreated. For example, a fold called the left inferior temporal gyrus processes information regarding body image and shows decreased volume.[64]

In summary, neglect affects multiple circuits in the developing brain. The circuitry considered above emphasizes the limbic ("deep-brain") network. Stress causes accelerated development of the amygdala, leading to abnormal regulation of emotion and stress responses. Sequels to these deficits include various forms of internalizing psychopathology (Fig. 16, sequence on left).[65]

FIGURE 16

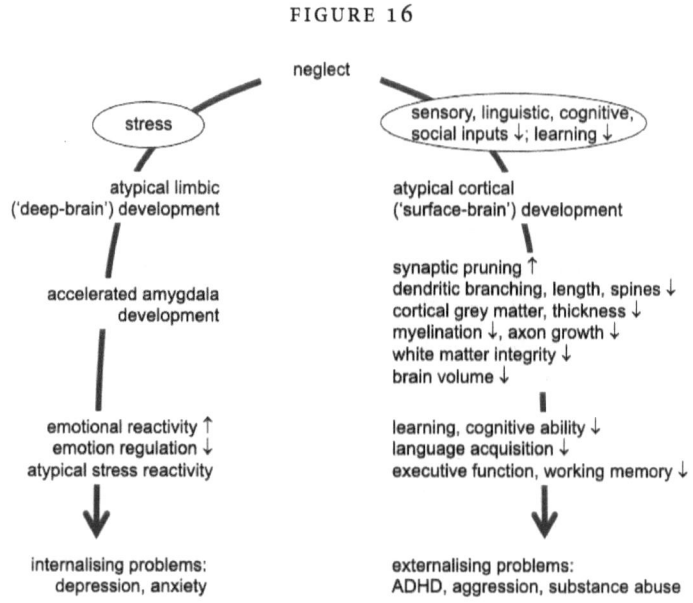

Effects of childhood neglect on development of brain.

Abstracted from McLaughlin et al., "Neglect as a Violation," 462–71; Nelson and Gabard-Durnam, "Early Adversity and Critical Periods," 133–43.

Studies of childhood neglect, as described above, reveal major effects on socioemotional and cerebral development, but some children have been

64. Monteleone et al., "Effects of Childhood Maltreatment," 301–9.

65. McLaughlin et al., "Neglect as a Violation," 462–71; Nelson and Gabard-Durnam, "Early Adversity and Critical Periods," 133–43.

exposed to conditions of deprivation that are even closer to those of the "forbidden experiment." The effects of time spent in understaffed, severely neglectful orphanages (such as those of the Communist era of Romania), and of subsequent adoption into stable families, have been studied in both the UK and the US.

First, the European study. Children who spent more than six months in an orphanage before adoption (relative to children adopted before six months) showed persistently higher incidences of ASD, social disinhibition, inattention, and over-activity. Intellectual ability (as measured by IQ) and ToM were suppressed. There was evidence of epigenetic change (DNA methylation) in the late-adopted group. With time from placement in foster care, such children showed recovery in cognitive performance, although they achieved less educationally. However, a surge of emotional difficulties occurred during young adulthood.[66] Imaging has shown that children adopted from such orphanages showed "profound and enduring" decreases in total brain volume, which became increasingly marked with duration of deprivation. Every month that passed before children were removed from the orphanage and adopted into an enriched family context was associated with a further three milliliters of lost brain volume. These physical changes correlated with suppressed IQ and elevated ADHD risk.[67]

The American study assessed whether the effects of neglect persisted as the children aged from eight to sixteen years. Deficiencies in attention, working memory, and problem-solving persisted through adolescence to sixteen years. Such deficiencies compromise executive function—the ability to focus on issues, to hold relevant information in mind, and to achieve goals. Deficiencies in executive function (in childhood) mediate between neglect (in infancy) and general measures of psychopathology that manifested in sixteen-year olds. The cognitive deficits can, in many cases, be linked with abnormal electroencephalograms (which may reflect the volume of connecting nerve tracts in the brain cortex).[68]

An MRI method (*diffusion tensor imaging*) has been used to investigate the structural integrity of neural connections (white matter tracts) in brain. These are cell extensions, such as axons, that mediate communication

---

66. Kumsta et al., "Severe Psychosocial Deprivation," e830; Sonuga-Barke et al., "Child-to-Adult," 1539–48.

67. Mackes et al., "Early Childhood Deprivation," 641–49.

68. Wade et al., "Global Deficits in Executive Functioning," 1687–94; Wade et al., "Long-Term Effects," 1808–13.

between cells. Neglect impaired the integrity of white matter tracts, especially of the fronto-striatal circuitry and the corpus callosum. White matter abnormalities may reflect defects in the myelination (insulation) of axon fibres. This damage was associated with the development of depression and anxiety. Girls, but not boys, who were fostered into supportive families at two years, showed improvements in emotional symptoms between eight and twelve years.[69]

Children reared in orphanages are deprived of sensory, linguistic, cognitive, and social stimulation. The absence of such inputs may suppress the development of cortical ("surface-brain") circuits. Neglect may lead to extreme pruning of synapses (connections between brain cells), loss of dendritic spines, and suppression of dendritic branching and length. Structural MRI studies showed that institutionalized children had decreased volumes of gray matter, with subsequent thinning of the brain cortex, and of white matter. Loss of myelination leads to loss of white matter integrity and of communication between brain regions. Brain volumes are reduced. The result is loss of learning, language acquisition, cognitive functions, and (via loss of working memory) executive function (the ability to act purposefully) (Fig. 16, sequence on right). After adoption into supportive families, by eight years of age, only white matter volume recovered to normal levels.[70] Extended time in neglectful Romanian orphanages, linked to mental health deficits, even affected the basal levels of inflammation in the children's bodies, and their genetics. Children who develop internalizing psychopathology (anxiety, depression) or general psychological difficulties (such as poor regulation of emotion) may acquire chromosomal abnormalities. The tips of chromosomes (or *telomeres*), required to maintain chromosome stability, become shortened. The mechanisms connecting mental difficulties with inflammation and telomere shortening are not known, but the long-term impacts include elevated risks of developing cardiovascular disease, diabetes, and cancer—and early mortality.[71]

All sorts of claims are made for genetic control of our being. However, genes do not *dictate* the formation of the brain and the way people relate to each other, make love, defend their territories, organize their societies,

---

69. Bick et al., "Effect of Early Institutionalization," 211–19; Bick et al., "Early Deprivation," 140–53.

70. Tibu et al., "Reduced Working Memory," 1850; Bick and Nelson, "Early Experience," e1387; McLaughlin et al., "Neglect as a Violation," 462–71.

71. Tang et al., "Externalizing Trajectories," 104408; Wade et al., "Telomere Length and Psychopathology," 140–48.

practice virtue, or visit savagery upon each other. The multimillion-year-long evolution of genes supporting neural systems can produce only a neural primordium, poised to respond to social inputs that are vulnerable to change. Genes alone produce a human organism. Genes require the influence of loving-kindness to produce a human person. Genes are not sufficient to make us think rationally. Even less are genes sufficient to enable us to think compassionately or justly. Our genetic inheritance by itself "is not enough to enable us to think and act well. Nothing in evolutionary biology leads us to believe that genes make us good. . . . Deep down we are thoroughly compromised, and must make an effort at good, finding the strength to do this, if we ever do find it, somewhere other than in our genes."[72]

I have often been asked the question, "are we still evolving?" The answer is, "Of course—but imperceptibly slowly." Of infinitely greater urgency is the fact that the nurturing of each generation, and the continued vitality of society and of a moral humanity, are extremely vulnerable to cultural, ethical, and religious variations. Societies may collapse precipitously in the face of excessive material expectation, preoccupation with hedonistic pursuits, substance abuse, ideological whim, social conflict, and the neglect of moral imperatives. All of these ethical issues threaten to overwhelm us now, and the gospel of Jesus speaks to all of them. The myth of genetic determinism is a fantasy.

4. Beyond genes: creating social brains

The organization of matter in human brains is not a simple outcome of genetic specification. Brains develop in response to dispositions, values, and visions that science cannot measure. Our interpersonal relationships—both the reality of their existence and the quality of their expression—are invisible to science. The inventory of cues regulating cerebral gene expression might include as core elements love, joy, peace, patience, kindness, goodness, faithfulness, humility, self-control—what St Paul listed as "the fruit of the Spirit."[73]

At this stage we need to clarify some terms. How do contemporary categories of *mind* and *brain* relate to St Paul's description of humans as

---

72. Briggs et al., *It Keeps Me Seeking*, 180.
73. Gal 5:22–25.

constituted by "*body, soul* and *spirit*"?[74] Paul's terminology has given the impression that we made up of three separate components. But the idea that we have a body that is inhabited by an immortal soul or spirit derives from the philosophy of the Greeks (Plato and the later gnostics), not from the faith of the Hebrews. As brain scientist Donald MacKay wrote in 1978, the "teaching of chapter 1 of Genesis is that man 'became' a living soul, not that a 'soul' was coupled to his body as an extra *part*."[75] Biblically, we *are* a soul; we don't *have* one. In MacKay's terms, when we talk of body, mind, and spirit, we are speaking of three "levels of significance" by which we can describe the complex unity that is each one of us. Mental activity is *embodied* in brain just as spiritual activity is *embodied* in mentality.[76]

Our soul or spirit is an emergent property of brain. We do not possess an immortal soul. Christians who have absorbed Plato's postulate of an immortal soul might wonder: "what then of my hope for immortal life?" The answer is at the center of Christian faith: our hope beyond this life is not for the survival of a soul, but for the *resurrection of the body*, the transformation of the whole person. And this is guaranteed, by the faithful Creator God, as an element of God's continued creative activity.[77]

During the last few hundred years, "soul-body" talk has changed to "mind-brain" talk.[78] The nature of the unitary reality of mind and brain is indicated by Malcolm Jeeves who wrote, "cognitive processes are embedded in our brains" even as "cognition and behaviour sculpture our brains."[79] And it is now well recognized that our social environment, habitual behavior, beliefs, and hopes mold our brains. Our brains and minds (including

---

74. 1 Thess 5:23.

75. See Donald MacKay, "Brain Research and Human Responsibility," in Henry, *Horizons of Science*, 180.

76. See Donald MacKay, "Brain Research and Human Responsibility," in Henry, *Horizons of Science*, 181.

77. See Donald MacKay, "Brain Research and Human Responsibility," in Henry, *Horizons of Science*, 183–84; for Tom Wright on Plato; *Surprised by Hope*, 36, 80, 160; on resurrection as new creation, *Surprised by Hope*, 228, 259; "throughout the Jewish and early Christian writings in which resurrection plays a central role we find it correlated closely with belief in the one god as creator," *Resurrection of the Son of God*, 544; also 353, 358–59, 548, 680–81, 729–30.

78. See Malcolm Jeeves, "The Emergence of Human Distinctiveness: The Story from Neuropsychology and Evolutionary Psychology," in Jeeves, *Rethinking Human Nature*, 177–78.

79. See Malcolm Jeeves, "The Emergence of Human Distinctiveness: The Story from Neuropsychology and Evolutionary Psychology," in Jeeves, *Rethinking Human Nature*, 187.

our spiritual awareness) are formed by bottom-up (genetic) and top-down (personal) realities.[80] Everything that we have considered in this chapter relates to the formation of the entire, undivided person, including those neurally embedded mental aspects of our being that have traditionally been known as *soul* and *spirit*.

Science cannot directly engage with or measure the personal aspect of our existence. But mind leaves its formative mark on the matter that constitutes brain. The physical anatomy and biochemistry of our brains are molded by the non-quantifiable properties of the non-material love expressed by the non-objectivizable persons who have nurtured us. No wonder that physicist Andrew Steane insists that the world is deeply personal.[81] Several imperatives follow.

Bringing up our children

The development of children's prosocial behavior (their *socialization*) is not innate but learned. A virtue such as *helping* is facilitated not merely by verbal encouragement and rewards, but by the way children observe those who have learned to be helpful before them.[82] The *problem-solving determination* of eighteen-month-old infants is enhanced by watching adults persist with a problem.[83] Even *attending to faces* is itself learned by visual exposure to faces, which enables the formation of a dedicated brain region, located in the superior temporal sulcus.[84] Genes can provide only the conditions that make *learned* social behavior possible.

The most God-like, creative thing humans can do is to provide the conditions of love and support that optimally support neural and mental (including social) development in their children. From birth (if not during development *in utero*, when they learn to recognize their mothers' voices),[85] children's brains are formed by the environment of love, faith, and hope in which they are nurtured. We are enabled to love, show compassion, and

---

80. See Malcolm Jeeves, "The Emergence of Human Distinctiveness: The Story from Neuropsychology and Evolutionary Psychology," in Jeeves, *Rethinking Human Nature*, 180–81.
81. Steane, *Faithful to Science*, 1, 50, 114.
82. Dahl "How, Not Whether," 72–76.
83. Leonard et al., "Infants Make More Attempts," 1290–94.
84. For example, as shown in macaques: Arcaro et al., "Seeing Faces," 1404–12.
85. Ferrari et al., "Ultrasonographic Investigation," 354.

pursue moral visions only because we learned our humanity from others. Reproduction itself is hardly creative; the slugs and wombats do it. From what has been presented above, it is misleading to call it *procreation*. What is God-like, truly creative, is the way in which parental love and attentiveness are poured into children (especially in those exhausting early years!), generating neural networks and minds, dendrites and character, synapses and patterns of kindness, that underlie a lifetime of goodness.

Self-perpetuating cycles of parental neglect have produced multitudes of children endowed with enormous genetic potential, but whose mental and socioemotional development is disrupted. Childhood maltreatment is a global epidemic. Studies in Germany and the United States found that almost one quarter of people in the general population have experienced some form of childhood maltreatment. In Germany the most common forms of abuse were emotional (7.1 percent) and physical (9.0 percent) neglect.[86] When neglect is experienced during sensitive or critical periods of brain development, the neural and mental damage inflicted in the first few years of life will be poorly reversible. However, studies with Romanian (neglected) orphans who were subsequently placed into high-quality foster care have shown that at least some of the negative effects are ameliorable. Neglected-then-fostered children who were exposed to adversities as adolescents developed fewer externalizing psychopathologies (aggression, ADHD) than did children who were not fostered.[87] There is hope.

In 2020, California became the first state to screen for childhood abuse. This programme is based on the expectation that "early detection and early intervention improve outcomes."[88] Debate exists, however, over whether the state can sustain such initiatives, about how to intervene in cases of chronic domestic violence, and about how to identify those children who are resilient in the face of adversity. Loving families create healthy children at no expense to the state. But the breakdown of family structures costs the state billions of dollars in health and mental-health bills. The quality of home life is what ecologists call an *externality*—a value that exists outside the market system and that is therefore often ignored. Herein lies a priority for pastoral mission in a broken society.

---

86. Witt et al., "Child Maltreatment in Germany," 47; Lippard and Nemeroff, "Devastating Clinical Consequences," 20–36.

87. Wade et al., "Stress Sensitization," 5771.

88. Underwood, "Screen for Childhood Trauma," 498.

Developing brains

The survival and viability of society

The nature-versus-nurture, genes-versus-environment dichotomy is dead. Genes are necessary but insufficient when it comes to the creation of social brains. It follows that the possession of human genomes cannot guarantee the perpetuation of human society. The evolution of genes or changes in gene frequencies—or indeed targeted editing of the germline—can have infinitesimally small effects on overall human social well-being.

Intense socioemotional input is required for optimal language acquisition, cognition, ToM, mental health, gray- and white-matter formation, and brain volume. It follows that the geneticistic claims sometimes made for genes (that natural selection is responsible for human reciprocity, ethics, virtue, love, . . .) must be seen as ungrounded mythology. Genes in human brains produce virtuous and loving human persons *only* when their expression is regulated by the nurture of those who have themselves learned and practised virtue and love. The data reviewed above indicate that a rich social environment optimizes expression of those genes that underlie the operation of the social brain.

Westerners live and think in the shadow of Enlightenment individualism. There is great wisdom in the African proverb *umuntu ngumuntu ngabantu*, which may be translated, "a person is a person through other persons."[89] Perhaps Westerners have lost the sense that the potent dynamic of communal cohesion creates persons. We seem to live under the presupposition that "every man is an island," a bundle of rights to be heroically defended. But such individualism must be seen as idiosyncratic to Enlightenment ideologies and to be self-defeating. From an African perspective, the saying, "a person is a person through persons" is "opposed to all kinds of individualism" and "collectivism of a European kind." It stresses that community is not "an aggregated sum of individuals." There is an "ontological independence to human society." African thought starts with society and moves to individuals, in the sense that society is more than the sum of myriad atomistic parts. It is only in the context of human society that we can be human beings at all.[90]

An English-language equivalent might be "humans making humans human."[91] Such communitarian thinking should be native to Christians,

---

89. De Gruchy, *Christianity and Democracy*, 191.
90. Villa-Vicencio and De Gruchy, *Doing Ethics in Context*, 29.
91. Evans, *What Is a Human?* 159.

blessed as they are by membership in the body of Christ. John Polkinghorne has said that "the notion of person can be discriminated from that of individual by the former adding to the latter's internal states a network of external relationships."[92] A person is a focus of love and care, given and received; an Enlightenment individual is a paranoid bundle of rights. Colin Gunton has also emphasized the communitarian basis of personhood: "To be a person is to be a distinct and particular entity, albeit one whose being is constituted only through relatedness."[93]

Descartes famously stated that "I think therefore I am." It may be more meaningful to affirm that *"I am known* therefore I am." Ultimately, "I think" only because "I am known." Indeed, I can think scientifically only because I am known personally. But the immateriality of "knowing" means that it can be overlooked by scientists and journalists (and consumers), who focus on measurable quantities. C. S. Lewis seemed to point to the vulnerability of our continued existence as social beings in his Narnia stories. When Aslan called the Talking Beasts into existence, he gave them Narnia and himself, but warned them: "The Dumb Beasts whom I have not chosen are yours also. Treat them gently and cherish them but do not go back to their ways lest you cease to be Talking Beasts. For out of them you were taken and into them you can return."[94] The implication is clear. Just as Narnia's Talking Beasts could lose their gift of sapience and moral agency, so human sociality could be lost through neglect of self-giving and self-forming relationality.

David Bentley Hart expresses a similar understanding. "When the aspiring ape ceases to think himself a fallen angel, perhaps he will inevitably resign himself to being an ape, and then become contented with his lot."[95] The perpetuation of *Homo sapiens* as human *persons* (rather than as merely genetically determined human organisms) is only as assured as our self-understanding as irreducibly relational beings.

Here is a thought experiment, modelled on the "forbidden experiment" of the unholy Roman Emperor Frederick II. Imagine that one could place a group of neonates in a desert island (that Lord of the Flies-type

---

92. Polkinghorne, *Science and Christian Belief*, 157; or, as Spencer states (discussing Jacques Maritain), a person (as opposed to an individual) is someone "distinct and inherently relational"; in *The Evolution of the West*, 132.

93. Gunton, *Christ and Creation*, 73.

94. Available at https://gutenberg.ca/ebooks/lewiscs-magiciansnephew/lewiscs-magiciansnephew-00-h.html (Ch X); sequel at https://gutenberg.ca/ebooks/lewiscs-lastbattle/lewiscs-lastbattle-00-h.html (Chs X, XIV).

95. Hart, *Atheist Delusions*, 230.

scenario, mentioned above) such that they could grow up in the absence of any personal and social input from previous generations. And imagine that they survived to produce a breeding population. They would not learn language or ToM, or develop a social brain. Our hypothesis is that, in that one isolated generation, language, rationality, sociality, and culture would be set back tens or hundreds of thousands of years—all with no change in the genetic endowment of the players. People have wondered about similar scenarios and their consequences in the case of feral children, who (supposedly) have been raised by animals in the wild and who act like animals. In general, it is challenging to authenticate genuine cases of this phenomenon.[96] However, the well-documented story of Genie, a deeply traumatised girl who was incarcerated, alone and from infancy, in a locked room in Los Angeles in the 1960s, points to the hauntingly tragic effects of isolation: the inability to acquire a fully human personality or to enter society. Following her discovery, Genie made painfully limited progress towards socialization, until the squabbling of scholars led to her institutionalization and disappearance from public view.[97] In our molecules-and-genes-besotted world, we should take seriously the hypothesis that humanness is profoundly sensitive to the creative role of immaterial, interpersonal knowing. Subjectivity is objectively real—but fragile.

Knowing God

The theme of knowing God is deeply rooted in the Hebrew Scriptures.[98] When it comes to the question of engaging with God, senior scientists state that God is not to be described analytically but known.[99] God is not a hypothesis to be tested but a person to be known.[100] The mental endeavor required to come to terms with the mysteries of quantum physics fits well

---

96. https://raisedwild.wordpress.com/; https://owlcation.com/social-sciences/Feral-Children-Fact-or-Fiction; https://rationalwiki.org/wiki/Feral_child.

97. https://www.psychologytoday.com/nz/blog/the-superhuman-mind/201707/the-feral-child-nicknamed-genie; https://www.theguardian.com/society/2016/jul/14/genie-feral-child-los-angeles-researchers.

98. Wright, *Paul and the Faithfulness of God*, 987–88; Old Testament instances of the theme of knowing include Isa 11:9; Jer 9:24, 31:33–34.

99. Steane, *Faithful to Science*, 21, 103.

100. Briggs et al., *It Keeps Me Seeking*, 17, 28, 348.

with the kind of theism of the hidden God who requires commitment to be known.[101]

And the claim is made also in the opposite direction: we are known by God.[102] The author of Psalm 139 perceived a close connection between God's knowledge of him and his lifelong development from unformed substance *in utero* to his thoughts, speech, and actions as an adult. You know me; you know everything I do; you know all my actions; you know what I will say; when my bones were being formed in secret . . . you knew.[103] In other words there is a connection between God's knowledge of me and my coming-to-be as a person. Accordingly, Steane describes his experience of Christian faith as a dawning realization that I am known by someone.[104]

Theologian Colin Gunton makes the connection between mutual knowledge—involving God and us—and the full development of our personhood. He has written, "We come to know ourselves most surely as we see ourselves in varying relations with God, our creator and redeemer."[105] In other words, the fullness of self-knowledge, of personhood, arises from engagement with God. Gunton continues, "without the knowledge of God as our creator and redeemer, we are unable to know ourselves as we truly are" and "we know God because and as the Father comes into free relation with us and the world though his Son and Spirit."[106] And molecular biologist Neil Messer states, "God creates human persons by calling them forth out of nothing to the dignity of fellowship. We come to know ourselves as selves by virtue of the encounters in which others call us by name. Our personal identity is to be understood in historical and relational terms."[107]

If knowing other humans confers upon us the richness of humanness, then it might be suggested, analogously, that knowing God confers upon humans the life of God's promised new age, the *zoe aionios*. The medium through which knowledge of the divine Mind (we could call it a spiritual ToM) is imparted is the divine Word, Jesus.[108] Key to this understanding is

---

101. Briggs et al., *It Keeps Me Seeking*, 344.

102. New Testament emphasis on God's knowledge of his people is found in Gal 4:9; 1 Cor 8:1–3; 13:12; 2 Tim 2:19.

103. Ps 139:1–5, 23 (knowing); cf 13–16 (creation, being).

104. Steane, *Faithful to Science*, 110.

105. Gunton, *Christ and Creation*, 73.

106. Gunton, *Christ and Creation*, 74.

107. Messer, *Christian Ethics and Selfish Genes*, 81.

108. Jesus is the divine Word (John 1:1, 14; 1 John 1:1; Rev 19:13); underlying St

Jesus' prayer, spoken on the night of his betrayal, in which he stated that *"eternal life is to know you,* the only true God, and to know Jesus Christ whom you sent."[109] Here is a clear statement that *eternal life* equates to *knowing* God, that *living* and *knowing* are inseparable, if not equivalent. Indeed, the "biblical understanding of life connects it with knowing—existential knowing. It thus implies entering into relationship—with God, with other persons and, to a lesser extent with things." The fullness of life then "consists in cognitive and responsive relationships"[110] with those who were persons before us: our parents, families, communities, and ultimately, the God who is love. Life is not a property of an object existing is lonely isolation.

Similarly, when St Paul articulated his deepest yearnings, he gave first place to knowing God, and linked that with the experience of knowing the power of Christ's resurrection (transformation within daily life), and ultimately with the hope of resurrection (transformation to the life of God's promised new age).[111] Wright's translation stresses the knowing-living connection: Paul's passion is "knowing him, knowing the power of his resurrection, and knowing the partnership of his sufferings . . . that I may arrive at the final resurrection of the dead."[112]

Our understanding of *being* and *living* as dependent on *knowing* is firmly anchored in biology. This connection has been developed in this chapter and has been articulated compellingly in recent surveys of the relationship between sociality and physical health. Current understandings are that for social animals, *knowing* is inseparable from *living* or *being*. Atzil and colleagues outline the thesis that social animals are those that depend on other individuals for effective regulation of their physiological processes. (Physiological regulation by others is called *allostasis*.) Social bonds are necessary for *survival*. *Knowing* (in a way appropriate to the capacities of different species) is needed for *living*. This hypothesis is supported by the developing understanding that there is an overlap of neural systems for sociality and allostasis or metabolic regulation. However, as Atzil and colleagues state, "empirical data suggest that humans are born without the neural infrastructure that supports adult sociality." It follows

---

Paul's claim that "we however have the mind of Christ" (1 Cor 2:16, GNT).

109. John 17:3; the "knowing-living" connection is enunciated clearly in 1 John 5:20.
110. Spanner, *Biblical Creation and the Theory of Evolution*, 71.
111. Phil 3:10–12.
112. Wright, *Paul and the Faithfulness of God*, 832.

that "neural circuits involved in social processing ... are not innate and ... early social experience effectively determines their functional outcome (as well as behavior) in adulthood." Thus the social environment is essential in determining mature brain structure and function and in forming social concepts (*mummy, face*), social competencies (cooperative interactions), joint attention, ToM, cognitive development, abstract concepts (love, pride, god), and culture. Ultimately, "the entire brain is wired with respect to the social environment."[113]

Christian faith has made the extraordinary discovery that God is no exception to the knowing-living interdependence. C. S. Lewis wrote that, "we learn from the doctrine of the Blessed Trinity that something analogous to 'society' exists within the Divine being from all eternity."[114] Biblical faith brings us to a God who cannot exist except in community. This God is essentially communitarian. To quote Gunton again: "The one who is known by virtue of his free and personal relatedness to the world is one who is a relational being in himself. God, that is to say, is a communion."[115] A God who is personal cannot exist as a lonely monad. No conception of a solitary god, a divine anchorite, can be God. "To be God is to be a communion of giving and receiving."[116]

The Eastern Orthodox theologian John Zizioulas has stated this insight clearly. He wrote of "the ontological reality of communion," that is, the reality of inter-personal knowing. He stated that "it is communion that makes beings 'be': nothing exists without it, not even God."[117] Communion, fellowship, knowing is an inseparable concomitant of life. The amazing concept of the *triune* God applies this understanding to the transcendent Creator, who in eternal joyful loving fellowship lives eternally. The nature of

---

113. Atzil et al., "Growing a Social Brain," 624–36. See also Snyder-Mackler et al., "Social Determinants of Health," eaax9553, who state that "Social adversity is linked to a remarkably broad set of conditions, including diseases as distinct as tuberculosis, diabetes, cardiovascular disease, and cancer." This connection is not limited to humans, but is seen in social animals (other primates, orcas and dolphins, hoofed animals such as horses and sheep, elephants, and hyraxes), in which there are "strong links between the social environment and mortality risk, that parallel those from long-term studies in humans." There is a general pattern of "greater survival with greater social integration," and "social environments both in early life and adulthood, are key determinants of lifespan variation in humans and other social animals."

114. Lewis, *Problem of Pain*, 17.

115. Gunton, *Christ and Creation*, 74.

116. Gunton, *Christ and Creation*, 89.

117. Quoted in Polkinghorne, *Science and Christian Belief*, 159.

Developing brains

God as Trinity greatly illuminates the perspectives it gives on our humanity. The divine knowing-is-living is extended to us as creatures. As Hutchings and McLeish say, "the Bible presents God as being relational as part of his very essence. The Trinity created us to *join in* with this relationship. We almost unbelievably, are invited into the Trinity relationship."[118] And in so knowing, we acquire the *zoe aionios*, the life the new age.

Human genes generate a neural substrate that becomes organized into a social brain only following reception of scheduled environmentally (socially) sourced morphogenetic signals. Human brain development is not autonomous but is contingent upon *species-expectant experience*,[119] the anticipation of necessary developmental cues that arise outside the individual. Longitudinal studies indicate that human flourishing ("complete human well-being") requires social inputs. These include participation in a religious community.[120] We are incomplete in ourselves, and this is reminiscent of St Augustine's realization that "God . . . you have made us for yourself, and our hearts are restless till they find their rest in you."[121] A Christian interpretation of the requirements for flourishing is that knowing God is a vital instance of fully human species-expectant experience: growth towards the full potentiality of each individual awaits the transformative experience of encounter with God.

A hope-filled observation is that, in adulthood, the human brain has been observed to retain a degree of plasticity—the capacity to undergo reorganization—during training in socio-affective skills, such as compassionate attitudes, and in socio-cognitive skills, such as ToM. This has been shown by structural MRI studies of brains of people who have engaged in mental exercises for three-month periods. Areas of the cerebral cortex respond to training by undergoing increases in thickness.[122] From this analogy, it may be posited that the experience of knowing God has an enduring capacity to change, mold, and reconfigure our brains and minds. Some may find this approach excessively brain- or matter-focused. I am not qualified to speculate on all the ways by which the Spirit of God may transform people and

---

118. Hutchings and McLeish, *Let There be Science*, 157.

119. McLaughlin et al., "Neglect as a Violation," 462–71; Nelson and Gabard-Durnam, "Early Adversity and Critical Periods," 133–43.

120. VanderWeele, "On the Promotion," 8148–56; human flourishing includes also physical and mental health, meaning, purpose, character, virtue, and close social relationships.

121. Lane, *Lion Concise Book of Christian Thought*, 43.

122. Valk et al., "Structural Plasticity of the Social Brain," e1700489.

leave the divine imprint on their minds. But the way by which relationship forms brain and mind is at the very least a powerful analogy.

To conclude, human brains require human genes. But the development of the human social brain, and the ability to function in a human society, are contingent upon species-expectant interpersonal knowing. Jesus extended the formative effect of "knowing" beyond human society: "Now that you have known me, you will know my Father also."[123] The structure of my brain—from which my personhood, values, loves, and yearnings arise—will endure beyond the dissolution of my body to find new form in the new creation. It has been formed by God's knowledge of me and by my painfully clouded and incomplete knowledge of him.

---

123. John 14:7.

4

Immunity as unity in community

Theology in immunology

Abstract

The immune system consists of an innate arm (that is largely pre-programmed in its activity), and an adaptive arm (that learns on the job). Over phylogenetic time, ancient repetitive elements have contributed in many ways to genetic function underlying immunity. Conventionally inherited genes underlie the capacities of innate immunity, but inherited genes underlie only the *potential* capacities of adaptive immunity, which requires extensive education before it can engage specifically with the endless variety of molecules thrown up by the environment. For example, in B cells, *three* antibody genes can generate an *uncountable* diversity of protective antibodies. This paradox arises from the fact that in each developing B cell, antibody genes are randomized, and potentially useful ones selected. This system demonstrates the sheer power of natural selection. It demonstrates the fallacy of genetic determinism, as antibodies develop only by engagement with an unspecifiable diversity of molecules originating beyond our bodies. The unity-in-diversity of immune cells provides a model of the collaborating members who constitute the body of Christ. The immune system is a health/non-health discriminator, modelling the church's role of working to bring wholeness to the world.

Key words

immunity, natural selection, genetic determinism, body of Christ, unity, diversity, life-giving, interactive, dynamic development, pathology, discrimination, wholeness

OUR IMMUNE SYSTEM IS the diverse community of specialised cells that protect our bodies from microbial invasion. It features in immunization, transplantation medicine, allergic and autoimmune disease, and cancer therapy.[1] Immune activity falls into two broad classes. One class is said to be *innate*: we are born with it. The other is *adaptive*: it learns how to function only by engaging with molecules (antigens) in our environment.

Over evolutionary time, immune systems have developed by the Darwinian process of *natural selection*. Random variation (by mutation) arises in the genome. Variants are screened by environmental pressures, and variants that promote an organism's survival and reproductive success are perpetuated (or *selected*). Potent sources of variation are genome-modifying units of parasitic DNA: endogenous retroviruses (ERVs) and transposable elements.[2] They have continually modified immune system function, in both its normal and pathological operations, as illustrated below.

1. Innate immunity

The *innate immune system* uses stereotypical means to control infectious agents or effect healing following injury.[3] Cells are pre-programmed to engulf and destroy particles (such as bacteria) by the phylogenetically ancient process of *phagocytosis*. They release weapons of mass destruction (reactive forms of oxygen, proteases, and toxic peptides) to kill microbes—often with collateral damage to surrounding tissue.

The immune system and the ever-changing microbial world are locked into an arms race. The immune system possesses the capacity to evolve rapidly because randomly accumulated ERVs and transposable elements provide motifs in the genome that can be recruited at short notice

---

1. Pulendran and Davis, "Science and Medicine of Human Immunology," eaay4014.
2. Maraska et al., "Sophisticated Transcriptional Response," 3201.
3. Huber-Lang et al., "Innate Immune Response," 327–41; Zundler et al., "Immune Cell Circuits," 129–36.

into regulatory circuits. These motifs bind proteins called *transcription factors* that regulate the activity of genes, including those with immunological functionality.[4]

Many ERVs contribute to circuits that control genes involved in innate immunity. Interferons (IFNs) are proteins that orchestrate defence against viruses. In humans, IFN-γ induces the production of a protein known as AIM2, which is a component of a structure (the *inflammasome*) that detects viral DNA and triggers protective inflammatory responses. The *AIM2* gene is activated by signals that emanate from a nearby ERV-related MER41 element (Fig. 17, top). This MER41 sequence entered primate genomes in an ancestor of the anthropoid primates. The insertion site is depicted in Fig. 17, bottom.

FIGURE 17

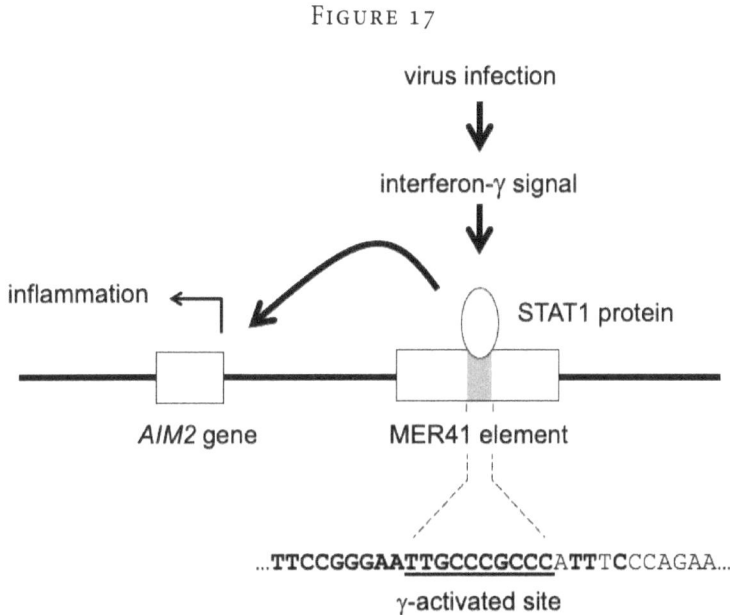

---

4. Maraska et al., "Sophisticated Transcriptional Response," 3201.

MER41B		TGTCAGAGGC...TAACA
human	...TGTATATA	TG**CTTTT**GAGGC...CAACA**CTTTT**AGATACCCTC...
chimp	...TGTATATA	TG**CTTTT**GAGGC...CAACA**CTTTT**AGATACCCTC...
gorilla	...TGTATATA	TG**CTTTT**GAGGC...CAACA**CTTTT**AGATACCCTC...
orang	...TGTATATA	TG**CTTTT**GAGGC...CAACA**CTTTT**AGATACCCTC...
gibbon	...TGTATATA	TG**CTTTT**GAGGC...CAACA**CTTTT**AGATACCCTC...
baboon	...TGTATATA	TG**CTTTT**GAGGC...CAATG**CTTGT**AGATACCCTC...
macaque	...TGTATATA	TG**CTTTT**GAGGC...CAATG**CTTGT**AGATACCCTC...
snub-nosed mo	...TCTATATA	TG**CTTTT**GAGGC...CAACG**CTTGT**AGAAACCCTC...
marmoset	...TGTATATA	TG**CTTTT**GAGGC...CAACA**CTTTT**TGATGCCCTC...
Ma's night mo	...TGTATATA	TG**CTTTT**GAGGC...CAACA**CTTCT**AGATGCCCTC...
capuchin	...TGTATATA	TG**CTTTT**GAGGC...CAACA**GTTTT**AGATGCCCTC...
tarsier	...TGTGTGTG	TG**CTTTT**AGATGCCCTA...
galago	...TGTA ATC	TG**CTTTC**GGATCCCCTC...
gray mouse lemur	...TGTATATATGT G**CTTTT**AGATGCCCTG...	
aye-aye	...TGAAATG	TG**CTTTT**AGATGCCCGC...
colugo	...TG TATA	TG**CTGTT**ACATGCCCTC...
Chinese tree shrew	...TGTGTGCC	TG**CTTTG**AAGTGCTCTC...
naked mole rat	... TCTACA	TG**C TTG**ACATGCTCTC...

ERV that drives AIM2 gene expression.

Top: Sequences in an ERV (a MER41 element) recruit a transcription factor (STAT1) that induces the *AIM2* gene, involved in inflammatory responses.

Bottom: the insertion site of the MER41 element. The target site and its tell-tale duplications, that bracket the ERV, are shaded and in bold type. (The example is from Chuong et al., "Regulatory Evolution," 1083–87.)

Many genes that participate in innate immunity are regulated by sequences in MER41 elements. Convergently, similar ERVs have been co-opted in other mammals (bats, carnivores, cattle) to provide enhancers for IFN-inducible responses.[5] The recruitment of ERV-derived sequences as modifiers of immune function is a recurring story.

Similar findings have been obtained with innate immune cells called *dendritic cells*, involved in immune surveillance. In response to bacterial endotoxin, many genes are activated from sequences present in ERVs and transposable elements. Some of these are ancient, such as unique MIR elements shared by humans *and* mice. Others are more recent, belonging to subtypes found only in primates *or* rodents.[6]

---

5. Chuong et al., "Regulatory Evolution," 1083–87.
6. Donnard et al., "Comparative Analysis of Immune Cells," 381–94.e7.

Inflammation may spiral out of control when infection spreads through the vascular system. In patients with *septic shock*, many ERV loci are expressed in a way that reflects immune perturbations. Such ERVs may generate double-stranded RNA, and trigger IFN-mediated innate immunity. One such ERV has resided in the genome since an ancestor of monkeys and apes (Fig. 18).[7]

FIGURE 18

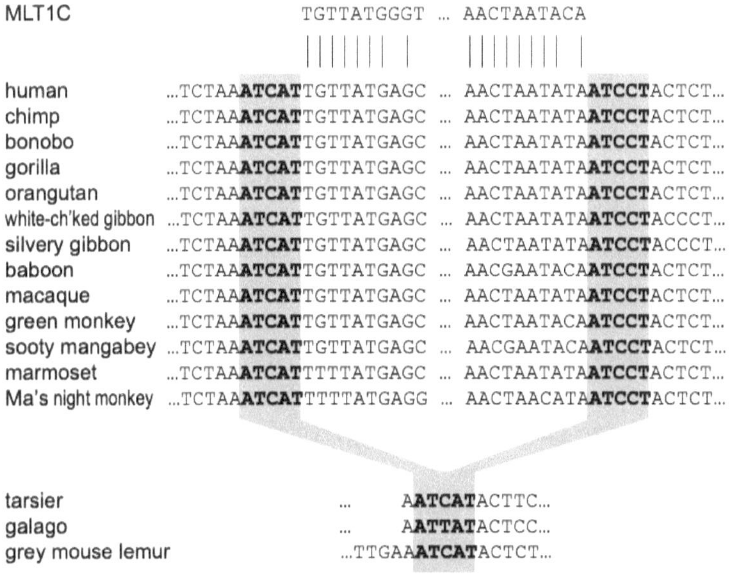

```
MLT1C                     TGTTATGGGT ... AACTAATACA
                          |||||||| |     |||||||| |
human                ...TCTAAATCATTGTTATGAGC ... AACTAATATAATCCTACTCT...
chimp                ...TCTAAATCATTGTTATGAGC ... AACTAATATAATCCTACTCT...
bonobo               ...TCTAAATCATTGTTATGAGC ... AACTAATATAATCCTACTCT...
gorilla              ...TCTAAATCATTGTTATGAGC ... AACTAATATAATCCTACTCT...
orangutan            ...TCTAAATCATTGTTATGAGC ... AACTAATATAATCCTACTCT...
white-ch'ked gibbon  ...TCTAAATCATTGTTATGAGC ... AACTAATATAATCCTACTCT...
silvery gibbon       ...TCTAAATCATTGTTATGAGC ... AACTAATATAATCCTACCCT...
baboon               ...TCTAAATCATTGTTATGAGC ... AACGAATACAATCCTACTCT...
macaque              ...TCTAAATCATTGTTATGAGC ... AACTAATATAATCCTACTCT...
green monkey         ...TCTAAATCATTGTTATGAGC ... AACTAATACAATCCTACTCT...
sooty mangabey       ...TCTAAATCATTGTTATGAGC ... AACGAATACAATCCTACTCT...
marmoset             ...TCTAAATCATTTTTATGAGC ... AACTAATATAATCCTACTCT...
Ma's night monkey    ...TCTAAATCATTTTTATGAGG ... AACTAACATAATCCTACTCT...

tarsier                              ...    AATCATACTTC...
galago                               ...    AATTATACTCC...
grey mouse lemur             ...TTGAAATCATACTCT...
```

Insertion site of an ERV activated during septic shock.

The example is from Mommert et al. "Dynamic LTR Retrotransposon," 96.

Pharmacological activation of ERV transcription in cancer cells might be of therapeutic use. The rationale behind this idea is that ERV-derived RNA molecules might be recognized by inflammasomes as indicating viral invasion. Such *viral mimicry* should activate innate immunity, and promote immune rejection of tumors.[8] Therapeutic treatment of patients' blood cell cancers (using the drug 5-azacytidine) stimulates production of ERV-derived RNA, followed soon after by gene transcripts that generate proteins

---

7. Mommert et al. "Dynamic LTR Retrotransposon," 96.
8. Ohtani et al. "Switching Roles for DNA," 1147–57.

effecting innate immunity. The drug-ERV RNA-innate immunity cascade was shown to occur only in those patients who responded to the therapy.[9]

2. Adaptive immunity

The adaptive immune system has the capacity to generate highly specific protective responses against antigens that have never been encountered before. Adaptive immunity entails the ability to *learn* and *remember*. It is constituted by two classes of cells. B cells are produced and mature in the bone marrow, and make antibodies. T cells develop in the thymus, and regulate immunity (helper T_H cells) and kill abnormal cells (cytotoxic T_C cells).

Our genome possesses *three* genes that specify the production of antibodies (one heavy chain and two light chain genes) but, amazingly, our B cell population produces *innumerable* antibody proteins, each of which recognizes a different antigenic shape (or *epitope*). Estimates of the total number of antibody proteins that may be produced vary from at least 10^{11} in mice to 10^{16} to 10^{18} in humans.[10] T cells similarly possess *four* genes encoding proteins that recognize epitopes, but during their development, each T cell generates *one* receptor protein, so that the community of T cells detects an astronomically large number of different epitopes (10^8 in any one individual; say 10^{15} to 10^{20} in total).[11] How can this *generation of diversity* arise?

Consider the *IGH* gene that specifies production of the *heavy chain* of antibody molecules. Three separate segments of DNA encode that part of an antibody molecule that specifically recognizes target molecules. Each of these segments is present in multiple alternative versions (Fig. 19). When each B cell develops, the antibody gene is rearranged such that any *one* of each of the segments (V, D, and J) is selected to specify the amino acid sequence of the antibody recognition site. The V-D and D-J joining points are spliced together by an error-prone mechanism, that introduces mutations into the gene. This vastly increases the number of possible protein sequences made.[12]

---

9. Ohtani et al., "Activation of a Subset," 2441–50; Jones et al., "Epigenetic Therapy," 151–61.

10. Chen et al., "BCR Selection," 421–25; Briney et al., "Commonality," 393–97.

11. Muller et al., "Evolutionary Perspective," 505–28.

12. Wang et al., "B-cell Development," 1–22.

FIGURE 19

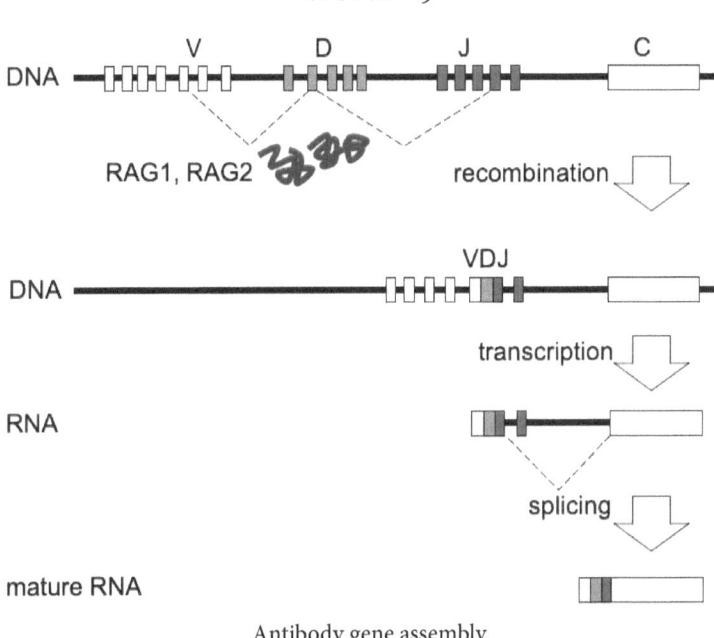

Antibody gene assembly.

The diagrams depict (from top), the germ-line organization of the *IGH* gene (the actual number of V and D segments is severalfold greater than indicated); a rearranged gene in one B cell; the RNA copied from that particular gene; and the mature spliced RNA used to make the antibody protein.

Two enzymes are absolutely required for the joining of the V, D, and J segments. These DNA-shuffling enzymes are known as RAG1 and RAG2 (encoded by the *recombination activating genes*). People who inherit scrambled forms of these enzymes cannot make antibodies and their T cell equivalents. They manifest *severe combined immunodeficiency* and are highly susceptible to infections.[13]

For years, scientists have noted that the RAG1 and RAG2 proteins are similar to transposable element-encoded genes known as *transposases*. These latter enzymes enable their respective transposons to hop around host genomes by a cut-and-paste mechanism. People speculated that RAG1 and RAG2 were derived from a transposase. In 2016, a transposon was discovered in amphioxus (a tiny fish-like invertebrate) that possessed transposases with striking similarly to RAG1 and RAG2. The long-hypothesized

---

13. Gennery "Recent Advances," 148.

transposon-encoded progenitor of our *RAG1* and *RAG2* genes had been identified! The two DNA-rearranging enzymes belonging to the amphioxus transposon were dubbed protoRAG.[14]

The implication is unavoidable: transposon-derived *protoRAG* genes were co-opted to serve as vertebrate *RAG* genes. This process of domestication occurred in an ancestor of the jawed vertebrates. Scientists have subsequently elucidated key amino acid changes that transformed protoRAG into the RAG enzymes. These alterations in protein structure changed the enzyme from a genome-disrupting *transposase* into an antibody gene-assembling, life-sustaining *recombinase*.[15]

Other ERVs and transposable elements have provided genomic sites that contribute to regulation of adaptive immunity. For example, an ancient MIR element that regulates production of the pro-inflammatory interleukin 6 gene in T_C cells is present in mice and primates, including humans—co-descendants of the one individual in which *this* MIR was added to the mammalian germ-line.[16]

Another signalling molecule, PD-L1, regulates T cell activity. Different versions of PD-L1 are produced. One of these arises when gene activity is modified by a fragment of an ancient LINE2 transposable element that is present in species as distantly related as humans, elephants, and armadillos. It spliced itself into the genome we have inherited in an ancestor of eutherian mammals.[17]

Every one of the four million ERVs and transposable elements that populate our genomes arose by random process. But many of these inserts now contribute to the elaborate regulatory circuitry that underlies immune function. They exemplify the power of natural selection over evolutionary timescales.

The broadly protective activities of innate immunity, and the *potential* for adaptive immune function have been honed by evolution over hundreds of millions of years. In contrast, the *actual* specific directedness of adaptive immunity develops in the lifespan of each individual. "With innate immunity, the prior self-/not-self-filtering of reactivity plays out over evolutionary time, whereas acquired immunity plays out over somatic

14. Huang et al., "Discovery of an Active RAG," 102–14.

15. Zhang et al. "Transposon Molecular Domestication," 79–84; Lieber, "Transposons to V(D)J recombination," 668–70.

16. Ye et al., "Specific Subfamilies," 7905–16.

17. Ng et al., "Soluble PD-L1," e50256.

time."[18] *Somatic time* is the few decades that comprise our lifespan. We will consider below the capacity of adaptive immunity to evolve over the duration of days and weeks.

3. Adaptive immunity: somatic evolution by natural selection

In each individual, natural selection in microcosm underlies the development of adaptive immunity, paralleling natural selection in macrocosm that underlies the evolution of species. Both evolutionary histories show the power of *chance* (random mutations that generate diversity) constrained by *necessity* (lawful selection of those variants that confer survivability). The evolutionary development of adaptive immunity in *each person's lifetime* is Darwinian.[19]

Random mutation generates the capacity of each person's immune system to recognize an unlimited range of epitopes. The RAG proteins, together with other DNA-altering enzymes, *randomize* antibody and T cell receptor genes. Some of these genes turn out to be useful: they encode proteins that could provide protection against invading pathogens. Other genes (two-thirds of them) are misassembled and non-functional. And other genes are harmful: they encode proteins that might react destructively against the body's own tissues. Formation of antibody genes by recombination "is inherently random and error-prone, generating diversity, but often assembling genes that are non-productive or that encode potentially autoreactive antibodies."[20]

It follows that randomization must be followed by quality control (*selection*) that perpetuates the protective genes, discards the misassembled genes, and eliminates the pathogenic genes. Selection of stochastically generated gene variants underlies adaptive immunity during the life history of every individual.

A newborn B cell has three options. First, cells that make functional, potentially protective, non-self-directed antibodies are *positively selected*. Each cell with its unique antibody survives as a valued member of the

---

18. Forsdyke., "Two-Signal Half-Century," e12746.
19. Muller et al., "Evolutionary Perspective," 505–28.
20. Nemazee, "Mechanisms of Central Tolerance," 281–84.

immune repertoire. If challenged by a microbial molecule, it generates a clonal population of antibody-secreting descendants (Fig. 20).[21]

FIGURE 20

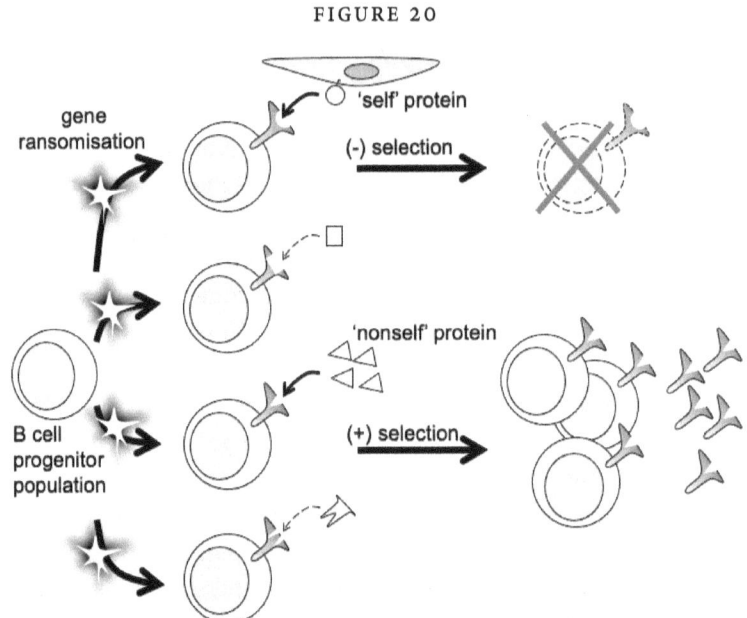

Natural selection of antibody-forming cells.

Pre-B cells randomize their antibody genes as they develop into B cells. Every new B cell makes a cell-bound antibody with a distinctive binding site (Y-shaped symbols). If this antibody strongly recognizes a self molecule, the cell dies (negative selection). Otherwise, the cell will survive and, if it encounters a threatening non-self molecule, will generate a clone of antibody-secreting cells (positive selection). The antibody-secreting clone will undergo hypermutation to hone the affinity of antibody-antigen interactions.

In this clone of cells, the antibody gene continues to mutate, generating modified antibodies, some of which may bind more tightly to the microbial molecule. *Somatic hypermutation* leads to *affinity maturation* of antibodies.[22] That is, there is an ongoing evolutionary process within functional antibody-forming clones of cells, involving mutation coupled to

21. Nemazee, "Mechanisms of Central Tolerance," 281–84.
22. Stebegg et al., "Regulation of the Germinal Centre," 2469.

selection, leading to progressively tighter binding between antibodies and the antigens by which they have been elicited (Fig. 21).

FIGURE 21

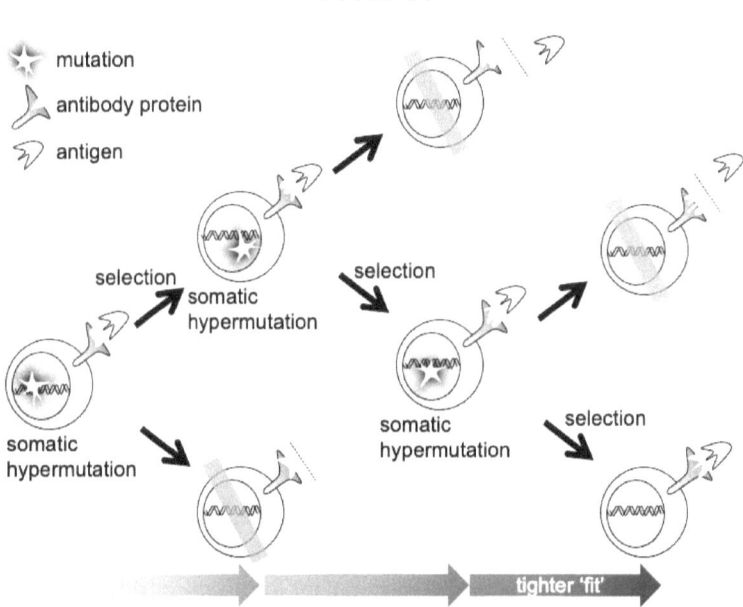

On-going natural selection: somatic hypermutation of antibody genes leads to antibody affinity maturation.

Positive selection has been shown in mice colonized with different populations of commensal gut bacteria. Antibodies with particular V-H combinations and mutational modifications are selected by particular bacterial species.[23] Selection and evolution of B cell clones occur in humans immunized with defined strains of influenza virus.[24] A single antibody may recognize self and non-self molecules with similar shapes. But over time, somatic hypermutation and affinity maturation generate derivative antibodies with lower affinity for the self and higher affinity for the non-self molecules.[25]

Second, if gene rearrangements generate non-functional antibodies or potentially harmful anti-self antibodies, cells may undergo further

23. Chen et al., "BCR Selection," 421–25.
24. Turner et al., "Human Germinal Centres," 127–32.
25. Burnett et al., "Conformational Diversity," 22341–50.

antibody gene rearrangements (undergo *receptor editing*). Further iterations of gene randomization represent attempts to generate antibodies of greater utility and less capacity for autoimmune damage to self.[26] Immunologists like theological metaphors. They have described the mechanism of reiterated mutagenesis as "autoantibody redemption,"[27] which provides a path of escape from self-reactivity.

Third, if genes remain non-functional or retain anti-self reactivity, even after further iterations of randomization, they will be eliminated. The ultimate negative selection step is cell death.[28] Otherwise, anti-self antibodies might cause autoimmune diseases—the *horror autotoxicus* imagined by Paul Ehrlich a century ago.

Similarly, as T cells develop in the thymus, a vast range of receptors (each with its unique binding site for molecular shapes) is generated. Again, many potentially damaging receptors with anti-self recognition are produced. Cells with anti-self receptor specificity are subject to negative selection and destroyed.[29] Those with potential anti-non-self function are subject to positive selection and armed for defensive roles.[30]

Colling described how we possess "billions of preformed B cells" that "appear to accomplish the impossible—protecting us from virtually *anything* that might come our way.... A random design system of this nature thus provides the most effective mechanism for accomplishing the goal of lifelong protection with the highest degree of certainty."[31] Similarly, of the T cells entering the thymus, 99 percent are negatively selected and die.[32] As Colling says, "this rigid selection protocol that destroys so many of our hopeful T cells is, in fact, crucial to our survival."[33]

From a theological perspective, it appears that natural selection instantiates the freedom-constrained-by-lawfulness that makes created reality so fruitful. Colling describes this system as "higher order random

---

26. Nemazee, "Mechanisms of Central Tolerance," 281–84.

27. Burnett et al., "Conformational Diversity," 22341–50.

28. Nemazee, "Mechanisms of Central Tolerance," 281–84; Wang et al., "B Cell Development," 1–22.

29. Breed et al., "Measuring Thymic Clonal Deletion," 3226–33.

30. Miller, "Function of the Thymus," eaba2429.

31. Colling, *Random Designer*, 180.

32. Colling, *Random Designer*, 70–71.

33. Colling, *Random Designer*, 72.

design" and God as the Random Designer.[34] Random processes, embedded in created regularity, are integral to the way God's purposes are achieved. The process of natural selection, "repeating over and over in an endless and infinite series of trials, propels life toward the Creator's ultimate purpose."[35] Immunologists have called the problem-solving goal-directed strategy by which B and T cells acquire the ability to recognize uncountable different epitopes the *generation of diversity*, GoD. There is more truth in that than many recognize.

Some people doubt that, through evolutionary history, natural selection has the capacity to generate the amazing diversity of living organisms. Perhaps some find the concept distasteful because *free randomness* and a *purposive God* are often considered to be incompatible ideas. But in *each one* of us, natural selection operates continually as a powerful mechanism for generating new immunological capacities. Generation of diversity strategies occur also in sexual reproduction and in neural development.[36] They are used by technologists to develop novel enzymes and antibodies (*directed evolution*)[37] and powerful computer programmes (*genetic algorithms*).[38] The process of science itself (creative hypothesis-generation sifted by experimental selection) is Darwinian.[39]

To some people, natural selection carries objectionable connotations. It has been reified into a monument to inefficiency and wastefulness, as if mortality in a physical universe was avoidable or reprehensible. (Do people who so decry the "wastefulness" of natural selection entertain tacit yearnings for immortality?) But mortality is a given, and natural selection may be interpreted as a feature of the irrepressible autopoietic[40] exuberance of life. An effervescent newness rises from creaturely mortality. For those who believe in a God who brings life out of death,[41] this insight is unsurprising.

---

34. Colling, *Random Designer*, 181–82.
35. Colling, *Random Designer*, 72.
36. Muraille, "Diversity Generator Mechanisms," 223.
37. Packer et al., "Methods for the Directed Evolution," 379–94. As an interesting case, antibodies of greatly increased binding affinities have been generated artificially, by using transposable elements to generate sites randomly in antibody genes, at which deletions and random insertions were introduced, followed by selection. See Skamaki et al., "In Vitro Evolution," 27307–18.
38. Rolston, *Genes, Genesis and God*, 34–37.
39. Rolston, *Genes, Genesis and God*, 168, 170.
40. Rolston, *Genes Genesis and God*, 12, 52.
41. For example, Rom 4:17; 8:11.

The products of natural selection cannot be said to be *designed*—a non-biblical concept in any case. However, the strategy is powerfully life-sustaining. It invites *interpretation* of the process as purposive.[42] As persons, we are acutely aware of those terrible occasions when random genetic variation manifests as disease and blights the lives of (especially) young people. We will address this problem in the next chapter, but now we will note simply that (scientifically speaking) such sufferings seem to be intrinsic to a world in which biology is possible, and that (theologically speaking) God has determined to extirpate all such evils from his creation, and in Jesus has entered into creation's pain to achieve this end.

4. Development through learning: the failure of genetic determinism

Two systems in our bodies require interactions with the outside world for their operation. First, the development of the *social brain* requires interpersonal relationship. Psychopathologies arise when children are neglected (chapter 3). Second, the *adaptive immune system* requires exposure to microbial products for its ability to control harmful agents and to tolerate the self antigens in our bodies (where immunological *tolerance* indicates *specific unresponsiveness* to particular molecular shapes).[43]

The *microbiota hypothesis* posits that aspects of modern urbanized life have modified microbial communities in our bodies, perturbing the balance between beneficial symbionts ("Old Friends") and potentially harmful pathobiont microbes. It has been proposed that this state of imbalance (dysbiosis) affects immunity, and underlies the current epidemic of allergic and autoimmune diseases.[44] Development of a "microbial theory of health" should lead to the adoption of "targeted hygiene"—lifestyle factors that favor good microbes over bad and so optimize immune development.[45]

---

42. Gingerich, *God's Planet*, 95; see Peter Harrison, "Evolution, Providence, and the Problem of Chance," in Giberson, *Abraham's Dice*, 278-79.

43. Platt et al., "Five Dimensions of B Cell Tolerance," 80-93.

44. Caruso and Nunez, "Host-Microbiota Interactions," 411-26; Alexander and Turnbaugh, "Deconstructing Mechanisms," 264-76; Wargo, "Modulating Gut Microbes," 1302-3.

45. Sonnenburg and Sonnenburg. "Vulnerability of the Industrialized Microbiota," eaaw9225; Scott et al., "21st Century View," 1387-92.

Consider some examples. Transplants of allogeneic (genetically distinct) bone marrow cells are often used in leukemia therapy. Unfortunately, immune cells in the transplant may react against the tissues of the recipient. This is the potentially lethal *graft-versus-host* (GvH) response. Remarkably, GvH disease in some patients is suppressed by transfer of gut bacteria from unrelated donors. Alternatively, GvH disease is exacerbated by obesity-related changes in the gut microbiota.[46] The immune system is naturally reactive against foreign cells but can be re-educated by symbiotic microbes. Immune systems are controlled by genes *and* by microbial communities.

Babies delivered by cesarean section show abnormal microbial communities in their guts and are predisposed to developing diseases of immunity. The gut microbiota in C-section-delivered babies usually becomes indistinguishable from that of normally delivered babies by one year. However, the persistence of a C-section microbial signature to one year of age is associated with the development of asthma at six years. Thus, it appears that the presence of a dysbiotic state contributes to an increased risk of immunological disease. However, following caesarean delivery, a neonate's gut microbiota can be normalized by adding a sample of mother's gut bacteria (a pinch of fecal matter, if you like) to the first milk feed.[47] And in Finnish urban day-care centres, children who played in enriched biological environments (on soil or forest litter, and engaged in planting activities) showed more diverse microbial communities in skin and gut, and decreased inflammatory immune activity relative to children who played in wholly artificial spaces. Arid, human-made environments lead to un-educated immune systems and predispose to immune-mediated diseases.[48] Clinical trials will be needed to establish whether exposures that normalize microbial communities in cesarean-delivered and day-care-attending children will indeed provide protection against the later development of immunological diseases. Undoubtedly, such studies are being planned, but

---

46. Biernat et al., "Fecal Microbiota Transplantation," 300060520925693; van Lier et al., "Donor Fecal Microbiota Transplantation," eaaz8926; Khuat et al., "Obesity Induces Gut Microbiota Alterations," eaay7713. Identified bacterial species (*Faecalibacterium, Ruminococcus 2, Akkermansia*) promote reconstitution of the immune system in leukemia patients following immune ablation and haematopoietic cell transplants, as shown by Schluter et al., "Gut Microbiota," 303–7.

47. Stokholm et al. "Delivery Mode," eaax9929; Korpela et al. "Maternal Fecal Microbiota Transplantation," 324–34.

48. Roslund et al., "Biodiversity Intervention," eaba2578.

it will take several years to establish whether these approaches to normalizing children's microbiotas lead to lower rates of immunological disease.

Some people speak as if we are mere gene machines, obedient robots that meekly obey the dictates of our genes. The strategy of immune system development refutes that dogma. Immunity, like the brain, develops from the ongoing interaction between genes and their indefinably complex environments. Immunologically, we are not self-sufficient monads, autonomous gene machines. Understanding of the benefits of microbial symbionts has been extended by a recognition of a *microbiota-gut-immunity-brain* axis. That microbes in the *gut* should affect our *mental state* is paradigmatic of the dependence of well-being on external relationships.[49] Integral to this axis are psychological considerations (such as anxiety and depression), which influence, and are influenced by, inflammatory abnormalities in the gut.[50]

In general, "immune system processes are influenced by social, neurocognitive and behavioural factors." Cognitive behavior therapy has beneficial effects on inflammatory cytokines (suppressing levels of interleukin 6, an inflammatory messenger molecule) and on cells mediating immunity (such as T_H cells). Benefits have been seen particularly in patients with autoimmunity and HIV/AIDS.[51] "The burgeoning field of psychoneuroimmunology" is replete with examples of how social and mental factors are reflected in cerebral and immunological processes.[52] Mind modulates the material mechanisms of the immune system. Mind-immunity/body relationships emphasize that we reside in both noosphere and zoosphere. The biblical picture of humanity is of a psychosomatic unity. Jeeves describes this understanding as dual aspect monism.[53] It is the whole, undivided person who is redeemed; it will be the whole person who will be transformed in resurrection.[54]

---

49. Pennisi, "Meet the Psychobiome," 570–73; Tong et al., "Nutraceuticals and Probiotics," 403–19; Teratani et al., "The Liver–Brain–Gut Neural Arc," 591–96; Willyard, "How Gut Bacteria," 22.

50. Labanski et al., "Stress and the Brain-Gut Axis," 104501.

51. Shields et al., "Psychosocial Interventions and Immune System," 1031–43.

52. See Jeeves, "The Emergence of Human Distinctiveness: The Story from Neuropsychology and Neurobiology," in Jeeves, *Rethinking Human Nature*, 188.

53. See Jeeves, "The Emergence of Human Distinctiveness: The Story from Neuropsychology and Neurobiology," in Jeeves, *Rethinking Human Nature*, 190.

54. Wright and Bird, *New Testament in Its World*, 300, 311–13, 493–94.

We are persons created by persons, matter molded by others' matter, formed through gene-environment interactions—whether that environment is material (such as commensal gut bacteria) or personal (chapter 3). Our others-dependence is emphasized by *image-of-God* terminology. Our development is not autonomous, but depends on God's grace "bestowed upon the whole of humankind as a community"—an understanding that acts "as a bulwark against the steady eroding of the understanding of humankind as having intrinsic value."[55] As Green states, "the nature of humanity derives from the human family's relatedness to God. The concept of the imago Dei, then, is fundamentally relational, or covenantal."[56] Green's chapter heading, "Humanity—created, restored, transformed, embodied," in the passive voice, indicates the initiative and continuous agency of God.

5. A paradigm of unity from diversity

The intricacies of the immune system and its myriad microbial collaborators constitute a paradigm of integrative function. The holism that defines this diversified cellular community models the church, the *ekklesia*, which St Paul describes in terms of an organic metaphor, the body, the *soma*, of Christ.[57] The complexity of the immune system parallels the interdependencies of the body and of life in the community of the Messiah. We can describe the church in terms of the intimate, intricate, and dynamic relationships that exist between the myriad players that comprise the immune system.

Unity

The cells of innate and adaptive immunity comprise a unified, co-operative whole. Innate immune cells process antigens, so regulating adaptive responses, which in turn orchestrate innate cell functions. Multiple cell types collaborate in the clonal selection of cells, which is "an emergent property, a new information system."[58] The advent of such collaborative immunological function represents a major transition in evolution, of the

---

55. Alexander, *Are We Slaves to Our Genes?* 202.

56. See Green, "Humanity—Created, Restored, Transformed, Embodied," in Jeeves, *Rethinking Human Nature*, 274.

57. Eph 1:23.

58. Muller et al., "Evolutionary Perspective," 505–28.

same momentous order as the development of multicellularity and animal eusociality. Like the brain, the immune system stores information in an open-ended way.[59]

Analogously, the indivisible body of Christ is a community of unprecedented integration, a true innovation. Paul emphasizes: "There is *one* body"; and "we are *one* body in union with Christ."[60] As Wright says, "The *ekklesia*, the Messiah's body, is nothing short of a new version of the human race. . . . The unity of God's people in the Messiah is the most obvious worldview-symbol Paul has."[61]

The ecclesial body's integration, despite its disparate (and previously incompatible) component parts, is a revolution in human relationality: "all of us, whether Jews or Gentiles, whether slaves or free, have been baptized into the one body by the same Spirit."[62] It follows that any "distinctions of class and wealth . . . flies in the face of Paul's entire vision of the one church, the central symbol of its own worldview."[63] The body of Christ, unlike the civic body of the Stoics, rejected every ethnic and social distinction by which civic life was marked.[64] And it must stand in trenchant prophetic contradistinction to every divisive "ism" that acts to fragment human society and destroy the solidarity of the creatures who bear God's image. We have considered how many tribal people, like the ancient Hebrews, consider the social group as having ontological precedence over the individual (chapter 3). The unity of the cells of the immune system is lost in the destructive autonomy of leukemia and lymphoma cells.[65] Somewhat analogously, the fundamental imperative of unity in Christ's body[66] has been systematically rejected through church history.

Diversity

Many types of cells constitute the immune system. "Each drop of blood provides a snapshot of many lineages, as well as dozens of differentiation

---

59. Muller et al., "Evolutionary Perspective," 505–28.
60. Eph 4:4; Rom 12:5 (GNT).
61. Wright, *Paul and the Faithfulness of God*, 396, also 426.
62. 1 Cor 12:13; reiterated, Eph 2:16; 3:6.
63. Wright, *Paul and the Faithfulness of God*, 1346.
64. Wright, *Paul and the Faithfulness of God*, 1333–34.
65. Thurner et al., "Role of Specific B-Cell," 604685.
66. John 17:11, 20–23.

and activation states."[67] Diversity or variety at all levels of biology, from immune systems to ecosystems, is associated with vitality and resistance to adversity. If living systems are to prove resilient in the face of diverse environmental challenges, they will need to be constituted by a commensurate diversity. This correlation has been expressed as the "law of requisite variety."[68]

In human terms, the multiple types of people who constitute the body of Christ attest to a high valuation of individuality, and of the particular contributions made by each person. "Christ is like a single body which has *many parts*. . . . For the body itself is not made up of only one part but of many parts. . . . As it is, there are many parts but one body."[69] A body constituted of one part "would be a monstrosity."[70] Diversity in the body is functional differentiation, richness, vitality. The various contributions of members are required for the good of all.

Fee notes that Paul emphasizes the "need for unity *and* for diversity in the believing community, both of which are the work of 'the one and the same Spirit' (1 Cor 12:11)."[71] The heterogeneous group of people comprising the body of Christ "must submit their diversity to the unifying work of the Spirit. Homogeneous churches lie completely outside Paul's frame of reference."[72] The fissiparous and exclusivistic tendencies and practices of Jesus' followers in a deeply fragmented society represents an abject failure to live up to their calling. As David Wenham says: "there needs to be within the body both love and the exercise and recognition of different gifts and ministries."[73]

Life-giving control

Immune system operations require meticulous control. A master regulator is the *major histocompatibility complex* (MHC), a genetic locus that produces many proteins with vital functions in immunity. It encodes proteins that function in surveillance of the universe of potential molecules. It is

67. Pulendran and Davis, "Science and Medicine of Human Immunology," eaay4014.
68. W. R. Ashby in Muraille, "Diversity Generator Mechanisms," 223.
69. 1 Cor 12:12–27; Rom 12:4–8.
70. Fee, *Paul, the Spirit, and the People of God*, 71.
71. Fee, *Paul, the Spirit, and the People of God*, 69.
72. Fee, *Paul, the Spirit, and the People of God*, 70.
73. David Wenham, *Paul: Follower of Jesus or Founder of Christianity?* 185.

required for the ability of the immune system to discriminate between tissues that are self and those that are non-self. It promotes rejection of organ transplants and induces GvH reactions.[74] Key MHC genes exist in so many variants that each person's assemblage is unique. This diversity may contribute to the resilience of populations to epidemics of pathogens. The MHC arose with jawed vertebrates[75]—the epoch of RAG protein domestication and of the origins of adaptive immunity. Children who inherit mutations that ablate MHC function are highly vulnerable to infections.[76]

Analogously, the controlling presence of Christ defines the constitution of his body. The authority of Christ, and submission to that authority, are the non-dissociable markers of membership in the body of Christ. He completes,[77] rules and saves,[78] cares for,[79] and enlivens[80] his body.

According to Wright, the metaphor of "the Messiah's body" encapsulates the idea of "corporate christology."[81] The Messiah is "the representative of his people," the one who draws them together, "with the main point being the unity of that company, and in particular their unity across traditional boundary-lines."[82] The phrase *en Christo* ("in union with Christ," GNT) parallels the *body* metaphor. It stresses the participation of the members in the life of Christ.[83] Those who are *en Christo* derive their life from him.[84]

The Spirit of the Messiah provides the body's all-pervading controlling dynamic: the immanent source of life, energy, and purpose.[85] The Spirit

74. Kamal et al., "Genetics, Histocompatibility Antigen," in *StatPearls* (online).

75. Heijmans et al., "Comparative Genetics," 243–60.

76. Abolnezhadian et al., "Novel Mutation in RFXANK," 225–31; Cai et al., "Novel RFXANK Mutation," ofaa314.

77. Eph 1:23; or as J. B. Phillips translates it, "For the Church is his body, and in that body lives fully the one who fills the whole wide universe." In other words, the body is not the completion of Christ, but is completed *by* Christ. This expression is favoured also by Stott, *God's New Society*, 64–66.

78. Eph 5:23.

79. Eph 5:29–30.

80. Col 1:18.

81. Wright, *Paul and the Faithfulness of God*, 825.

82. Wright, *Paul and the Faithfulness of God*, 834.

83. Wright, *Paul and the Faithfulness of God*, 825; David Wenham, *Paul: Follower of Jesus or Founder of Christianity?* 188–89.

84. The close association of the concepts of being in Christ and of possessing life are indicated, for example, in Gal 3:27; 5:10; 1 Cor 4:15, 17; 15:22, 31; Rom 6:23; 8:2; Eph 1:1; Phil 1:26; 3:3; 4:10; Col 1:10; Phlm 1:6; 1 John 4:16; 5:20.

85. 1 Cor 12:7–13.

empowers his members to expose and reject evil and bring healing and regeneration.

Interaction

White blood cells mediate core immunological functions. They migrate as individuals, unlike brain cells that are locked into stable networks. Nevertheless, immunological cells connect with each other intimately and with bewildering complexity[86] at multi-component communication points called *immunological synapses*.[87] These collaborating cells manifest a physical, information-sharing, and life-sustaining togetherness.

Interacting immune cells provide a model of how members of Christ's body fit together, are held together,[88] and are called together (guided by the peace of Christ).[89] A concept pervasive though Paul's writing is that the Messiah's people are in continual relation with one another/each other. ("*Everything* is done *allelon*.")[90] The members of the body of Christ are in constant, necessary, and empathetic communication. "If one part of the body suffers, all the other parts suffer with it; if one part is praised, all the other parts share its happiness."[91] Hauerwas and Willimon indicate that every self must be communally created.[92] God deals with us only in ways that are "social, communal, familial, colonial."[93] Indeed, "nothing the gospel asks of us . . . is expected of us as loners."[94]

Dynamic development

We are not born with a functioning adaptive immune system. It develops only through intimate and ongoing interaction between the internal world

---

86. Stebegg et al., "Regulation of the Germinal Centre," 2469.

87. Binder et al., "CD2 Immunobiology," 1090; Demetriou et al., "Dynamic CD2-Rich Compartment," 1232–43.

88. Eph 4:16; Col 2:19.

89. Col 3:15.

90. For example, Rom 12:5; are members together (enjoined to truth-telling), Eph 4:25; Fee, *Paul, the Spirit, and the People of God*, 66.

91. 1 Cor 12:26.

92. Hauerwas and Willimon, *Resident Aliens*, 65.

93. Hauerwas and Willimon, *Resident Aliens*, 92, 129.

94. Hauerwas and Willimon, *Resident Aliens*, 136.

of self, and the ever-changing biotic (especially microbial) world of nonself. The immune system is communal in the way it progressively learns, adapts, and remembers throughout life.[95]

The body of Christ is also an ever-developing community. The capacities that Christ provides are intended "to build up the body of Christ."[96] "So when each separate part works as it should, the whole body grows and builds itself up through love."[97] As Alexander says, being a bearer of God's image is "a dynamic ongoing developmental process carried out in relationship in which God delegates responsibilities through the human social community."[98] And Joel Green describes development within the body: human "(trans)formation is fully embodied within a nest of relationships, a community."[99] Indeed, "human formation is a process."[100] Disciples are formed "in a process of conversion [entailing] a reconstruction of one's self within a new web of relationships, . . . an ongoing transformation of one's theological and moral imagination that necessarily locates and immerses one in the multiethnic community of God's people."[101]

Development includes the death of cells that are no longer required. New-born B cells and T cells are self-reactive and are eliminated. In the thymus, cells with misassembled receptors, and with strongly anti-self reactivity undergo minutely regulated "death by neglect" and "clonal deletion" mechanisms, respectively.[102] Analogously, during the process of spiritual maturation, freedom from self requires death to the influence of self. Paul writes: "You have also died because you are part of the body of Christ."[103] The apparent paradox that ongoing death is a means to life is a theme of biblical thought[104] as it is in biology.

---

95. Stebegg et al. "Regulation of the Germinal Centre," 2469.

96. Eph 4:12.

97. Eph 4:16; Col 2:19.

98. Alexander, *Are We Slaves to Our Genes?* 203–4.

99. See Joel Green, "Humanity—Created, Restored, Transformed, Embodied," in Jeeves, *Rethinking Human Nature*, 277.

100. See Joel Green, "Humanity—Created, Restored, Transformed, Embodied," in Jeeves, *Rethinking Human Nature*, 279.

101. See Joel Green, "Humanity—Created, Restored, Transformed, Embodied," in Jeeves, *Rethinking Human Nature*, 285.

102. Breed et al., "Measuring Thymic Clonal Deletion," 3226–33.

103. Rom 7:4.

104. John 12:24–25; Rom 6:5–11; 2 Cor 5:14–15; Gal 2:20.

Pathology

Features of Western civilization (cesarean births, enriched diets, over-use of antibiotics) have been connected with derangement of immune systems. We are confronted with epidemics of allergies,[105] chronic inflammatory diseases,[106] autoimmune conditions,[107] and colorectal cancer.[108] Changing environments are disordering immune reactivity.[109]

St Paul saw the irreducible unity of the body of Christ as the supreme symbol of the new creation. Consequently, "anything which fragments the unity of the lord's single 'body is a crime against the lord himself."[110] Paul fulminated against divisive pathologies, which destroyed the body of Christ: immorality,[111] idolatry,[112] and a snobbish disdain for disadvantaged members at the eucharistic meal.[113] Malaise arose in members who had "stopped holding on to Christ who is the head of the body."[114] Similar pathologies compromise the vitality of the contemporary body of Christ.

Ultimately, the metaphors of the body and of the immune system coalesce into one. Immunological health and well-being cannot be confined to classical immunological componentry, but pervade the entire body. It is now known that environmentally sensitive immunological dysfunction manifests in the gamut of chronic diseases, including cardiovascular disease, diabetes, and liver disease. Such body-wide syndromes are *immunometabolic*, based on underlying *metaflammation* (or low-grade inflammatory stress).[115] In the same way, all the members of the body of Christ

---

105. Renz and Skivaki, "Early Life Microbial Exposures," in press.

106. Furman et al., "Chronic Inflammation," 1822–32.

107. Konig, "The Microbiome," 101473.

108. Janney et al., "Host-Microbiota Maladaptation," 509–17.

109. Fitzgibbon and Mills, "The Microbiota and Immune-Mediated Diseases," 326–37; Chen et al., "Interplay of Intestinal Microbiota," 1–11.

110. Wright, *Paul and the Faithfulness of God*, 1347.

111. 1 Cor 6:15.

112. 1 Cor 10:14–17; our "sharing in the body of Christ" (v. 16), may refer to both the sacrament of Christ's physical body, and the unified *ekklesia* of Christ (as in v. 17); David Wenham, *Paul: Follower of Jesus or Founder of Christianity?* 185–86.

113. 1 Cor 11:27–29.

114. Col 2:19.

115. Hotamisligil, "Inflammation, Metaflammation and Immunometabolic," 177–85; Sanna et al., "Causal Relationships," 600–605.

share each other's pain[116] and the decisions of each member ripple for better or worse through the whole, and beyond.

6. Beyond self and non-self

"Self/non-self" terminology is conventional immunological parlance. But it misrepresents the discriminatory functions of the immune system. The assumption is that self should be tolerated and non-self should be rejected. But innocuous substances such as allergens and dietary components are non-self and should be wholly tolerated. (Ask any allergy-sufferer. Uncalled-for immune reactivity against pollens is a cause of much unhappiness.) And myriad non-self microbes inhabiting our bodies are symbiotic—they are essential to our well-being, and should be positively welcomed.[117] Appropriately functioning immune systems learn to tolerate such symbionts.

We should discard the idea that the immune system discriminates self from non-self in favor of the idea that the immune system discriminates "non-harm" (our own cells, symbiotic microbes, and innocuous molecules) from "harm" (pathogenic cells and microbes). Adaptive immunity is a "safe/non-safe," "health/non-health" discriminator.

Nathaniel Comfort, a historian of biology, has criticized immunological self/non-self parlance for its influence on conceptions of individual identity. The boundaries between self and non-self are now seen as very porous. "The biological self has been reframed as a cluster of communities, all in communication with each other."[118] We are not self-sufficient. Our openness to the outside word has led some scientists to describe us as *holobionts* or *metaorganisms*,[119] irreducibly cooperating communities of human and microbial cells.

The "self/non-self" terminology sits uneasily with the body of Christ, which does not exist to maintain boundaries between an in-group (self) and an out-group (non-self). Rather, the body of Christ consists of persons who are incomplete in themselves. Our sense of self is given "in relation to the people of God, and this in relation to the covenant and promises from the God of Israel."[120]

116. 1 Cor 12:25–26.
117. Muller et al., "Evolutionary Perspective," 505–28.
118. Comfort, "How Science Has Shifted," 167–70.
119. Muraille, "Diversity Generator Mechanisms," 223.
120. See Joel Green, "Humanity—Created, Restored, Transformed, Embodied," in Jeeves, *Rethinking Human Nature*, 289.

We might learn from the immune system and suggest that the body of Christ exists to differentiate between "non-harm" and "harm." Scripture uses various terms to describe the dualities between which discrimination is appropriate. There is light and darkness; life and death; the Spirit and human nature ("flesh").[121] Humans face increasing intensities of intolerance, prejudice, and untruthfulness. The church's immunological role is to act with unity and discrimination to resist evil and promote God's healing *shalom*.

In a world wracked by COVID-19 (and numerous other threats), the church "incarnate as Christ's body must live, breathe and unite its members amidst the diversity of human history and culture." Its mission is two-fold: "to feed and sustain those who are in the body"; and "to proclaim the Word . . . to bring more people to Christ."[122]

---

121. Rom 8:3–17; Gal 5:16–26; Eph 2:1–5; 5:8–14; the pneuma and the psyche, which underlie and animate the eschatological *soma pneumatikon* and the biological *soma psychikon*; 1 Cor 15:44–49; Wright, *Paul and the Faithfulness of God*, 1400–1402; Joel Green, "Humanity—Created, Restored, Transformed, Embodied," in Jeeves, *Rethinking Human Nature*, 290–93.

122. Evener, "Spirit and Truth," doi: 10.1111/dial.12594.

5

Created histories

Eschatogeny recapitulates phylogeny

Abstract

The revolution in comparative genomics has shown that random mutations underlie the spectacular development of the diversity of life and the evolution of humanity. *Precisely* the same classes of mutations underlie genetic diseases such as cancer. This commonality of mechanism does not seem to be compatible with the idea that God micro-manipulates his world in such a way as to determine the nature of mutations (God is not the immediate cause of cancers). Nor can we accept the proposal that cancers arose only following a cosmic fall (mutations with the potential to disrupt biological integrity long preceded the advent of humanity). Rather, an appropriate understanding of evolutionary process as history recognizes its ambiguity, contingency, and genuine ontological freedom. The operation of random, autonomous process (*chance*) in the context of directing order (*necessity*) leads evolution along particular trajectories, so that phylogenetic history invites a teleological interpretation. Creation remains incomplete, and it will fully reflect the nature of God only at the eschaton. The work of Jesus, God's Messiah, entails that he represents and takes upon himself Israel's history, and that of all humanity. Analogously, Jesus also bears in himself all biology and indeed the cosmos and takes it to its consummation. To misquote a great Christian evolutionary biologist, nothing in evolution makes sense except in the light of eschatology.

Key words

genomics, evolution, cancer, suffering, creation, history, providence, eschatology

ANALYSIS OF DNA SEQUENCE data has led to the identification of complex mutations that arise from the concerted actions of DNA-modifying enzymes. Each such complex mutation arises as an essentially singular, non-repeatable event. If a particular mutation is shared by multiple cells (as in a tumor), multiple individuals, or multiple species, we may conclude that those cells or organisms are descended from the one cell in which that singular mutation arose. Those tumors are said to be *monoclonal*; the multiple individuals or species are *monophyletic*. In each case, they are related by descent from one ancestor. Inventories of such mutations delineate the route of evolutionary histories—whether of tumors or of biological taxa.

In this chapter, we revert to where I started on my vocational journey as a cancer cell biologist. Over my working lifetime, I learned about clonal mutations and retroviruses from my reading of tumor biology. This journey took me, by surprise, into the use of complex mutations—ERVs and then transposable elements—for delineating phylogenetic relationships. We are, emphatically, an evolved species. But in the last few years, as a result of the genome sequencing revolution and the desire to understand how cancers develop, diversify, and acquire more aggressive features, the worldwide biomedical community has engaged in a renewed programme to investigate cancer genomics and evolution.

Many thousands of cancer genomes have been sequenced. The same mutational processes described hitherto—propagation of retroviruses and of transposable elements—have now been shown to provide markers of *cancer* development, in exactly the same way as they provide markers of our *evolutionary* development. In other words, there are parallels between *oncogeny* and *phylogeny* (see later). Markers of cancer evolution document the pain-, separation-, and death-inducing propensities of cancers. Markers of biological evolution document the marvellous diversity of living forms. People who think about the creative work of God encounter a sharp dissonance in the opposing consequences of the activities of genetic parasites. How do we see the work and purposes of a good God in this apparent paradox?

1. ERVs and transposable elements as phylogenetic markers

To reflect on the constructive and destructive effects of genomic parasites, we will compare their roles in biological evolution and cancer. To start with, we will reflect on some representative phylogenetics data. Alignments of mutant sequences from multiple species are depicted in Figs. 22–24. Target site duplications generated by the enzyme-mediated cascade of events are highlighted. These genomic features arose from molecularly defined events that occurred in progenitors that we share with other species.

The insertion sites of retroviral genomes are depicted in Fig. 22. Each is a potent phylogenetic marker. The LTR12c insertion (top) is present only in African great apes, and it arose in an ancestor of the African great apes. Species that retain a recognizable, undisturbed, progenitor sequence branched out on their own evolutionary trajectories before the mutation arose. This particular ERV is of interest because, although it arose in the standard retroviral manner as a piece of genomic flotsam, it has acquired a function in the host genome. The retroviral sequence includes motifs that help regulate a nearby gene, *RAE1*, the protein of which acts to export RNA molecules from cell nuclei.[1]

---

1. Jung et al., "Activity Analysis of LTR12C," 22–28.

CREATED HISTORIES

FIGURE 22

```
LTR12c                    TGTGAGAGGTG...TTCCGGACACA
                          ||  ||||  |  ||||||||||||
human              ...TAAGTCACATTGAGAGATGAC...TTCCGGACACAACATCACCTC...
chimp              ...TAAGTCACATTGAGAGGTGAC...TTCCAGACACAACAT    CCTC...
bonobo             ...TAAGTCACATTGAGAGGTGAC...TTCCAGACACAACAT    CCTC...
gorilla            ...TAAGTCACATTGAGAGGTGAC...TTCTGGACACAACATCACCTC...


orang                           ...TAAGTCACATCACCTC...
gibbon                          ...TAAGTCACATCACCTC...
baboon                          ...TAAGTCACATCACCTC...
rhesus macaque                  ...TAAGTCACATCACCTC...
crab-eating macaque             ...TAAGTCACATCACCTC...
green monkey                    ...TAAGTCACATCACCTC...
marmoset                        ...TAAGTCACATCATCTC...
night monkey                    ...TAAGTCACATCACCTC...


LTR12c                    TGTGAGAGGTGA...TCCGGACACA
                          |||||||||||  |||||||||||
human              ...GAAAACACTATTGAGAGGTGA...TCCGGACACCCTATCAGAGAT...
chimp                                      ...TCCGGACACCCTATCAGAGAT...
bonobo                                     ...TCCGGACACCCTATCAGAGAT...
gorilla            ...GAAAACACTATTGAGAGGTGA/TCCGGACACCCTATCAGAGAT...
orang              ...GAAAACACTATTGAGAGGTGA/TCCGGGCACACTGTCAGAGAT...


gibbon                          ...GAAAACACTATCAGAGAT...
baboon                          ...GGAAACACTGTCAGAGAT...
macaque                         ...GGAAACACTGTCAGAGAT...
green monkey                    ...GGAAACACTGTCAGAGAT...
snub-nosed monkey               ...GGAAACACTGTCAGAGAT...
tarsier                         ...GAAAACACAATCAGAGAT...
galago                          ...AAAAGTATAATCAGAGAT...
grey mouse lemur                ...GAAAGCACAATCATAGAT...
cat                             ...GAATACAGGATCAGAGAT...
horse                           ...AAAGACATGATCAGAGAT...
dolphin                         ...ACAGACATGGTCAGAAAT...
Brandt's bat                    ...AAAGACGTGCTCAAAAAG...
```

Evolution and Eschatology

```
ERV-K(HML-6)                    TGTTGCAGGCCGAA...
                                |||||  |||||||||
human        ...GTCCCCATGTTTGTGTGTTGGAGGCCGAA...TTTGTGGGTCATGC...
chimp        ...ATCCCCATGTTTGTGTGTTGGAGGCCGGA...TTTGTGGGTCATGC...
bonobo       ...ATCCCCATGTTTGTGTGTTGGAGGCCGGA...TTTGTGGGTCATGC...
gorilla      ... TCCCCATGTTTGTGTGTTGGAGGCCGAA...TTTGTGGGTCATGC...
orang        ...GTCCCCATGTTTGTGTGTTGGAAGCCAAA...TTTGTGGGTCATGC...
gibbon       ...GTCCCCATGTTTGTGTGTTGGATGCTGAA...
baboon       ...GTCCCCTTGTTTGTGTGTTGGAGGCCAAA...TCTGTGGGTCATGC...
drill        ...GTCCCCTTGTTTGTGTGTTGGAGGCCAAA...TCTGTGGGTCATGC...
green monkey ...GTCCCCTTGTTTGTGTGTTGGAGGCCAAA...TCTGTGGGTCATGC...
snub-nosed m ...GTCCCCTTGTTTGTGTGTTAGAGGTCAAA...TCTGTGAGTCATGC...

marmoset            ...G       TGTTTTTGGGTCACGC...
squirrel monkey     ...G       TGTTTTTTGGTCATGC...
capuchin monkey     ...G       TGTTTTTTGGGACATGC...
tarsier             ...GTCCTAATGGTTGTGTGTCA    G...
colugo              ...ATCCCCATGTTTGTGGTTCATGT...
cat                 ...GTCCCCGTGTGTGTGGCTCCTGT...
elephant            ...TTCCCCATGTTTGTGGGCCATGT...
armadillo           ...GTCCATATGTCTGTGGGCCTTGT...
```

Insertion sites of ERVs with contrasting effects.

Top: The retroviral sequence (starting "TGAG...") lies between the duplicated target site "ACAT" in African great apes. Other species retain the undisturbed progenitor sequence (Jung et al., "Activity Analysis of LTR12C," 22–28).

Middle: The retroviral sequence (starting "TGAG...") lies between the duplicated target site "CTAT" in great apes (Jang et al., "Transposable Elements Drive Widespread Expression," 611–7).

Bottom: The retroviral sequence (starting "TGTT...") lies between the duplicated target site "TTTGTG" in Old World monkeys and apes. Other species retain the undisturbed progenitor sequence. The insert was described in Pisano et al., "Comprehensive Characterization," e00110–19. Sequences are from the NCBI (using BLAST), http://dfam.org/entry/DF0000402/model (LTR12c), and http://dfam.org/entry/DF0000501/summary (ERV-K(HML-6)).

Another ERV of the same class (LTR12c, middle) is found in the genomes of all the great apes. Right hand sequences have been lost in chimps, and there have been internal rearrangements in gorilla and orang relative to human (indicated by the forward slash "/"). The repetition of sequence motifs in genetic text, such are present in our LTR12c element, may give rise to deletions or duplications. (The same phenomenon is known from textual criticism, in which deletion and duplication "mutations" of blocks of text are known as *haplography* or *diplography* respectively). This ERV has also been recruited into a particular functional role—but a frankly undesirable one, as it may perturb the activity of the *TP63* gene, and so contribute to cancer development.[2]

The ERV-K(HML6) insertion (Fig. 22, bottom) is a feature of the genomes of Old World monkeys and apes. In liver cancers, this ERV happens to influence the nearby *ZNF689* gene, in such a way as to promote cancer cell viability.[3] Three representative ERVs have thus acquired opposing personas. One is a now a valued part of our biology as humans; the others may be recruited to serve processes leading to cancer, physical debilitation, and death. The impact of ERVs on the genome largely depends on the genetic environment in which they insert themselves—and the choice of insertion site is a pretty random business.

Some six thousand ERVs are actively copied into RNA in cancers, both *specifically* in the tumor cells and *recurrently* (repeatedly in different tumors). That is, about 1 percent of the ERVs in our genome have the capacity to contribute to the RNA content of cells when those cells become cancerous. Such ERV-derived RNAs may contribute to disease development. Kidney tumors with higher concentrations of ERV1-derived RNA are associated with poorer patient outcome. Thus, in some cases, the activation of ERVs provides information about the aggressiveness of the tumors.[4] In other cases, ERVs are responsible for the production of tiny proteins (peptides), which might be recognized by cells of the immune system. Potentially these ERV-derived peptides, made only in cancer cells, could be exploited as targets for anti-cancer immunotherapy.[5] The random way such ERVs generate random peptides, visible to immune cells, could provide an interesting new therapeutic paradigm. By decorating cancer cells with wholly novel chemical shapes, they could unleash the power of immune defences against those cells.[6] To the cancer cell biologist, such ERVs, long-term residents in our genomes, present Jekyll-and-Hyde personae.

Transposable elements also yield to historical investigation—although those histories may have markedly divergent consequences. The Alu-J

---

2. Jang et al., "Transposable Elements Drive Widespread Expression," 611–17.

3. Pisano et al., "Comprehensive Characterization," e00110–19.

4. Zapatka et al., "Landscape of Viral Associations," 320–30.

5. Attig et al., "LTR Retroelement Expansion, 1578–90.

6. Ohtani, et al., "Switching Roles for DNA," 1147–57; Jones et al., "Epigenetic Therapy," 151–61,

insertion depicted in Fig. 23 (top) is of an ancient subtype, and provides a marker of the simian (New and Old World monkey-ape) branch of the primate family tree. The Alu element entered the primate germline in a simian ancestor. But it has been incorporated into the structure of a mysterious gene called *ANRIL*.[7] This randomly arising Alu element has been recruited as a part of a gene that seems to perform important roles in many physiological processes. Associated genetic variants influence the development of heart disease, diabetes, periodontal disease, and various cancers. Intriguingly, the *ANRIL* gene does not carry a code capable of making a protein, and is said to be *non-coding*. Thousands of similar, enigmatic non-coding genes have been discovered. Such genes are often cobbled together with genetic material of ERV and transposable element provenance.[8]

FIGURE 23

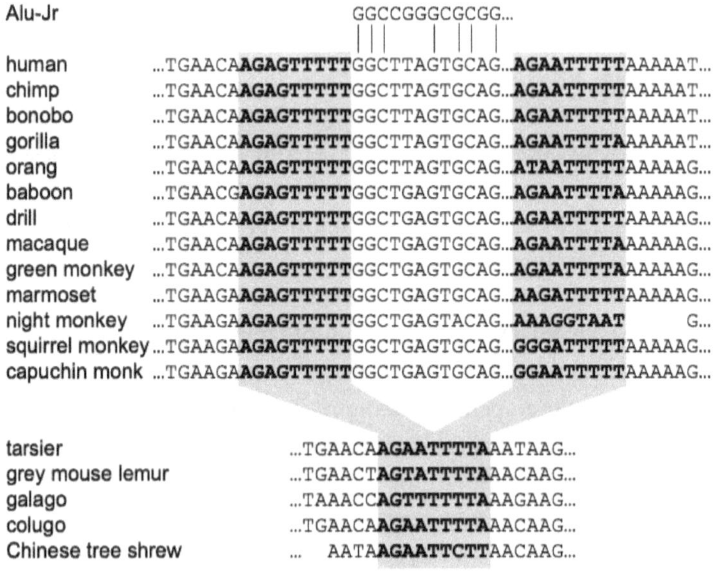

```
Alu-Jr                        GGCCGGGCGCGG...
                              ||| ||||
human            ...TGAACAAGAGTTTTTGGCTTAGTGCAG...AGAATTTTTAAAAAT...
chimp            ...TGAACAAGAGTTTTTGGCTTAGTGCAG...AGAATTTTTAAAAAT...
bonobo           ...TGAACAAGAGTTTTTGGCTTAGTGCAG...AGAATTTTTAAAAAT...
gorilla          ...TGAACAAGAGTTTTTGGCTTAGTGCAG...AGAATTTTAAAAAT...
orang            ...TGAACAAGAGTTTTTGGCTTAGTGCAG...ATAATTTTTAAAAAG...
baboon           ...TGAACGAGAGTTTTTGGCTGAGTGCAG...AGAATTTTAAAAAG...
drill            ...TGAACAAGAGTTTTTGGCTGAGTGCAG...AGAATTTTTAAAAAG...
macaque          ...TGAACAAGAGTTTTTGGCTGAGTGCAG...AGAATTTTAAAAAG...
green monkey     ...TGAACAAGAGTTTTTGGCTGAGTGCAG...AGAATTTTAAAAAG...
marmoset         ...TGAAGAAGAGTTTTTGGCTGAGTGCAG...AAGATTTTTAAAAG...
night monkey     ...TGAAGAAGAGTTTTTGGCTGAGTACAG...AAAGGTAAT         G...
squirrel monkey  ...TGAAGAAGAGTTTTTGGCTGAGTGCAG...GGGATTTTTAAAAAG...
capuchin monk    ...TGAAGAAGAGTTTTTGGCTGAGTGCAG...GGAATTTTTAAAAAG...


tarsier                  ...TGAACAAGAATTTTAAATAAG...
grey mouse lemur         ...TGAACTAGTATTTTAAACAAG...
galago                   ...TAAACCAGTTTTTTAAAGAAG...
colugo                   ...TGAACAAGAATTTTAAACAAG...
Chinese tree shrew    ...    AATAAGAATTCTTAACAAG...
```

7. Holdt et al., "Alu Elements in *ANRIL*," e1003588.
8. Kapusta et al., "Transposable Elements are Major Contributors," e1003470.

CREATED HISTORIES

```
human   ...GGGACAAACAACTATTTTATTCTT[ ]AAAAAACTATTTTATTCTTAATCT...
chimp   ...GGGACAAACAACTATTTTATTCTT[ ]AAAAAACTATTTTATTCTTAATCT...
bonobo  ...GGGACAAACAACTATTTTATTCTT[ ]AAAAAACTATTTTATTCTTAATCT...
gorilla ...GGGACAAACAACTATTTTATTCTT[ ]AAAAAACTATTTTATTCTTAATCT...


orang              ...GGGACAAACAACTATTTTATTCTTAATCT...
gibbon             ...GGGACAAACAACTATTTTATTCTTAATCT...
baboon             ...GGGACAAACAACTATTTTATTCTTAATCT...
macaque            ...GGGACAAACAACTATTTTATTCTTAATCT...
green monkey       ...GGGACAAACAACTATTTTATTCTTAATCT...
snub-nosed monkey  ...GGGACAAACAACTATTTTATTCTTAATCT...
marmoset           ...GGGACAAACAACTATTTTATTCTTAATCT...
Ma's night monkey  ...GGGACAAACAACTATTTTATTCTTAATCT...
tarsier            ...GGGACAAACAACTGTTTTGTTTTTCATCT...
galago             ...GGGACAAACAACTATTTTATTCCTAGTCT...
colugo             ...AGGACAAACAACTATTTTATTCTTTATCT...
squirrel           ...GGGACAAACAACTATTTTATTCTTAGT T...
naked mole rat     ...GGGACAAACAACTGTTTAGTCTGGATCT...
rat                ...GGAACAAAAGACTGTTTATACTAAACCC...
cat                ...GGGACAAACAACTATTTTACTTTTAATCT...
elephant           ...GGGACAAACAACTATTTTGTTTTTAATCT...
```

Insertion site of transposable elements with contrasting effects.

Top: the Alu sequence (starting "GGCTTA..." in the human genome) lies between the duplicated target site "AGAATTTTT" or similar in Old and New World monkeys and apes. This Alu element, part of the *ANRIL* gene, was shown in Holdt et al., "Alu Elements in *ANRIL*," e1003588.

Bottom: the L1PA2 sequence (represented by square brackets) lies between the duplicated target site "AAACAACTATTTTATTCTT" or similar in African great apes. Asian apes (orang-utan, gibbon), monkeys, prosimians (tarsier, galago), and non-primate genomes retain the undisturbed progenitor sequence. The L1PA2 insert activates the *SYT1* gene in cancers, and was identified by Jang et al., "Transposable Elements Drive Widespread," 611–17; Jiang and Upton, "Human Transposons are an Abundant," 16. Sequences were from the UCSC Browser (human) and the NCBI (using BLAST).

Recently, scientists have shown that many ancient transposable elements in our genome, long silenced by epigenetic means, can be aberrantly activated during cancer development. These long-term genomic residents have been co-opted, in the altered genomic environment of developing cancers, to provide sequence motifs that act as gene regulators that drive disease. Perhaps we should identify them as gene *dysregulators*, since their effects are entirely disruptive. They inappropriately activate nearby growth-enhancing genes and so promote cancer development. Whereas

Fig. 23 (top) depicts the location of a transposable element that provides useful genetic innovations, Fig. 23 (bottom) identifies one that manifests life-destroying capacities: the sequences depict a L1PA2 transposable element that acquires the capacity to drive the *SYT1* gene in at least 10 percent of cancers.[9] This represents a carcinogenic effect. An insertion event may contribute to evolution of species (a generative, adaptive role) *or* of cancers (a degenerative, maladaptive role). *Same process—opposing outcomes.*

We have described how genes may be copied-and-pasted (*via* an RNA intermediate) by enzymes originating from transposable elements (chapter 1, Fig. 6). The insertion sites of two such retrocopies are shown in Fig. 24. *APOBEC3* genes encode proteins that provide protection against genetic pathogens such as retroviruses. Our genomes have a cluster of such genes on chromosome 22. But the messenger RNA of one of these, *APOBEC3G*, has been copied-and-pasted to produce a derivative retrocopy, known as *APOBEC3I*, located on chromosome 12.[10] Investigation of its genetic history reveals that it arose in the genome of an ancestor of monkeys and apes—that is, in an simian primate ancestor (Fig. 24, top). Does the new gene retain its original function? The short answer appears to be *no*. It has accumulated many crippling mutations. Biological systems are pulsatingly opportunistic, and it is possible that some new function has arisen—but the original enzymatic function possessed by APOBEC3 has been well-and-truly disabled in this retrocopy. It was generated, and has since degenerated, by a concatenation of random events.

But the *UTP14C* gene, copied from the unique *UTP14A* progenitor, is a striking example of how a vital new gene may arise from a random mutational event.[11] The *UTP14C* gene also arose in a simian primate (monkey-ape) ancestor (Fig. 24, bottom). It exemplifies gene birth by a wholly random duplication event, followed by selection of desired features. The copied *UTP14C* daughter gene has acquired *essential* new functionality. It is involved in processing RNA and is needed for the production of sperm and for male fertility. Human reproduction now depends on a random event that occurred in an ancestor of monkeys and apes. The two inserts (Fig. 24) arose through the same random copy-and-paste process, but the events have issued in wholly different outcomes.

9. Jang et al., "Transposable Elements Drive Widespread," 611–17; Jiang and Upton, "Human Transposons Are an Abundant," 16.

10. Yang et al., "Retrocopying Expands the Functional Repertoire," e58436.

11. Rohozinski, "Lineage-Independent Retrotransposition," 171049.

CREATED HISTORIES

FIGURE 24

```
A3G transcript           ...TCCAGACAAAGA...AAATCTTTCTGTA

human          ...GGGGAC**AAATTT**CAGACAAAGA...AAAACTTCTA**AAATTT**GGTGAA...
chimp          ...GGGGAC**AAATTT**CAGACAAAGA...AAAACTTCTA**AAATTT**GGTGAA...
bonobo         ...GGGGAC**AAATTT**CAGACAAAGA...AAAACTTCTA**AAATTT**GGTGAA...
gorilla        ...GGGGAC**AAATTT**CAGACAAAGA...AAAACTTCTA**AAATTT**GGTGAA...
Bornean orang  ...GGGGAC**AAATTT**CAGACAAAGA...AAAACTTCTA**AAATTT**GGTGAA...
gibbon         ...GGGAAC**AAATTT**CAGACAAAGA...AGAACTTCTA**AAATTT**GGTGAA...
baboon         ...GGGTAC**AAACTT**CAGACAAAGA...AAAACTTCTA**AAATTT**GGTGAA...
macaque        ...GGGTAC**AAACTT**CAGACAAAGA...AAAACGTCTA**AAATTT**GGTGAA...
green monkey   ...GGGTAC**AAACTT**CAGACAAAGA...AAAACTTCTA**AACTTT**GGTGAA...
marmoset       ...GGGGAC**AAACTT**CAGACAAAGA...AAATCTTCTA**AAATTT**GGTGAA...
Ma's night mo  ...GGGGAC**AAACTT**CAGACAAGGA...AAAACTTCTA**AAATTT**GGTGAA...
squirrel monkey...AGGGAC**AAACTT**CAGACAAGGA...AAAACTTCTA**AAATTT**GGCAAT...
capuchin mo    ...GGGGAC**AAACTT**CAGACAAAGA...AAAACTTCTA**AAATTT**GGTGAA...


reconstructed target          ...GGGGAC**AAATTT**GGTGAA...
colugo                        ...      **AAATTT**GGTGAA...


UTP14A mRNA               ...TTTCCTTCGGCTT...
human          ...AAGAA**AATGGATGAC**TAGCCTTCGGCTT...**AATGGATGAC**CATTA...
chimp          ...AAGAA**AATGGATGAC**TAGCCTTCGGCTT...**AATGGATGAC**CATTA...
bonobo         ...AAGAA**AATGGATGAC**TAGCCTTCGGCTT...**AATGGATGAC**CATTA...
gorilla        ...AAGAA**AATGGATGAC**TAGCCTTCGGCTT...**AATGGATGAC**CATTA...
orangutan      ...AAGAA**AATGGATGAC**TAGCCTTCGGCTT...**AATGGATGAC**CATTA...
gibbon         ...AAGAA**AATGGATGAC**TAGCCTTCGGCTT...**AATGGATGAC**CATTA...
baboon         ...AAGAA**AATGGATGAC**TAGCCGGGCGCGG...**AATGGATGAC**CATTA...
macaque        ...AAGAA**AATGGATGAC**TAGCCTTCAGCTT...**AATGGATGAC**CATTA...
green monkey   ...AAGCA**AATGGATGAC**TAGCCTTCAGCTT...**AATGGATGAC**CATTA...
marmoset       ...AGGAA**AATAGATGAC**CAGACTTCGGCTT...**AATCGATGAC**CATTA...
night monkey   ...AGGAA**AATAGATGAC**CAGACTTCAGCTT...**AATGGATGAC**CATTA...
capuchin mon   ...AGGAA**AATAGATGAC**CAGACTTCGGCTT...**AATGGATGAC**CGTTA...

galago              ...AAGAA**AATGAATGAC**TGATA...
gray mouse lemur    ...AAAGA**AATGGATGAC**TGACA...
colugo              ...AGGAA**AATGGACAAC**TGATG...
Chinese tree shrew  ...AGGAA**AATGGATGAC**TGAAA...
horse               ...AGAAA**AATGGATGAC**TGATA...
pig                 ...AAGAA**AATGAATGAT**TGATA...
elephant            ...AGGAA**AATGGATCCC**TGATA...
manatee             ...AGGAA**A  TGCCTGA**    TA...
```

Insertion sites of retrocopied APOBEC3I (top) and UTP14C genes.

Top: The *APOBEC3I* sequence (starting "CAGACA...") lies between the duplicated target site "AAATTT" in simian primates. The original target site could not be identified with confidence. The *APOBEC3I* retrocopy was identified by Yang et al., "Retrocopying Expands the Functional Repertoire," e58436., and the genomic coordinates found by BLAST search with the *APOBEC3G* coding sequence (https://www.ebi.ac.uk/ena/data/view/AGS14892&display=fasta).

Bottom: The *UTP14C* sequence (starting "TAGCCTT...") lies between the duplicated target site "AATGGATGAC" or similar in monkeys and apes. Prosimians and non-primates retain the undisturbed progenitor sequence. Co-ordinates of the insert in the human genome were from Rohozinski (2017). Sequences were from the UCSC Browser (human), the NCBI (using BLAST), and https://www.ncbi.nlm.nih.gov/nuccore/NM_001166221.1?report=GenBank (*UTP14A* messenger RNA).

Analyses of *multiple instances* of each class of mutations, which span a range of evolutionary ages, have revealed our relatedness to other primate (and non-primate) species and taxa. Examples of the different classes of mutation presented above (Figs. 22–24) disclose precisely the same primate phylogenetic tree (Fig. 25). The dendrograms are defined by insertions of retroviral DNA of the ERV9 subtype,[12] of transposable elements,[13] and of genes copied-and-pasted by enzymes of transposable element provenance.[14] Such representative data provide a fully consistent outline of primate phylogenetic relationships.

FIGURE 25

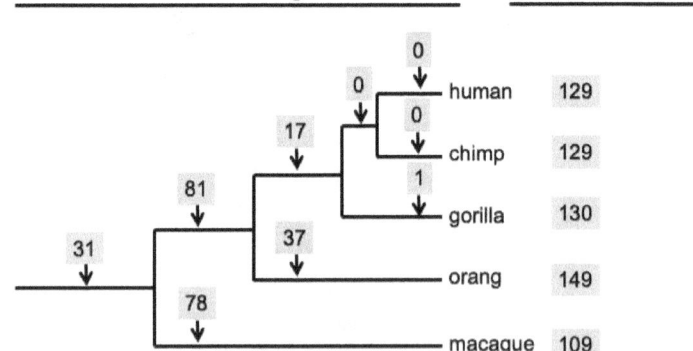

12. Gemmell et al., "Phylogenetic Analysis," e1004964.
13. Noll et al., "PAC-Genome Presence/Absence," 257–86.
14. Noll et al., "Ancient Traces of Tailless Retropseudogenes," 889–900.

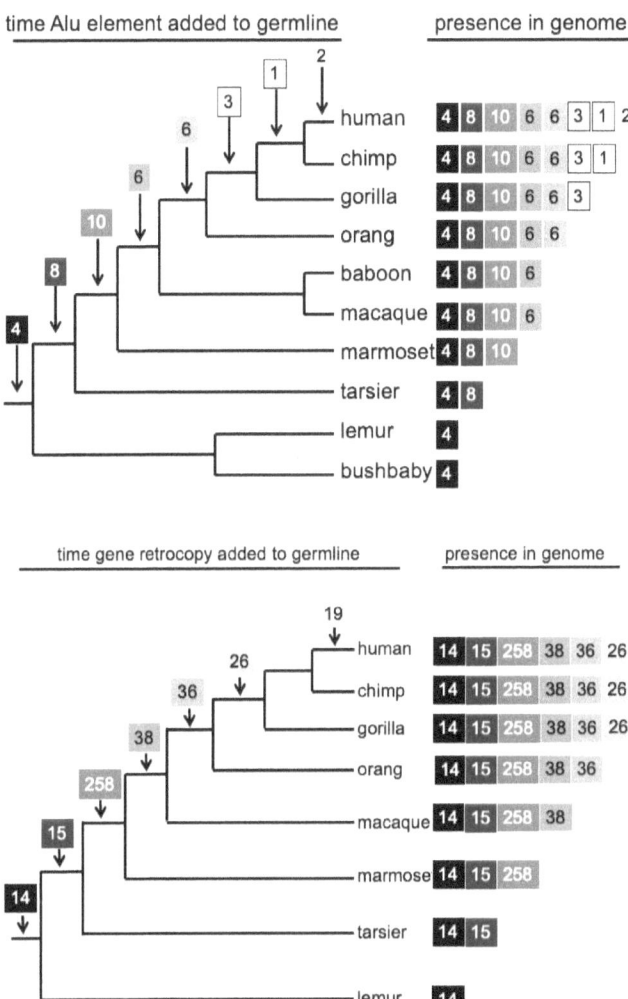

Phylogenetic trees constructed from insertions of endogenous retroviruses (ERV9 type, top), transposable elements (Alu elements), and retrocopied genes

Numerals to the right indicate the total number of inserts identified in each species Numerals above the cladograms indicate the number of individual inserts spliced into the germline at each stage of primate history. For example, eighty-one ERV9 inserts entered the primate germline in ancestors of the great apes, after the Old World monkey (represented by the macaque) lineage had branched off. From Gemmell et al., "Phylogenetic Analysis," e1004964; Noll et al., "PAC-Genome Presence/Absence," 257–86; Noll et al., "Ancient Traces of Tailless Retropseudogenes," 889–900.

We have built up a picture of accumulating mutations that, at the least, comprise a genetic barcode that specifies the route of our evolutionary ascent (Fig. 25). They provide a record of the exhilarating development of beautiful species, including the complex wonder that is *Homo sapiens*. In addition, some of these randomly inserted units of DNA have acquired notable new functions (Figs. 22–24; and previous chapters describing new genes arising with placental, neural, and immunological functions). Other inserted units of DNA may be activated in abnormal cells to drive cancer development. We can resolve the steps by which new genetic components arose, and were incorporated into the circuitry of genetic systems, by interlinear genome comparisons.

2. Retroviruses and transposable elements as oncogenetic markers

Until recently, genome sequencing has been a vast undertaking. Deciphering the genomic information of representatives of different species has been a major research project. But advances in genome sequencing technology entail that mammalian genomes now can be sequenced in a few hours. The sequencing revolution is now applicable to the genomes of *individuals*, including their cancers. This approach has enabled medical geneticists to elucidate the evolutionary histories of cancers from individual patients.

In general, *all* the cells that constitute a cancer share a set of mutations, indicating that those cells are descended from the single cell in which each such mutation occurred. That is, cancers are typically *monoclonal*. As further mutations progressively arise, they define the order of appearance of cancer subclones. The same three complex mutation types discussed above arise also in *cancer* genomes, during the history of individual patient's clinical cancers. The clonal insertion sites, in each of three human cancers, of a retrovirus (HTLV-1),[15] a transposable element,[16] and a gene copied by enzymes of jumping gene provenance[17] are depicted in Fig. 26. The insertion sites clearly show the classical target site duplications that bracket retroviral and transposable element insertions. These are characteristically six bases long in the case of HTLV-1, but of variable (but greater) length in the case

---

15. Retrovirus Integration Database (RID), https://rid.ncifcrf.gov/tmp/hg19-chr1-2741420-strand+.html.

16. Scott et al., "Hot L1 Retrotransposon," 745–55.

17. Cooke et al., "Processed Pseudogenes Acquired Somatically," 3644.

CREATED HISTORIES

of transposable element-mediated events. The molecular processes that re-modelled the genomes belonging to distant ancestors (millions of years and generations ago) are the same as those that arise in our cells today—and that, on occasions, contribute to disease.

FIGURE 26

```
HTLV-1                    TGACAATGAC...
                          |||||||||||
retroviral       ...GTTCTGAGGTCATGACAATGAC...AGGTCACCTGGG...

normal                ...GTTCTGAGGTCACCTGGG...



cancer      ...CAGTTCACTTGATAGTTTT[LINE-1]CACTTGATAGTTTTGAGAG...

normal            ...CAGTTCACTTGATAGTTTTGAGAG...



cancer      ...GTTTGCATAATTTTC[FOPNL pseudogene]CATAATTTTCAACTT...

normal            ...GTTTGCATAATTTTCAACTT...
```

Insertion sites that define clonality of cancers in individual patients.

The inserts (top to bottom) are of a retrovirus (HTLV-1), a transposable element, and a transposable element-mediated *FOPNL* gene retrocopy. From Retrovirus Integration Database; Scott et al., "Hot L1 Retrotransposon," 745–55; Cooke et al., "Processed Pseudogenes," 3644.

Such insertion mutations act as markers of monoclonality and subclonal branching in particular cancers. The use of multiple instances of such mutation classes in defining the evolution of individual patient's cancers is shown for retroviral DNA in a patient's leukemia,[18] transposable

---

18. Oksenhendler et al., "Persistent Risk," 859–62.

elements in a pancreatic cancer,[19] and genes copied-and-pasted by enzymes of transposable element provenance in a lung cancer[20] (Fig. 27).

FIGURE 27

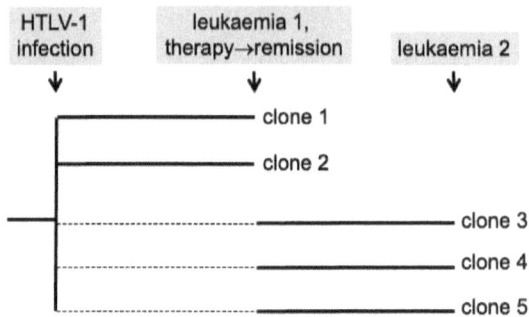

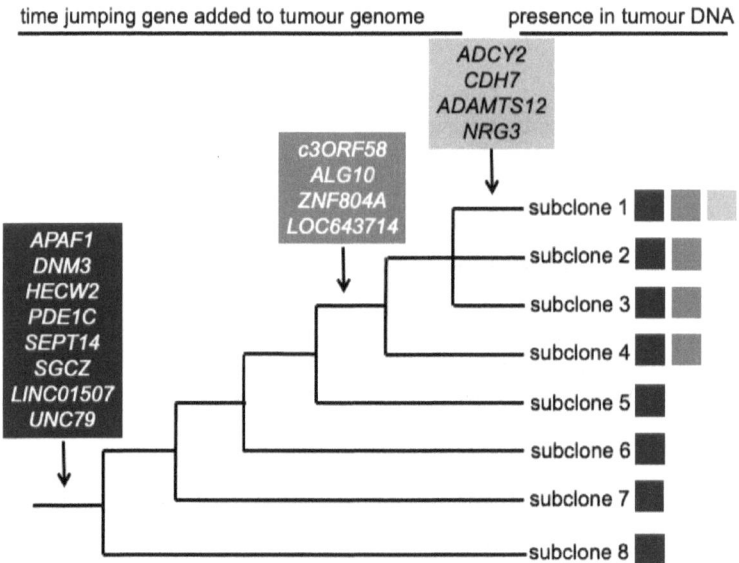

19. Rodic et al., "Retrotransposon Insertions," 1060–64.
20. Cooke et al., "Processed Pseudogenes," 3644.

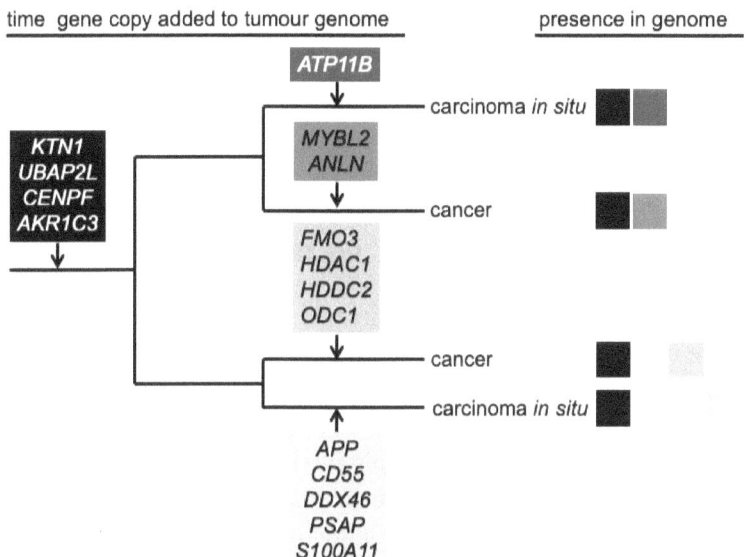

Cancer phylogenetic trees constructed from insertions of HTLV-1 retroviral DNA (top), transposable elements, and retrocopied genes.

The cancers are, respectively: a leukemia, comprised of five major clones, a pancreatic cancer, for which symbols indicate nearby genes, and a lung cancer, for which symbols indicate the gene duplicated. From Oksenhendler et al., "Persistent Risk," 859–62; Rodic et al., "Retrotransposon Insertions," 1060–64; Cooke et al., "Processed Pseudogenes," 3644.

These examples of complex, uniquely arising mutations demonstrate with stark clarity that the types of mutations and the mechanisms of genetic change that define species and their relationships during *biological evolution* are *precisely* the same as those mutations that occur in tumor cells and that define clonal diversification during *tumor evolution*. It must be stressed also that there are many other classes of mutation that can act as collaborating markers of phylogenetic and oncogenic development.[21]

Cancer evolution reverses the direction of biological evolution. Paradoxically, the same classes of genetic event mediate *diametrically opposing* evolutionary trajectories. Oncogeny reverses phylogeny.[22] "Malignancy grants somatic cells freedom from the constraints of the multicellular

---

21. Such as nuclear sequences of mitochondrial origins; see Ju et al., "Frequent Somatic Transfer," 814–24.

22. Johnston et al., "Origin of the Cancer Cell," 831–34.

organism," and takes them back to a unicellular mode of behavior.[23] Biological evolution has led to increasing complexity, differentiation, and integration of living forms; cancer evolution leads to decreasing complexity, loss of differentiation, and dis-integration.[24] Cancer cells are atavistic throwbacks to a unicellular state.[25]

3. Challenge for theology

Biological evolution inspires awe. It has led to the stupendous diversity of life, the intricacy of the myriad interactions between species that sustain the integrity of the biosphere, and the wonderful appearance of sentient beings. A product of this history that is of great significance is a creature that is said to bear God's image.[26] This awe may be tempered, however, by the co-evolution of pathogenic microbes (and of their sophisticated toxins) and of nasty parasites. Biological evolution—the evolution of species—carries a degree of ambiguity.

There is, however, nothing ambiguous about the evolution of cancers. Cancers are inherently destructive. Malignant disease elicits a sense of revulsion. The suffering experienced from the growth of cancers does not invite considerations of purpose—although sufferers may use their experiences of sickness as opportunities for growth in love and fortitude.

In the overall scheme of things, ERVs and transposable elements have contributed enormously to the construction of genetic functionality,[27] even as they have contributed to its destruction, as seen in cancers and other genetic diseases.[28] The very same properties that make transposable elements useful on evolutionary timescales contribute to disease on individual human timescales. We have highlighted this issue by events in our DNA, but our ambivalence to nature is not restricted to genetics. Geophysicist

---

23. Glassman et al,. "Cancer, Evolution and Birth," 13–16.
24. Chen and He, "Convergent Cancer Evolution," 4–12.
25. Bussey et al., "Ancestral Gene Regulatory Networks," 6160–62.
26. Gen 1:26–28.
27. Warren et al., "Evolutionary Impact," 505–31; Joly-Lopez and Bureau, "Exaptation of Transposable Element," 34–42; Platt et al., "Mammalian Transposable Elements," 25–43; Schrader and Schmitz, "Impact of Transposable Elements," 1537–49.
28. Hancks and Kazazian, "Roles for Retrotransposon Insertion," 9; Kazazian et al., "Mobile DNA," 361–70; Payer et al., "Transposable Elements in Human Genetic Disease," 760–72; Burns, "Our Conflict," 51–70.

Bob White points to the fact that shifting plates comprising the earth's crust are essential for life to exist, but they also cause earthquakes and tsunamis that devastate whole communities.[29] How is God involved in the *opposite* outcomes of the *one* lawfully constituted (divinely ordained) process?

It seems that the achievement of something resoundingly good[30] may be attained only at the cost of undesirable side-effects. C. S. Lewis wrote that "not even Omnipotence could create a society of free souls without at the same time creating a relatively independent and 'inexorable' Nature."[31] If we are to be truly free, nature has to be untamed. It follows that, in Lewis' words, "the possibility of pain is inherent in the very existence of a world where souls can meet."[32] And of course, this principle pertains also to the evil in persons. Lewis, again: "the mere existence of a self—the mere fact that we call it 'me'—includes, from the first, the danger of self-idolatry."[33]

More recently, the physicist-theologian John Polkinghorne has stated, "The created order looks like a package deal. Exactly the same biochemical processes that enable cells to mutate, making evolution possible, are those that enable cells to become cancerous and generate tumors. You can't have one without the other. In other words, the possibility of disease is not gratuitous, it's the necessary cost of life."[34] This remarkable scholar has keenly anticipated the insights of genomic science that have been described above. He wrote as if he were fully aware of the latest information about transposable elements: "the same process that allows new life to develop also permits some cells to become cancerous."[35]

The divine assessment of creation as "very good" does not imply that all evil and disease is excluded. Creation was good "as a beginning."[36] Jonathan Clarke, with a geologist's sense of time, proposed that: "the goodness here is the goodness of function, just as we would declare each stage towards the completion of a house as good, even though it is still a building

---

29. See Chris Mulherin, "Natural Disasters are Not a Result of the Fall: An Interview with Bob White," in Ashby, *Reckless God?* 91–95.
30. Gen 1:4, 10, 12, 18, 21, 25; indeed, very good, v. 31.
31. Lewis, *Problem of Pain*, 17.
32. Lewis, *Problem of Pain*, 77.
33. Lewis, *Problem of Pain*, 69.
34. Polkinghorne, *Quarks, Chaos and Christianity*, 45.
35. Polkinghorne, *Quarks, Chaos and Christianity*, 94.
36. Konig, *New and Greater Things*, 166.

site."[37] The goodness of creation indicates *fitness for purpose*.[38] According to John Walton, such purpose might include the construction of a cosmic temple in which God is worshiped, and the provision of a home for humanity.[39] In the unfolding story of God and his world, creation is the stage on which that God and those humans will work out their relationship. The Bible calls this divine-human partnership the *covenant*. The ultimate goal of this engagement is that "I will be their God and they will be my people."[40] No one ever said this would be easy!

The nineteenth-century physicist C. A. Coulson reflected deeply on the contradictions in biology. Outside his study sparrows engaged in love-play (how idyllic!); and other birds feasted on insects (how disconcerting!). Science presents to us both "greatness" and "wretchedness." Coulson said that "we are not permitted to have the one without the other also" and deemed this to be a "specifically Christian revelation." Coulson quoted the entomologist Jean-Henri Fabre, who said that "all of nature is obedient to a supreme law of sacrifice."[41] Specifically referring to evolution, Coulson saw it as "the travail of God's energy.... No wonder it is shot through with pain and sacrifice and blood."[42]

Natural selection operates during evolutionary history to maximize fitness, the ability to thrive and to reproduce over successive generations. Rolston writes: "one could even employ a religious metaphor: fitness is 'dying to self for newness of life' in a generation to come."[43] Evolutionary progression comes at a cost. But sacrificial self-giving is at the very heart of the gospel. "Since the beginning, the myriad creatures have been giving up their lives as a ransom for many. In that sense, Jesus is not the exception to the natural order, but a chief exemplification of it."[44] Rolston concludes that

---

37. See Jonathan Clarke, "Droughts and Flooding Rains: Disasters are Part of the Planet's Functioning," in Ashby et al., *Reckless God?* 89.

38. Knight, *I AM: This Is My Name*, 82: "And God saw that creation was *good for* his purposes"; Briggs et al., *It Keeps Me Seeking*, 73, 207.

39. Walton, *Lost World*, 72-92 (regarding temple); 51, 66, 149-50 (regarding goodness).

40. From Lev 26:12 to Rev 21:3; see Konig, *Eclipse of Christ*, 56-58, 87, 95, 100-101, 153, 240.

41. Coulson, *Science and Christian Belief*, 133-34.

42. Coulson, *Science and Christian Belief*, 135.

43. See Rolston, "Care on Earth: Generating Informed Concern," in Davies and Gregersen, *Information and the Nature of Reality*, 224.

44. Rolston, *Genes, Genesis and God*, 307.

"the cruciform creation is, in the end, deiform, godly, just because of this element of struggle, not in spite of it."[45]

It seems that a world that generates sentient life *must* be one in which suffering can occur, in the same sense that 2 + 2 must equal 4. Divine omnipotence cannot produce the impossible. Suffering is not gratuitous. It is necessary. And it is not only creation itself that must experience suffering. It seems that a creating God has to suffer. The God who declared creation to be resoundingly good knew what he was in for. From the beginning, the cross was written into history. Creation could never arrive at its consummation—become perfect—apart from the self-immolation of the divine Son of God.

Atheistic faith denies directionality to the evolutionary story that connects simple cells to complex cerebra. Christian faith affirms the purpose of God in creation, a purpose that must encompass the evolutionary history of humanity, the creature that is the object of his redeeming love.[46] But given that the genetic mechanisms of biological evolution (Figs. 22–24) and tumor evolution (Figs. 26–27) are the same, can we justifiably affirm the creative purposes of God in the former process (phylogenesis), but expressly deny it in the latter (oncogenesis)? Three broad approaches to this theological conundrum are considered below.

God causes every event, and all is his will

The sovereignty of God is a foundational understanding in biblical theology—albeit one that may be variously nuanced. It may be interpreted to mean that all that happens is the will of God, the immediate outcome of divine action. If we attribute the direct action of God to each genetic event that occurs during biological evolution, we must do it equally to each event that occurs in tumor evolution. In this way, God in inscrutable love and wisdom becomes directly responsible for the phylogenesis of species and pathogenesis of cancers and of other genetic diseases. We could describe such a deterministic control of matter as molecular Calvinism.

But this position does not seem to be acceptable. First, *an all-determining God is not compatible with the God of love*. The Reformed theologian Adrio Konig has questioned how people can entertain the idea that "the God of love could be held responsible for all the glaring misery on earth."

45. Rolston, *Genes, Genesis and God*, 306.
46. Eph 1:3–14.

Moreover, to speak of God's *allowing* such wretchedness is tantamount to saying that he is *responsible* for it.[47] Oord has proposed that God's love for his creation precludes coercion or interference in its operations (see section: "The contingency of histories points to an underlying genuine ontological freedom"). We must take seriously "the *meaningless* elements of our present history, which admits that *not* everything that happens is the will of God." Many things occur that are contrary to his will.[48]

It is unacceptable to posit that God mobilizes and directs jumping genes when they unleash cancer development or when their activities mediate genomic derangements during cancer evolution.[49] But to be consistent, we cannot then attribute those *same* jumping gene activities to God when they contribute to new genetic functionality, as has been documented in stem cell, placental (chapter 2), neural (chapter 3), and immunological (chapter 4) tissue.[50]

Second, *a disease-determining God is not compatible with God's disease-eliminating actions in Jesus.* The Gospels taught that God was revealed in, and God's reign inaugurated by, Jesus the Messiah.[51] This new reality was effected by Jesus' love and compassion, teaching and healing, death and resurrection. Jesus' healings showed that God was at work to eliminate the diseases that devastate people and their communities. Matthew's Gospel described many healing events, and emphasized that healing was an inextricable focus of Jesus' work.[52] Further, Matthew interpreted the healing works of Jesus in terms of prophetic expectation,[53] as signs of the dawning kingdom of God,[54] and as concomitants of Jesus' climactic appear-

---

47. Konig et al., *Systematic Theology*, 324.

48. Konig et al., *Systematic Theology*, 327; elsewhere, Konig insists that God "does not do or occasion *everything* in history" and "much does happen that is against God's will," in *Here I Am*, 127, 165.

49. Scott et al., "Hot L1 retrotransposon," 745–55; Jung et al., "Immune Signatures," 1136–46; Xia et al., "LINE-1 Retrotransposon-Mediated," 642–47; Rodriguez-Martin et al., "Pan-Cancer Analysis," 306–18.

50. Zhang et al., "Transcriptionally Active HERV-H," 1380–88; Chuong, "Placenta Goes Viral," e3000028; Etchegaray et al., "Transposable Element-Derived Sequences," 1.

51. Wright, *How God Became King*, esp. ch. 5.

52. Matt 4:23–24; 10:1, 8; 14:14, 35–36; 15:30–31; 19:2.

53. Matt 8:16–17 cf. Isa 53:4–5; Matt 11:4–5 cf. Isa 35:5–6; 61:1; Matt 12:15–21 cf. Isa 42:1–4.

54. Matt 9:35.

ance as Messiah in the temple.[55] Luke's Gospel provided the same sense of fulfilment.[56]

Jesus' healings indicated that Israel's turbulent history had come to its climax, ancient prophecy was fulfilled, the Messiah was at work, the eschatological age had come, God's kingdom was being inaugurated.[57] Jesus' works of healing effected "the restoration to membership in Israel" of those who had been excluded; his healing activities "thus function in exact parallel with the welcome of sinners . . . as part of the inauguration of the sovereign and healing rule of Israel's covenant god." Jesus' healings brought the gift of *shalom*, wholeness.[58] They pointed "to the coming of the kingdom in all creation,"[59] suggesting that the removal of suffering from non-human organisms was integral to the creative purposes of God.[60]

The Gospels announced that the elimination of disease was intrinsic to the work of Jesus and to the inauguration of God's rule. It seems incoherent to posit that God expressly sends cruel diseases to afflict his creatures, and also becomes incarnate as a human being and submits to death on a cross in order to expressly eliminate cruel diseases from his creatures. We cannot allow that God so immediately manipulates the matter of his creation (such as the genetic matter) as to elicit the growth of cancers. The Gospels assure us that God is implacably opposed to diseases—they arise despite his purposes. Emphatically, God does not send osteosarcoma in children. Osteosarcoma in children is wholly abhorrent to a God who is love.

If we deny the direct action to God in the genetic events underlying cancer evolution, we must deny direct divine action in the same classes of genetic events that underlie biological evolution, and that led to the advent of humanity. This seems to preclude ideas of God's sovereignty as understood in terms of the immediate deterministic manipulation of molecular processes such as mutations in DNA. The idea of the micro-manipulating God of molecular Calvinism does not seem to work.

---

55. Matt 21:14; cf. Mal 3:1.
56. Luke 4:16–21; 7:18–23; cf. Isa 29:18–19; 35:5–6; 61:1.
57. McKnight, *The King Jesus Gospel*, 96–100, 103; Evans, *Fabricating Jesus*, 146–47; Keener, *Historical Jesus of the Gospels*, 240.
58. Wright, *Jesus and the Victory of God*, 191–93, 196–97.
59. Bauckham, *Bible and Ecology*, 166–67.
60. Mark 1:13 cf. the ecotopia of Isa 11; Bauckham, *Bible and Ecology*, 126–29.

God causes constructive genetic events in human evolution, but a cosmic fall underlies events in cancer evolution

Does Genesis teach a cosmic catastrophe, consequent upon human rebellion, which might have unleashed the destructive activities of transposable elements? The first eleven chapters of Genesis comprise a single literary unit, and include the story known traditionally as the fall. These narratives were not intended to be prosaic descriptions of historical events. Rather, they arose when the ancient Israelites incorporated familiar stories from the stock of motifs that circulated widely in the ancient Near East as part of pagan cosmogonies (or theogonies), and invested them with radically new content. They made the audacious claim that Israel's God was sovereign, without peers or competitors (chapter 1).[61]

Genre does not require a discrete fall event. The classical idea of the fall as a cosmic catastrophe consequent upon a first act of human disobedience is untenable as an interpretation of the story in Genesis 3. This story has many *literary* features that would resonate with the people of the ancient Near East, including actors whose names were Human (*Adam*) and Living One (*Eve*), a stock wise-guy snake, and an anthropomorphic depiction of God.[62]

The idea of the fall as a *historical event* involving a fundamental resetting of the patterns of nature often persists (Genesis 3), even though the creation stories (Genesis 1 and 2) are best read *figuratively* as part of Israel's subversive proclamation of the supremacy of her God (see chapter 1). Such divergent exegetical approaches are inconsistent. Speculation about a cosmic fall event is foreign to the genre of the text—as is increasingly argued by scholars working at the theology-science interface.[63] The genres of Genesis 1–11 do not require readers to accept a historical cataclysmic fall event of cosmic consequences.

---

61. See Robert Gordon, "The Week that Made the World: Reflections on the First Pages of the Bible," in McConville and Moller, *Reading the Law*, 229, 238-39; Gordon Wenham, *Exploring the Old Testament*, ch. 2, esp. 15-18; *Genesis 1-15*, xxxvii, xlv-l, liii, 36-40.

62. Harlow, "After Adam," 179-95.

63. Polkinghorne, *Reason and Reality*, 99-101; Southgate et al., *God, Humanity and the Cosmos*, 169-70; Messer, *Christian Ethics and Selfish Genes*, 184-94; Lamoureux, *I Love Jesus*, 81-84.

John Bimson has argued that a "cosmic fall" involving the non-human creation is not taught in the Bible.[64] He indicates that the curse on the ground (Gen 3:17–19) implies not a change in creation itself, but a change in Adam's situation, as he set out to cultivate wild nature rather than the fertile Garden. The depiction of a future ecotopia ("the wolf will live with the lamb"; Isa 11:6–10) refers not to the reversal of carnivorous behavior, but to the safety of God's people who live under the Messiah's rule. Hebrew nature poetry (Pss 104; 145; Job 38:39—39:30) rejoiced in the magnificence of God's great predators. And in the New Testament, the "frustration" of creation (Rom 8:20) referred not to its "fall" but to its incompleteness, as it awaits the attainment of its goal. Creation will be fulfilled only when transformed—at last—in the consummated kingdom of God.

It seems unlikely that the teachers of Israel would have speculated on the origin of sin at some datable event in remote history. Such empirical aspects of anthropology are a modern preoccupation.[65] Perhaps the quintessentially metaphorical fall story addresses the universal experience of estrangement from God and its horrendous sequelae—incessant inter-tribal slaughter, but now in our own day recognized as human hubris issuing in personal, social, and ecological disaster. These are desperately pertinent to the current death throes of our broken world. An analogy to this interpretative approach might be *The Lord of the Rings* as commentary on the quest to power as promulgated by Nietzsche and his spiritual ilk. Sauron's *ring of power* is entirely fictitious. But the human grasp for power in all its horror describes the human condition with compelling authenticity, with riveting truth. There is One who was not captivated by the ring.

The fall story may allegorize the consequences of Israel's disobedience to her God. Wright notes the parallels between the story of Genesis 3 and Israel's turbulent history.[66] For Israel, the occupation of the land, the giving of a solemn covenant, followed by apostasy, led to judgement and exile (a living death). For Adam and Eve, the placement in the Garden, the giving of a solemn command, followed by disobedience, led to judgement

---

64. Bimson, "Reconsidering a 'Cosmic' Fall," 63–81.

65. Wenham, *Genesis 1–15*, xlv–xlvi.

66. Wright, *How God Became King*, 66; Wright, *Resurrection of the Son of God*, 92–93; Wright, *Paul and the Faithfulness of God*, 787, 1052; Wright, *Surprised by Scripture*, 37. Wright indicates that there is no evidence the story was so used (*Resurrection of the Son of God*, 122). However, biblical scholar Peter Enns strongly favors the idea that the Adam and Eve story is an allegory of Israel's often tragic history: see Giberson and Collins, *Language of Science and Faith*, 211–12.

and banishment (a living death). Genesis 3 may be commentary on God's judgement of Israel for its disobedience. The teaching point of this story is historically located; but having understood this, its relevance to hedonistic, libertarian, post-truth, twenty-first-century humanity is obvious.

Such considerations cannot question the central biblical assertion of our sinfulness. As Colin Gunton states, if we wish to maintain the truth of the concept of human fallenness, "we are not bound . . . to hold to a belief either in the literal story of Adam or in the form the doctrine of sin has often taken in the past"[67]—which presumably entails a cosmic catastrophe. In other words, our fallenness has no necessary connection to destructive, disease-causing transposable elements. We are fallen, sinful, guilty before God, because as biological creatures we have not risen, and indeed we could not rise, into the fellowship of the triune God. "Flesh and blood cannot share in God's kingdom."[68] Gunton continues, "had there been no fall, it would still have been the Father's good pleasure to come into personal relation with us through the incarnation of his Son."[69] That all people have sinned and fallen short of God's glory is a non-negotiable reality of the human condition.[70] If the rejection of a discrete, cosmos-deranging fall event in history has any effect on our understanding of the human plight, it must be to relocate the issue of our fallenness from a nebulous remote past (with all the ungrounded speculation that that idea has occasioned), to the immediate, urgent, personal present.[71]

The idea that the work of Jesus restores only what was lost in a past fall—a story that is essentially cyclic—is foreign to the directional thrust of the biblical narrative. "The view of history the Bible postulates can in no way whatever be depicted as a great cycle back to the original creation."[72] The Bible presents "a linear movement of history . . . moving forward towards judgment and new creation."[73]

---

67. Gunton, *Christ and Creation*, 45.

68. 1 Cor 15:50; note that "for Paul, 'flesh and blood' was a way of referring to ordinary, corruptible, decaying human existence, . . . the present physical humanity, subject to decay and death." Wright and Bird, *New Testament in Its World*, 313.

69. Gunton, *Christ and Creation*, 96.

70. Rom 3:23.

71. A critical discussion of various conceivable fall hypotheses is provided by Alexander, *Creation or Evolution*, 254–76.

72. Konig, *New and Greater Things*, 166–67.

73. Wright, *Surprised by Scripture*, 105.

The second-century theologian Irenaeus propounded a perspective that is compatible with the historical vista described here. The fall story of Genesis 3 described a misstep in the ever forward-moving trajectory of God's plan for a new creation. Steenberg has stated that "Irenaeus finds in Genesis 1–3 not the story of perfection/fall leading to redemption, but of imperfection, growing and maturing into the fullness of life, which is ultimately the life of Christ." Steenberg adds that the Jewish reading of the fall story interprets it as a "myth about human maturation," and this approach "allows us to discern the degree to which Irenaeus' reading of human protology [the doctrine of origins] agrees with that of various Hebrew interpreters with regard to these concepts of development and growth."[74] Irenaeus goes beyond Jewish writers, of course, in his insistence that it is the death and resurrection of Jesus that achieve human reconciliation with God.

Polkinghorne stated that "Evolutionary cosmology is consistent with an Irenaean picture of growth into fulfilment, rather than an Augustinian picture of decline from paradise."[75] Harrison describes Irenaeus' position in similar terms: "the material world had been created as a venue for the moral development of human beings." The first humans were imperfect from the start. It was inevitable that they would fall, but this was not "an unmitigated disaster," because the Creator has intended all along "to allow his creatures to err, and like children under the guidance of a benevolent parent, to mature gradually" to attain the condition purposed for them.[76]

The vastness of human history does not sit easily with a single fall event. The genetic mechanisms illustrated in Figs. 22–24 are common to both biological and cancer evolution. The retroviral and transposable element activities that currently occur during cancer evolution (Figs. 26 and 27) manifestly involve the same biochemical mechanisms (as evinced by target site duplications, for example) as those that occurred in ancestors of African great apes, Old World primates, and anthropoid primates. As such, retroviruses and transposable elements have operated seamlessly for tens of millions of years, *long preceding* the appearance of humans—or indeed of primates.

74. Steenberg, *Irenaeus on Creation*, 143; Steenberg continues: "strands of interpretive tradition have long existed in which there is played no part by what is now, in widespread Christian theology, the usual reading of Genesis 1–3 as the story of 'paradise lost' and the corruption of primitive human perfection" (144–45).

75. Polkinghorne, *Reason and Reality*, 99–100.

76. Harrison, *Bible, Protestantism and the Rise of Natural Science*, 14.

Perspectives invoking a cosmic fall (with the introduction of disease, suffering, and death) imply that a major discontinuity in the way matter operates must have occurred at some point in the past. There is no sign of a discontinuity in genetic mechanism indicative of destructive mutations appearing only in recent human history, consequent upon a crisis in obedience.

Created free histories will conform fully to God's will only at the eschaton

As highlighted in this book, the very same genetic process that have made us what we are (placental, big-brained, social primates) generate also devastating genetic diseases and destructive cancers. Are retroviruses and transposable elements (de)generative, (dis)integrative, and (mal)adaptive? We can only answer *yes*. Created history is ambiguous.

But this situation is not new. The created histories of Israel and of the church are similarly ambiguous (chapter 2). The Hebrew Scriptures provide a story of a people discovering the wonder of a loving, holy, and redeeming God, a story that has enriched humanity more than we can ever comprehend. Cahill has reminded us that the experiences of ancient Israel have facilitated the "slow evolution of our entire system of values." So many of our best words—"individual, person, vocation; time, history, future; freedom, progress, spirit; faith, hope, justice—are gifts of the Jews."[77] But those same Scriptures tell a tale of idolatry, moral failure, and national and religious disaster. Created Israel was no model of perfection. Nor, for that matter, is the created church, constituted as it is by fractious, self-seeking, often faithless people (chapter 2).

Unless we have an eschatological perspective to reality—the belief that there is an overarching direction to the sequence of events—"the primary reality is the ambiguous world of historical experience."[78] History reduces to an unfathomable admixture of the beautiful and the ugly. Reality is an uninterpretable jumble. We need a big picture to make sense of it.

The ambiguities of history lead us to recognize the presence of evil. Events involving inanimate matter and inhumane minds can devastate people's lives. When such devastation happens, is it appropriate to subsume under the single heading of *evil* both those physical processes (that destroy

---

77. Cahill, *Gifts of the Jews*, 96, 241.
78. R. A. Markus in Judge, "Religion of the Secularists," 307–19.

without intent), and those moral acts (that destroy by wilful injustice, violence, and cruelty)?

John Polkinghorne thinks so.[79] He asks how "a world of cancer and concentration camps" can be the creation of a good God. Earthquakes, or more correctly, human disaster arising from earthquakes (as this planet supports life only because earthquakes are possible) and leukemias, are forms of physical evil.[80] Oord recognizes that the cruel blows inflicted by natural processes (a rock randomly crashing through the windscreen) and by the violence and hatefulness of people (rape and murder) are equally to be recognized as evils.[81]

Colin Gunton states that Genesis 3 "makes it quite clear that moral and physical ills are interdependent, so that redemption from them will likewise involve a healing together of what we call moral and what we call physical."[82] Tom Wright warns that we must not "collude with the relatively modern break-up of the 'problem of evil' into 'natural evil' on the one hand and 'human sin' on the other."[83] A tsunami that wipes out a quarter of a million people in one day, and the inhumanity epitomized by Auschwitz are both to be recognized as evils.[84] Perhaps we could subsume under the category of evil anything that is contrary to the nature of the God of love and holiness.

The phylogenetic history documented in this chapter, and the histories of humanity, of Israel, and of the church, together raise questions regarding the presence of evil. These issues are particularly acute for people who believe in a God of love. The forms of evil are of different types, but they are evils nevertheless, and provide motivation to ask whether we might gain insight into the evils inherent in biological history from the study of evils in biblical history.

---

79. Polkinghorne, *Science and Providence*, 65, 67.

80. Polkinghorne, *Science and Christian Belief*, 83–85; *Quarks, Chaos, and Christianity*, 45.

81. Oord, *Uncontrolling Love of God*, ch. 1.

82. Gunton, *Christ and Creation*, 19.

83. Wright, *Paul and the Faithfulness of God*, 749; or as Wright and Bird say, "Evil—moral evil, societal evil, evil within the natural order itself—matters profoundly to God. It distorts and defaces his world," *New Testament in Its World*, 371.

84. Wright, *Surprised by Scripture*, 111; also 116, 127.

Evolution and Eschatology

i. Biological and human histories are contingent

The courses of histories are unpredictable, unforeseeable, not wholly determined. The possibility of evil is inherent in the histories of creations because such histories do not follow minutely specified routes.[85] Their twists and turns and dead ends might have been otherwise. Such contingency describes the way by which the complex mutagens (retroviruses, transposable elements) operate. It is not specified which agent in a genome will act next; or in what cell; or to what site in the genome a daughter element will be inserted; or when; or to what effect. *Contingency* defines biological development, in all its "uniqueness, singularity, specificity and unrepeatability."[86]

And in this contingent behavior, biological history shares the unpredictability of human histories. The historian Herbert Butterfield referred to such uncertainty as "the chanciness of human life and the precarious nature of man's existence in this risky universe." Butterfield warned against the presumption that modernity could buffer itself against the "contingencies and accidents of time."[87] We are in all things subject to the experience of contingency. How does this phenomenon relate to the underlying structures of our world?

ii. The contingency of histories points to an underlying genuine ontological freedom

John Polkinghorne says that we live in a world of genuine becoming.[88] He has drawn a vital analogy between the progressive unfolding of biological history, and that of persons and societies. There is *free process* in cosmic and biological history, just as there is *free will* in human history.[89]

Polkinghorne's proposal that histories are genuinely free is supported by other Christian physicists. Briggs, Halvorson, and Steane acknowledge "that much that goes on in the world is not what God would wish. So this world has this independence from God, while nevertheless only being able

---

85. Polkinghorne, *Science and Christian Belief*, 66.
86. John Haught in Conway Morris, *Deep Structure*, 228–30.
87. Butterfield, *Christianity and History*, 93–94.
88. Polkinghorne, *Science and Creation*, 39, 41; *Science and Christian Belief*, 81.
89. Polkinghorne, *Science and Providence*, 65–68; *Reason and Reality*, 84; *Science and Christian Belief*, 79, 83–85; *Quarks, Chaos, and Christianity*, 46–47.

to be there because God decides that it will continue."[90] Biological systems and human persons act freely, in their own ways (mutations in the former case, conscious volition in the latter), according to the respective capacities that God has endowed upon them. Biology and humanity would cease to be what they are if God were to rescind their freedom. As Steane says, "having given to humanity the ability to make choices, the option of overriding those choices does not exist; it would be the equivalent of taking away the very humanity that is essential to who we are."[91]

Adrio Konig argues that the depth of suffering in this world precludes any idea that God controls all the events of history. Much that happens in the world is an affront, a grief to God. Konig has written, "from the overwhelming witness of Scripture, it is perfectly clear that, if in one way or another we smuggle the chaos and misery of the world into his eternal purpose, it does not advance God's honour. It dishonours him!"[92] The happenings of this world are free, and many things that arise are deeply opposed to the purposes of God.

Creation must be free; random mutations, like human agents, are ontologically free.[93] Oord has suggested that, because of his love for creation, God *cannot* deprive it of freedom.[94] He calls this relationship between God and a free-but-always-dependent creation *essential kenosis*, where *kenosis* refers to the self-giving nature of God. This idea states that "God's eternal nature is uncontrolling love. Because of love, God necessarily provides freedom/agency to creatures; . . . randomness in the world and creaturely free will are genuine."[95]

Retroviruses on the one hand and persons on the other are free agents, independently exercising the powers of agency that are appropriate to their nature as molecular biological systems or self-conscious persons. But does this reduce God to an effete spectator of history—an eighteenth-century, absentee, deist abstraction? Biblical faith entails that God works in providence and miracle and responds to prayer.[96] However, Christians

---

90. Briggs et al., *It Keeps Me Seeking*, 220.
91. Steane, *Faithful to Science*, 220.
92. Konig et al., *Systematic Theology*, 322–26.
93. Oord, *Uncontrolling Love of God*, 40–41.
94. Oord, *Uncontrolling Love of God*, 169–75.
95. Oord, *Uncontrolling Love of God*, 94–95, also 151–91; the idea of kenosis is from the hymn of Phil 2:6–11, particularly verse 7.
96. Polkinghorne, *Science and Providence*, chs 3, 4, 6 (eg p 43); "a personal God . . .

have widely differing perceptions as to *how* God interacts with creation. As Mark Worthing says, theists hold to the complete spectrum of understandings of providence: from "God acts through natural causes only" to God determines "every single action and movement of every molecule."[97] People's understandings span the gamut from molecular Arminianism (the creatures are free) to molecular Calvinism (the creatures do what they are told). But Coulson asked whether we should choose between these understandings—between Kingsley's "absolute empire of accident and a living, immanent, ever-working God." He concluded that we should not regard these perspectives as alternatives: "the two accounts of the development of the natural order are not to be regarded as exclusive."[98] Scientific descriptions cannot by their nature speak of divine action, purpose, or compassion; God's purposes and actions are hidden to the scientist but everywhere in operation.

Polkinghorne has wondered whether God might influence the world by inputting information into quantum process.[99] Any such influence, however, is not apparent in the opposing consequences of genetic mechanism. For if God directs a transposable element so as to produce new functionality, why does God not deflect a transposable element when its activity might be oncogenic? We should not reduce or equate God's action to any physical process. Perhaps we should be content to acknowledge that God's acts reflect a higher rationality than is perceptible to us, and God's actions, such as miracles, may represent the lawfulness of the still-to-be-completed kingdom of God.[100] God's actions may be proleptic instantiations of the as-yet-undiscovered lawfulness of the new creation.

As Owen Gingerich says, God's involvement in creation is unnoticed, although not excluded by science. God acts but not always in ways most obvious to our blinkered vision.[101] And the three professors concur: God's acts do not "break" the laws of nature but reflect the "breaking-in" of higher laws. We should be content with the suggestion that "Our belief that God

---

must be capable of specific response to specific circumstance," *Reason and Reality*, 56.

97. Worthing, *Unlikely Allies*, 38.

98. Coulson, *Science and Christian Belief*, 97.

99. Polkinghorne, *Reason and Revelation*, 45–47; *Quarks, Chaos, and Christianity*, 69–72; *Science and Christian Belief*, 68, 77.

100. Polkinghorne, *One World*, 75–76; *Science and Providence*, 51.

101. Gingerich, *God's Universe*, 111, 121.

acted in history is not conditioned on our having some quasi-scientific story about how He did it."[102]

We do not capitulate to deism if we believe that God continuously upholds creation and ordains at every instant of time that the creatures exercise a lawful independence (a position of faith along with any other position). Moreover, no one can be a deist if he or she holds to the conviction that God has profoundly altered, indeed is transforming, the course of cosmic and human history in the incarnation and work of Jesus. Ultimately, as the three professors write: "the world is not merely the outworking of impersonal forces, but also the arena of personal encounters and stories. If humans can enact personal encounters without breaking out of the patterns we call 'laws of nature', then so can God."[103]

iii. The future is not fully determined: history is open

Polkinghorne posits that the freedom devolved upon creation entails that the future is open.[104] He has written, "I do not believe that the future is up there waiting for us to arrive. If the future plays so significant a role in the present, it is not because we are witnessing the unfolding of an inexorable plan, but rather because final fulfilment, though arrived at through the contingencies of history, is guaranteed by the steadfast love of a God ceaselessly at work within that history."[105] To Polkinghorne, the unpredictabilities of history "are signs of a genuine ontological openness."[106] As another physicist, Paul Ewart, asserts: "chance is both real and has a creative role to play in achieving God's purposes."[107] Indeed, he marvels at its exploratory function: "the operation of chance in evolution is entirely consistent with a creative purpose. It [chance] is seen as the most efficient and effective way of

---

102. Briggs et al., *It Keeps Me Seeking*, 287, 295.

103. Briggs et al., *It Keeps Me Seeking*, 108.

104. Polkinghorne, *Science and Creation*, 41, 43–44, 48–49; *Quarks, Chaos, and Christianity*, 73.

105. Polkinghorne, *Science and Christian Belief*, 66, also 61; *Quarks, Chaos, and Christianity*, 42.

106. Quoted in Oord, *Uncontrolling Love of God*, 128.

107. Ewart, "Necessity of Chance," 111–31.

realising the potentialities inherent in the nature of the created material."[108] And Oord: "history is open and creatures join God in writing it."[109]

Such perspectives may appear unsettling to people who have been brought up to believe (despite all appearances in this broken world) that God controls everything. And yet created history is on the move.

> The openness [reflecting random change] is positive. It is the sort of process which does not dictate where things will go in detail, but gives an opportunity for things to explore, to find their own way into the space of possibility. . . . Randomness is often portrayed as some sort of defect or problem. But randomness could also be named openness. It is freedom from micro-management. Is there, in fact, any difference between randomness and openness, in cases where the material has no conscious agency?[110]

To Holmes Rolston, as far as evolution is concerned, "the exact routes it takes are open and subject to historical vicissitudes."[111] For John Haught, in the word's dramatic unfolding, there is a "contingent openness to indeterminate future outcomes."[112] And to my inspirational theology professor, Adrio Konig, "Creation was brought into being to be open to the future and to move towards it."[113] We are wont to say that nothing happens by chance. We should recognize that in a free world, we are indeed subject to happenstance. But if our history is free, and the end is open, how can we hope for anything but chaos and carnage?

iv. History proceeds by the operation of free events in the context of directing order

In cosmic and biological history, there is flexibility-within-constraint. The operation of random movement that is channelled along well-laid routes has been described as the interplay between *chance and necessity*. Chance could be expressed as happenstance, the way that things happen to be. Chance (epitomized by retroviral insertions and transposable elements)

---

108. Ewart, "Necessity of Chance," 111–31.
109. Oord, *Uncontrolling Love of God*, 111.
110. Briggs et al., *It Keeps Me Seeking*, 203.
111. Rolston, *Genes, Genesis and God*, 208.
112. See John Haught, "Purpose in Nature: On the Possibility of a Theology of Evolution," in Conway Morris, *Deep Structure*, 228–29.
113. Konig, *New and Greater Things*, 169.

generates novelty and underlies the possibility of change and development. *Necessity* refers to the lawful regularity that governs what is possible and how things develop. Necessity tests, selects, and preserves those novelties that can contribute to new forms and functions.[114] Polkinghorne proposes that, theologically, *chance* represents the divine gift of freedom, and *necessity* represents the divine gift of faithfulness, regularity, consistency.[115] The God who is both loving and faithful has given to his creation the twin gifts of independence *and* reliability.[116]

Chance (the random generation of variety) in the context of lawful necessity (the constraints that ensure that potentially fruitful variants are perpetuated) can lead to "inescapable conclusions" because although the "path is subject to chance, its end is not."[117] The openness that we have noted above is not absolute. It is limited. History has a limited set of destinations. Thus, random events such as mutations are the driving force of evolution, but the variants that survive and propagate are restricted to clearly demarcated habitable channels presented by the environment. "Although individual steps in evolution may be random, the overall direction is constrained by the way the world is."[118]

It is not only physicists but biologists also who have commented on the directedness of evolution. Chance or happenstance in the context of lawful consistency may generate evolutionary predictabilities if not inevitabilities. Conway Morris posits that "the evolutionary destinations—say humans—are very far from being fortuitous, and by implication unpredictable. To the contrary, the evidence suggests that in reality rather than being an open-ended process evolution is deeply constrained."[119] Organisms can evolve adaptive solutions independently. This tendency of living organisms to independently generate a stock suite of adaptations when presented with common challenges (or opportunities) is called *convergence*.

Capacities thrown up randomly are stringently tested for their compatibility with biophysical givens: "the lines of evolutionary vitality

---

114. Polkinghorne, *The Way the World Is*, 8, 11; *One World*, 50–55; *Science and Creation*, 47–50; *Quarks, Chaos, and Christianity*, 39–40; *Science and Christian Belief*, 76–77; Oord, *Uncontrolling Love of God*, 32–39.
115. Polkinghorne, *Reason and Reality*, 82–83.
116. Polkinghorne, *Quarks, Chaos and Christianity*, 42.
117. Polkinghorne, *One World*, 68.
118. Briggs et al., *It Keeps Me Seeking*, 63.
119. Conway Morris, "Predictability of Evolution," 1313–37.

thread through a landscape that leaves evolution with surprisingly few choices. The basis of this view relies on the phenomenon of evolutionary convergence."[120] In general, evolutionary process has an "uncanny ability ... to navigate to the appropriate solution through immense 'hyperspaces' of biological possibility"[121] in such a way that "something like ourselves is an evolutionary inevitability."[122]

The fruitful synergism between chance and necessity may be seen also in the passage of human histories. Human behavior may be pretty arbitrary, but in many cases the outcomes may be anticipated. Human history is subject to moral law; its course is affected by the lawful constrains of people's fate-effecting deeds.[123] Scripture stresses that our choices, good or bad, do influence future generations.[124] We do reap what we sow.[125] We may consider, for example, whether the rejection of marriage in the West, say since the 1960s, *must* result in generations of rootless and broken children; and whether uncontrollable consumerism *must* overwhelm the resilience of the biosphere and lead to ecological catastrophe. The mid-nineteenth-century historian Herbert Butterfield observed that morality itself was part of the structure of human history.[126]

v. Biological and human histories may be read as stories embodying meaning and purpose

Our worldviews are expressed in *stories*. Wright states that stories are more fundamental than facts; that "metaphors and stories are in fact *more* basic within human consciousness than apparently factual speech."[127] When we reflect on New Testament history—and it may be suggested, the historical sciences—it is stories that answer "the great worldview questions: who we are, where we are, what time it is, what's wrong, what the solution might be,

---

120. Conway Morris, "Evolution: Like Any Other Science," 133–45.
121. Conway Morris, *Life's Solution*, 327.
122. Conway Morris, *Life's Solution*, xv.
123. Keillor, *God's Judgements*, 69.
124. Exod 34:6–7; Lev 26; Deut 5:8–10.
125. Gal 6:7–8; Rom 8:5–6.
126. Butterfield, *Christianity and History*, 68; and ch. 3.
127. Wright, *New Testament and the People of God*, 84, 130.

and what we should be doing about it."[128] Stories encapsulate our worldviews. They specify the way we view and interpret facts.

Amazing new realities emerge during evolution. Rolston asserts that this great sequence of innovations "can only be related as a story. Stories do progress."[129] Our story begins with physics, progresses through chemistry, then through biology, and ultimately diversifies into the multiple stories found in culture. As enculturated creatures, we seek to *interpret* this story. Biological evolution is a story that becomes memorable, cumulative, and transmissible only with genes[130]—as has been abundantly illustrated in the case of the selected genetic mechanisms in this book. At the least, we have a continuous (genetic) record of our past; and its detailed textuality (written in DNA) and its haunting, astonishing character cry out for interpretation—and integration into the Great Story of the creating and redeeming God.

John Haught sees that the blend of contingency, law, and time that is inherent to evolutionary progression comprises a story. "Since meaning is generally embodied in the form of story, it is conceivable that the irreducibly narrative character of nature opens it up, in a remarkably deep sense, to being the embodiment of purpose. . . . The concrete *togetherness* of contingency, lawful necessity and deep time" are "inseparable aspects of nature's narrative setting."[131] We are challenged to seek deeper understanding, to reflect on the interconnectedness of events, to perceive meaning and discover purpose in our engagement with the evolutionary story.

The Jewish people told stories because such storytelling made sense of the whole of reality. Stories gave voice to their hope and subverted other ways of interpreting the world.[132] "One of the major differences between them and some other cultures, however, was that their controlling stories had to do with actual events in history."[133]

As Hauerwas and Willimon state, "the Bible is fundamentally a story of a people's journey with God. Scripture is an account of human existence as told by God." The people of Israel found their identity by telling the story

---

128. Wright and Bird, *New Testament in Its World*, 81.

129. Rolston, *Genes, Genesis and God*, 207.

130. Rolston, *Genes, Genesis and God*, 52, 355–56.

131. See John Haught, "Purpose in Nature: On the Possibility of a Theology of Evolution," in Conway Morris, *Deep Structure*, 223–25, 227–29, quote from 228.

132. Wright, *New Testament and the People of God*, 41–43.

133. Wright, *New Testament and the People of God*, 149–50.

of God's salvation from slavery—not by philosophizing about the relative merits of monotheism and polytheism. When telling their story, Israel came to see themselves "as a people on a journey, an adventure." People such as we, who learn from Israel's experience, discover that "God is taking the disconnected elements of our lives and pulling them together into a coherent story that means something."[134] When our stories (biological, biblical, and personal) are integrated, subsumed, encompassed into the one Great Story of God's dealing with us his creatures, we discover the intense wonder of our placement in the divine Great Narrative.

Stories have highlights that evince their significance. When we peer attentively at history, we find that it is not merely a sequence of uncoordinated events, with all the directionality of a meandering drunk. We may be able to see God's purposes in biological history at decisive turning points. These could include the development of cells, of multi-cellularity, and of neural networks. In human evolutionary history such turning points may be developments in dexterity, mentality, culture, and sociality.[135] As far as humans are concerned, "It is particular elements that give meaning to history. Expressed in terms of God's creative purpose, history's meaning is reflected in such characteristics as peace, love, righteousness, harmony, joy, and the glorification of God."[136] It is decisive new turning-points, new directions, that give meaning to history.[137] Coruscations of wonder engender confidence in a divinely conferred meaning to history. It is a strange sort of faith that dismisses evolutionary change as nothing more than uncoordinated sequences of brute fact, and to consider ourselves as the paradigm of the metaphysical doctrine of non-exceptionalism.

vi. The biological and human stories are incomplete

The troubling and painful ambiguities that we see in biological history, like those so disturbingly apparent in Israel's history, indicate that those stories await their denouement, their satisfying culmination. As long as malaria, emergent viral diseases, and cancers blight people's lives, we are witnesses and participants of nature's "still-unfinished story."[138] But the painful sense

---

134. Hauerwas and Willimon, *Resident Aliens*, 53, 54.
135. Rolston, *Genes, Genesis and God*, 208.
136. Konig, *New and Greater Things*, 170.
137. Konig, *New and Greater Things*, 173–75.
138. Haught in Conway Morris, *Deep Structure*, 229; and as quoted earlier, geologist

of waiting is familiar to those who have traveled with God, as attested in Scripture. St Paul states that in anticipation of a consummated story, creation groans, the people of God groan, and the Spirit groans.[139]

The story of Israel, recounted in the Hebrew Bible, "runs out without a sense of an ending, except one projected into the future. This story still needs to be completed." Out of the pain of its checkered history, the writers of Israel perceived that their "great story" was not yet complete, and remained full of ambiguity.[140] Our heroic God does not abandon creation but remains faithful and continues the story.[141] We wait on tip-toes. But we are not presented with an interminable wait, peering into the haze. And that is because Jesus the Messiah has come (as Gunton says) to "complete the story."[142]

vii. Completion of all stories is achieved in Jesus the Messiah

Creation has been endowed with a marvellous propensity to produce worshiping creatures such as we are. But that same freedom underlies the appearance of disease and suffering, human hubris, and perverted forms of worship. God's providential action is not obvious from observing nature or human history. Konig proposes that "the situation in which God's will will be done in everything is a *future* promise." We need, then, what Konig calls an *eschatological doctrine of providence*.[143] Histories will be lucid and unambiguous pointers to the goodness of God *only in the light of their completion*. Created reality, including our place in it, will be fully transparent to God's love only when the story is complete. Intimations of that perfection are now visible: "the cross is the heart of providence."[144]

As we twenty-first-century questioners agonize over the ambiguities of natural and human histories—this hotchpotch of goodness and evil—it is illuminating to discover that Christian faith arose in the attitudes of

---

Jonathan Clarke stated: "Creation is not yet finished . . . we are living on a building site," in Ashby et al., *Reckless God?* 89–90.

139. Rom 8:18–30.

140. Wright, *Testament and the People of God*, 216–19; *How God Became King*, 66–67; "creation is good but incomplete," *Surprised by Scripture*, 116, 119.

141. Hauerwas and Willimon, *Resident Aliens*, 57.

142. Gunton, *Christ and Creation*, 30.

143. Konig et al., *Systematic Theology*, 327–33.

144. Timothy Gorringe in Polkinghorne, *Science and Christian Belief*, 85.

quintessential evil that motivated the murder of Jesus. "The multiple ambiguities of God's actions in the world come together in the story of Jesus."[145] In the incarnation, when the very being of God entered matter, biology, and humanity, and in Jesus' proclamation of the kingdom of God, his death, and his resurrection, we have the hermeneutic key that gives hope and meaning to the ambiguities of phylogenetic, human, and Israelite history.

In the late 1800s, the embryologist Ernst Haeckel proposed that "ontogeny recapitulates phylogeny." That is, he postulated that the development of the *individual* (ontogeny) summarizes or re-enacts (*recapitulates*) the development of the *species* (phylogeny). The idea of recapitulation in embryology is now discredited and has been abandoned. But a concept of recapitulation has had a long hearing in theology. The second-century theologian Irenaeus developed a concept of theological recapitulation.[146] God's Messiah, Jesus, represents in himself and completes (sums up or *recapitulates*) the histories of the world. Jesus served as creation's, humanity's, and Israel's representative, and so all histories and their purposes are brought to fulfilment and resolution in him.

Konig presents a perspective like that of Irenaeus. Christ is himself the goal (*eschatos*) towards which all creation is directed.[147] It follows that the entire history of Jesus is eschatology.[148] Cosmic, biological, and personal elements must be included in any biblical eschatology.[149] All are represented by, and find their fulfilment in, Jesus the Messiah.

First, Jesus sums up the universe in himself.[150] Second, Jesus as Emmanuel is the representative human: he is "*the* human being, as God's covenant partner, not for himself but for us."[151] Thus Jesus represents and brings *human* history to its completion. Third, the Hebrew Scriptures describe Israel's miscarried history in which the covenant failed; but as the goal of Israel's history, Jesus "is himself both the fulfiller and the fulfilment of God's covenant with Israel"—indeed he is the covenant.[152] Jesus completes cosmic and biological history just as he completes human and Israelite history.

---

145. Wright, *Surprised by Scripture*, 120.
146. Steenberg, *Irenaeus on Creation*, 21, 39, 49, 85–86, 107–10, 136, 154.
147. Konig, *Eclipse of Christ*, 34–35; referring to Rev 1:17.
148. Konig, *Eclipse of Christ*, 15, 17, 23, 37–41, 44, 47.
149. Konig, *Eclipse of Christ*, 63.
150. Konig, *Eclipse of Christ*, 29.
151. Konig, *Eclipse of Christ*, 45, 56, 58.
152. Konig, *Eclipse of Christ*, 44, covenant failed; 56, the fulfilment of God's covenant

CREATED HISTORIES

Gunton also expresses ideas reminiscent of Irenaeus' theology of recapitulation. "Jesus is the one who relives the human story in direct inversion of the adamic pattern"[153] (where *adamic* pertains to Adam, understood here as the literary symbol of mortal, sinful humankind). Gunton posits different ways by which Jesus recapitulates created histories. In his incarnation, he took a body of the clay of the earth, of matter, truly "flesh of our flesh," so that "*this* part of the earth [could] be fully itself, to move to perfection. . . . Jesus is within the world as human, and yet as new act of creation by God."[154] In his baptism, his anointing as Messiah, he was shown to represent Israel, "the people of God under judgement," and yet offers to the Father "the perfection of a true human life."[155] In his death on the cross he represents a "sample of fallen flesh" that is now "purified and presented to God the Father."[156] The perfect life of Jesus is a "representative sample" of the created order, which is destined to be united with him. This unity between Creator and creation is the end, the final accomplishment, to which Jesus' recapitulation of histories is directed. Jesus represents matter (the free processes of which have generated beauty or disease), as well as humanity and Israel (the moral freedoms of which have produced goodness or evil). In his life and death of perfect obedience, Jesus offers a perfected instantiation of each to the Father. These multiple histories are focused and completed in Jesus.

Given the unity of histories, we could well expand and generalize Irenaeus' (and Gunton's) proposal. Jesus recapitulates in himself, brings to a head, perfects, *all* histories. Jesus represents in himself and completes the history of the physical creation, of non-human organisms, of humanity, and of Israel. We could say that "eschatology recapitulates all other created histories." Or that Christology recapitulates cosmology, biology, primatology, anthropology. Or even, to coin a word that links the history of Jesus with the created histories of biology and humanity: "eschatogeny recapitulates phylogeny." The history of Jesus, leading to his unchallenged rule of love over everything, perfects all other histories.

Tom Wright's perspectives echo those of Irenaeus. God's story in the world—culminating in the story of Jesus—"is the greatest story ever told,

---

with Israel; 59, he is the covenant.

153. Gunton, *Christ and Creation*, 29–30.
154. Gunton, *Christ and Creation*, 52–53.
155. Gunton, *Christ and Creation*, 53–57.
156. Gunton, *Christ and Creation*, 58–59.

and it will draw all our stories up into it."¹⁵⁷ In other words, the story of Jesus recapitulates all others. Humans were commissioned to care for the non-human creation, but failed. The people of Israel were called as God's covenanted people, to be a light, a channel of blessing to all humanity, but also failed, and indeed found that they were part of the problem. Jesus the Messiah was sent to be the representative of Israel, to bring Israel's history to its resolution, and to perform the redemptive task that Israel had so signally failed to do.¹⁵⁸ In his full obedience, Jesus redeemed Israel, and in so doing completed Israel's commission and redeemed humanity. In taking a body of a primate, indeed a body composed of atoms forged in the furnaces of dying stars,¹⁵⁹ Jesus also completed the task entrusted to humanity and redeemed the non-human creation, both animate and inanimate, and brought creation to its intended end in union with God.¹⁶⁰ This is summarized in Fig. 28.

Wright has emphasized this unifying perspective: God's self-disclosure in Jesus "is where Israel's history and with it world history reached their moment of destiny. . . . The story has been completed—the story of creation, the story of God's covenant with Israel. Now new creation can begin, as it does immediately afterward with Jesus' resurrection."¹⁶¹

God is going to do for the cosmos what he had done for Jesus at Easter.¹⁶² Resurrection showed that "what the covenant God had done for Jesus he would do not only for all his people but for the whole creation. He would 'swallow up death for ever.'"¹⁶³

---

157. Wright, *Surprised by Scripture*, 40, 90.

158. Wright, *Paul and the Faithfulness of God*, 825-33; Jesus "would do for Israel what Israel could not do for itself." (Wright and Bird, *New Testament in Its World*, 259; also 515).

159. "Every atom of carbon inside our bodies was once inside a dead star. We are made from the ashes of dead stars" (Polkinghorne, *Quarks, Chaos and Christianity*, 29); "We are all definitely star stuff" (Gingerich, *God's Universe*, 84).

160. Wright, *Surprised by Scripture*, 33-39, 118-20; see esp. Rom 8:17-26; *Paul and the Faithfulness God*, 740-64, 926-28; Wright and Bird, *New Testament in Its World*, 83.

161. Wright, *How God Became King*, 77, 79.

162. Wright, *Surprised by Hope*, 93, 99, 123, 136; God's intention was "to sum up in the Messiah all things in heaven and on earth"; Wright and Bird, *New Testament in Its World*, 78.

163. Wright, *Paul and the Faithfulness of God*, 756, quoting 1 Cor 15:54, alluding to Isa 25:8.

FIGURE 28

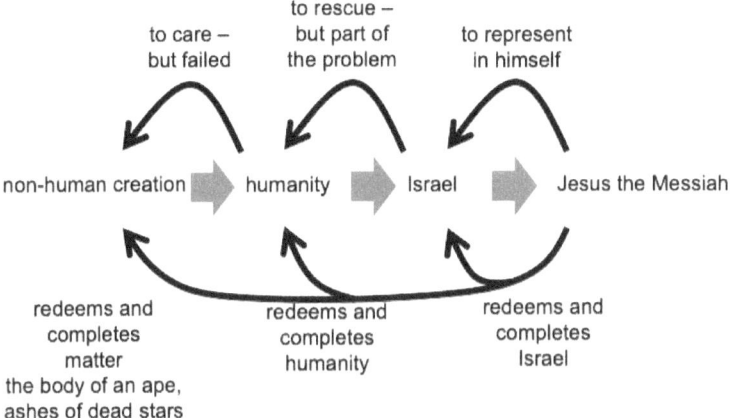

Jesus the Messiah takes all histories upon himself.

Jesus takes up all the parts of created reality as their perfect representative, bearing them to the cross and conferring upon them their fulfilment in the newness of the resurrection.

We summarize God's Great Narrative. The story of the physical and biological creation (that must include primate evolution), the story of humanity, and the story of Israel (as recorded in the Hebrew Scriptures) come to their denouement together, in their common focus on Jesus of Nazareth. People have long debated about whether this is the best of all possible worlds. Perhaps we may assume that the physical creation is indeed the best of all possible worlds (or among the set of best possible worlds) if God is to bring into being sentient, free agents who can participate in the divine life. But if that is so then we must appreciate that this best of all possible worlds is currently incomplete; there is a better possible state for this best possible world, and it is a state that is still to be realized. Its realization is an end that required God to take up matter and evil upon himself and pour out his divine life-force. According to the gospel, this is precisely what God does in the life and death of Jesus.

It seems that biological evolution could produce only an embodied creature enlivened by a biological nature—a *soma psychikon*—albeit, extraordinarily, one that could participate in the dimension of interpersonal relationship, including relationship with God. But God's completed creation required—and *always* required—the investment of the life of God himself in order to transform this biological creature into one that would be an embodied creature enlivened and energized by the Spirit of God—a *soma pneumatikon*.[164] Humanity as a completed product of history will possess the unprecedented and previously unimaginable *zoe aionios*, the life of the new age,[165] to which all of God's created histories pointed, the imperishable quality of the life of God himself.

This great transformation represented a climactic interruption of biological process. It required that one of the persons of the Holy Trinity should appear in human history (the incarnation), that he should live a selfless obedience culminating in death on a cross, and that a new paradigm of glorified humanness and a perfected creation should be born in the wholly unanticipated, colossal surprise of the resurrection. The evolutionary biologist Theodosius Dobzhansky said famously that "Nothing in biology makes sense except in the light of evolution."[166] We can adapt this as: "Nothing in evolution makes sense except in the light of eschatology."

Christians live in the hope that "creation itself would one day be set free from its slavery to decay and would share in the glorious freedom of the children of God."[167] Philosophers used to debate as to whether this current cosmos was the best of all possible worlds. Perhaps it is the best of all worlds in which God's eschatological program, achieved by God's Messiah Jesus, has yet to arrive at its glorious consummation.[168]

---

164. 1 Cor 15:44; Wright, *Surprised by Hope*, 43–44; *Resurrection of the Son of God*, 348–52; Wright and Bird, *New Testament in Its World*, 312–13.

165. For example, John 3:16.

166. Dobzhansky, "Nothing in Biology," 125–29; Dobzhansky would have agreed, because he was a Christian.

167. Rom 8:21 (GNT).

168. Rev 21:1–7.

APPENDIX 1

A glossary of some biological terms

activation (of genes): genetic information is stored in the DNA sequences of genes, which are themselves stored securely in the nuclei of cells. For genes to *do* something, they are copied into lengths of RNA. Gene activation is that state in which the DNA is accessible to a host of enzymes that perform the copying function, known as *transcription*.

anthropoid: pertaining to simian primates, that is, apes and monkeys.

antibody: a protein made by cells of the B-lymphocyte lineage, which includes a highly variable region that has the capacity to recognize and bind an antigen in a very specific way. Every newly generated B-cell expresses an antibody of one specificity—that is, an antibody with a unique version of the variable region, that recognizes one antigenic shape.

antigen: a molecule that (potentially at least) can be recognized by, and bound by, an antibody.

chromosome: a single DNA molecule, wrapped up in proteins and associated with numerous enzymes and transcription factors that control genetic functions. When a cell undergoes division, each chromosome is packaged into a visible body that can be stained with dyes (hence, *chromos-*, colored; *-soma*, body) and visualized using microscopes. During the rest of the cell's lifetime the chromosome is unravelled (and largely invisible) and is accessed by a host of proteins, allowing the DNA to direct cell activities.

Appendix 1

clone: a population of cells descended from one original cell. Clonal populations are generally identified by mutations that are common to the cells.

cortisol: a steroid hormone that mediates responses to stress.

cytokine: one of a family of protein molecules (such as interferons and interleukins) that signals to orchestrate immune responses.

DNA: deoxyribonucleic acid, the chemical that constitutes the genetic material of all life forms (except for some viruses, which use RNA). It consists of very long chains and encodes information in the form of chemical units known as bases, of which there are four: adenine (A), cytosine (C), guanine (G), and thymine (T). The order (or *sequence*) in which these bases occur along the DNA polymer embodies the information that underlies life processes. Experimental techniques for determining the order of these bases (*sequencing* methods) have revolutionized biology and our understanding of evolution.

deletion: a mutation in which a segment of DNA is lost.

dendrites: short, branched extensions of nerve cells, used to communicate with other cells.

domestication (of genes): the recruitment of a genetic entity in an ERV or transposable element to serve a new role in host cells (as when retroviral *env* genes are repurposed to serve as cell fusion-promoting *syncytin* genes).

enhancers: short DNA sequences to which gene-activating proteins bind, so as to control gene activity in a tissue- and time-dependent way.

epigenetics: systems that control the activity of DNA by heritable but reversible chemical changes to DNA (addition of methyl groups to cytosine) and to proteins associated with DNA (methylation and acetylation of histones, for example).

exaptation: recruitment of a novel function from a precursor that lacked that function (as when sequences present in transposable elements acquire new roles as enhancers or as non-coding RNA molecules in mammalian cells).

eutherian: pertaining to mammals with a well-developed placenta, as opposed to monotremes (that lay eggs), and marsupials (or metatherians, that have a rudimentary placenta).

A Glossary of Some Biological Terms

gene: a length of DNA that may be copied into one or more related RNA molecules. A gene usually consists of multiple discontinuous segments (*exons*, to be incorporated into mature RNA molecules) interrupted by spacer segments (*introns*), so that multiple combinations of exons can generate a family of RNA molecules. This arrangement allows a single gene to have multiple outputs.

genome: the total amount of genetic material belonging to an individual or species. In animals such as we are, the genome is sequestered in the cell nucleus (apart from the tiny chromosome of 15,000 bases that is found in organelles called mitochondria, the energy-generating factories of cells).

germline: the lineage of cells that generates germ cells (ultimately, eggs and sperm) and that is responsible for transmitting genetic information to future generations.

gray matter: tissue in the central nervous system that is enriched for the presence of cell bodies.

hominoid: pertaining to one of the ape species.

homoplasy: the situation that occurs when a feature shared by different species arose independently, and therefore cannot provide evidence of common ancestry. When an ERV or transposable element is shared by different species, it is almost certain that each arose in a unique event and was subsequently transmitted to multiple species. Such inserts are said to be essentially homoplasy-free and they provide powerful evidence of common ancestry.

insertion, a mutation in which a length of DNA is spliced into a DNA strand. Insertions include, but are not limited to, the additions of ERVs and transposable elements to chromosomal DNA.

messenger RNA: a class of RNA that contains the coding information required to direct the manufacture of proteins. It carries this information from genes (in the nucleus) to ribosomes (in the cytoplasm).

monoclonality (of cells): the condition in which a population of cells is descended from a single cell, typically defined by the common possession of a unique mutation.

Appendix 1

monophylicity (of species): the condition in which a group of species is descended from a single species, indeed from a single reproductive cell, as defined by common possession of a unique mutation.

mutation: a heritable change in the DNA sequence, ranging from single base changes and deletions or insertions, to large rearrangements of DNA molecules, in which lengths of DNA can be lost (*deleted*), inserted from elsewhere, duplicated, flipped 180° with respect to the surrounding DNA (*inverted*), or exchanged with expanses of DNA that normally reside elsewhere (*translocated*).

neural: pertaining to nerve tissue, as is found in the brain.

neuroplasticity: the ability of neural tissue in the brain to undergo reorganization (by forming new connections between cells) in response to injury and experience. It declines with age.

organoid: a cluster of cells in culture, which are cultivated in such a way as to express features of particular tissues (placental, neural, gut epithelium, for example).

non-self (in immunology): molecules (or antigens) which are not intrinsic to a person's body, to which the immune system may react (particularly if they are pathogenic or disease-causing).

pathobiont: a microbe that lives in or on our bodies which, under some conditions, may contribute to the development of disease.

repetitive element: a short length of DNA (typically up to about 10,000 bases long) that is recognizable because it is one of a family of such DNA units that are scattered haphazardly around the genome, and that were at some stage inserted into it. *Endogenous retroviruses* and *transposable* (or *mobile*) *elements* comprise the two main groups of repetitive element, although some families have characteristics of both.

retrovirus: a class of virus in which the genetic material is RNA. When cells are infected, this RNA is copied into DNA by an enzyme called *reverse transcriptase* (hence, *retro-*). The viral RNA-to-DNA strategy is opposite to what usually occurs in cells, in which segments of genomic DNA are copied into RNA molecules. The other main feature of retroviruses is that they insert their piece of DNA into the host cell genome.

ribosomal RNA: a class of RNA that is used to assemble ribosomes.

A GLOSSARY OF SOME BIOLOGICAL TERMS

ribosome: the multi-molecular complex, composed of four RNA molecules and seventy-nine proteins, on which the coding information in messenger RNA is translated into new proteins.

RNA: ribonucleic acid, a molecule very much like DNA, that carries out gene functions, and in some viruses, embodies genetic information.

self (in immunology): molecules (or antigens) that are an integral part of a person's body, to which the person's immune system should not react (be tolerant). Anti-self reactivity can result in autoimmune disease, such as rheumatoid arthritis and multiple sclerosis.

somatic: the myriad lineages of cells that perform specialist functions in the body (glands, muscles, nerves, . . .) and that do not transmit genetic information to future generations.

symbiont: any microbe that lives in or on our bodies, which contributes to our well-being, as we contribute to its. The relationship is symbiotic.

synapse: an intimate connection between cells across which cell-cell communication occurs.

transcription: the process of copying (*transcribing*) a DNA sequence into the corresponding RNA sequence (or, in the case of *reverse transcription*, of copying RNA into DNA).

transcription factors: proteins that interact with specific sites in DNA (such as enhancers and promoters) and that control the way the DNA is copied into RNA.

trophoblast: embryonic or fetal tissue that forms the covering of the placenta. The very outer layer (syncytiotrophoblast) is formed by the fusion of cells in the layer below (cytotrophoblast cells).

virus: an agent that consists of a piece of genetic material (DNA or RNA) wrapped up in protein, and often enclosed in a membrane made of lipid (fatty material). Viruses can replicate (reproduce) themselves *only* when they infect cells and make use of cellular building blocks. Viruses come in many forms, and cause many diseases, the one of interest at the time of writing being the coronavirus SARS-CoV-2.

white matter: tissue in the central nervous system that is composed largely of extensions from cells (axon fibres) that are involved in communication between cells.

APPENDIX 2

Procedure for researching the history of ancient repetitive elements

ANYONE WITH A MODEST background in biology and computing can search human and other species' genomes using publicly available databases.

First, select an ERV or a transposable element to investigate. We may obtain the genomic location (the *coordinates*) of a particular insert from a published source.[1] Inventories of a variety of inserted sequences, and their genomic coordinates, are readily available, generally in Open Access publications. As indicated in Table 3, these include ERVs and transposable elements such as Alu, SVA, MIR, AmnSINE1, and LINE-1 elements. In many of the studies listed in Table 3, lists of ERVs and transposable elements were curated because representative inserts were shown to have acquired special functions. For example, many MIR elements, which are very ancient, appear to have been co-opted to act as parts of genes (exons), of gene-activating motifs (enhancers), and of boundaries that divide DNA into distinct domains (insulators). Very ancient AmnSINE1 elements also commonly act as enhancers. And the LINE-1 elements listed have contributed to the construction of mysterious molecules called long noncoding RNAs. But this does not imply that all ERVs and transposable elements in the genome have acquired functions. Many may be relics of long-past events and are now quietly decaying into the background.

The inserts that arose relatively recently typically possess easy-to-recognize target site duplications. Very ancient inserts may not have

---

1. Published coordinates pertain to a particular edition (*build*) of the reference genome sequence, and it is vital to note the build relevant to a set of coordinates. Alternatively, we may use the UCSD Genome Browser to scroll around the human genome and select inserts at random.

recognizable target site duplications, as such sequences degenerate with time. However, with such ancient relics, unique boundaries between inserted and flanking sequences still serve to confirm that a given transposable element in the genomes of different species is *orthologous* (descended from a unique ancestral insertion event), and thus provide unambiguous demonstrations of monophylicity.

As described above, the enzymes of transposable elements may commandeer RNA molecules generated from the cell's DNA and, in completely unscheduled events, splice DNA copies of them back into the genome. There are extensive catalogues of such genes (of which thousands have been enumerated) that have been copied-and-pasted by the enzymatic machinery of transposable elements (retrocopies, Table 3).

Table 3. Publications providing genomic coordinates of classes of DNA insertions			
insert class	**insert subclass**	**element functionality**	**reference**
LTR element	endogenous retrovirus	gene regulatory networks	Brattas et al., "TRIM28," 1–11.
		near genes; uncertain	Karamitros et al., "Human endogenous," 10434–39.
		transcribed into RNA	Tokuyama et al., "ERVmap," 12565–72.
		not addressed	Pisano et al., "Comprehensive characterisation," e00110; Xue et al., "Identification," 10.

transposable element	various	gene regulation	Kitano et al., "Transposable elements shape," 274–84;
			Pehrsson et al., "Epigenomic Landscape," 5640.
	various	gene regulation, cancers	Jang et al., "Transposable elements drive," 611.
	Alu	gene regulation, decidua	Vrljicak et al., "Analysis of chromatin," 2467–77.
		possible enhancers	Zhang et al., "Genome-Wide," 1402–14
	SVA	gene regulation, neurons	Vasieva et al., "Primate-Specific," https://arxiv.org/abs/1602.07642
	MIR	gene exons	Lin et al., "Large-Scale," 2204–14.
		genetic enhancers	Jjingo et al., "Mammalian-Wide," 14.
		genetic insulators	Wang., "MIR," E4428-37.
	AmnSINE1	genetic enhancers	Nishihara et al., "Co-ordinately co-opted," e1006380.
	LINE-1	non-coding RNA	Chishima et al., "Identification," 23.
retrocopy	protein coding RNAs	some encode proteins	Navarro and Galante, "Genome-Wide Landscape," 2265–75.
	non-coding RNAs	none known	Noll et al., "Ancient Traces of Tailless," 889–900.

Second, having obtained the coordinates of an ERV or transposable element in the human genome, the next step is to obtain the sequence of the insert, and of several hundred flanking bases, both upstream (to the left) and downstream (to the right). Flanking sequences provide the genomic context that is necessary to define an insert as unique, which is essential if one is to establish orthology. Sequence information is conveniently obtained using the UCSC Genome Browser (https://genome.ucsc.edu/cgi-bin/hgGateway).

Third, get into serious history: is the ERV (or whatever) present in other species? Just as we can search for a word in a document using the "control F" function, we can use the human sequence as a "query" to search for the same insert and flanking sequences in non-human species using the NCBI database (https://blast.ncbi.nlm.nih.gov/Blast.cgi). The search

Ancient Repetitive Elements

method is called the *basic local alignment search tool* (BLAST). If a BLAST search comes back negative, BLASTN may be used to find more distantly related sequences. And if the insert is not present in another species, remove its sequence and one copy of the duplicated target site (to leave you with a putative *pre-insertion* sequence) and search the genome of that species with the pre-insertion sequence to ascertain whether the original, undisturbed progenitor sequence is still present.

Fourth, to characterize the genomic insert itself (class and "type" sequence of ERV or transposable element), the dfam database (http://www.dfam.org/browse) may be used. The type (or *consensus*) sequence for any one group of genomic insert is given under "Model." This database also provides the sequences of small cell-encoded RNA molecules that have undergone multiple transposable element-mediated copy-and-paste events, such as ribosomal RNA, transfer RNAs, and small nuclear RNAs.[2]

There are many advantages to performing this sort of exercise. First, as emphasized (chapter 1), complex mutations are essentially *homoplasy-free*; that is, it is exceedingly unlikely that a mutation that *appears* to be shared (identical location, target site, class of insert) had in fact arisen from independent events in two or more cells. When a complex mutation such as a transposable element insertion is found in multiple genomes, we can conclude confidently that *that* mutation was inherited by all species from the one unique cell in which it arose.

Second, DNA sequencing is performed robotically, and databases assembled computationally, so data cannot show bias or fabrication. As I have aligned orthologous sequences from multiple species (alignments presented in this book have not been published), I have experienced a sense of wonder at the consistent patterns that emerge.

Third, it is a fascinating exercise to inspect sequence data and identify inserted sequences, target sites and their duplications, and the taxa in

---

2. Finally, this is real science. It illustrates the difficulties of working out orthologies in the case of inserts located in highly repetitive environments. (For ease of analysis, it is best to select inserts that are not embedded in, or interrupted by, other inserts.) Sequences may be lost by large-scale genetic rearrangements. One may encounter non-canonical relationships as with *incomplete lineage sorting* in great apes. This is a phenomenon in which an inset that is polymorphic at the time of speciation may subsequently be lost or fixed randomly, and so provide variant phylogenetic trees. Incomplete lineage sorting is, however, rare, and usually occurs at nodes where speciation is rapid. Rarely, a transposable element with long target site duplications may exactly excise itself from the DNA through a process known as *non-allelic homologous recombination*. This occurs too infrequently to confound phylogenetic inference.

Appendix 2

which mutations arose. The BLAST search algorithm rapidly (typically in a few seconds) locates related sequences in the vastness of genomes of up to three billion bases. It is salutary to observe the high degree of similarity of the four great ape sequences—or even at times, the similarity of human with monkey sequences. We may also observe, in addition to the complex mutation being studied, base substitution or small indel mutations characteristic of one group of species (such as the Old World monkeys), which serve as incidental phylogenetic markers.

Bibliography

Abed, Mona, Erik Verschueren, Hana Budayeva, et al. "The Gag Protein PEG10 Binds to RNA and Regulates Trophoblast Stem Cell Lineage Specification." *PLoS ONE* 14 (2019) e0214110.

Abolnezhadian, Farhad, Razieh Dehghani, Sajad Dehnavi, et al. "A Novel Mutation in RFXANK Gene and Low B Cell Count in a Patient with MHC Class II Deficiency: A Case Report." *Immunologic Research* 68 (2020) 225–31.

Alexander, Denis R. *Are We Slaves to Our Genes?* Cambridge: Cambridge University Press, 2020.

———. *Creation or Evolution: Do We Have to Choose?* Oxford: Monarch, 2008.

———. *Genes, Determinism and God*. Cambridge: Cambridge University Press, 2017.

———, ed. *Has Science Killed God?* Faraday Institute. London: SPCK, 2019.

Alexander, Margaret, and Peter J. Turnbaugh. "Deconstructing Mechanisms of Diet-Microbiome-Immune Interactions." *Immunity* 53 (2020) 264–76.

Ander, Stephanie E., Michael S. Diamond, and Carolyn B. Coyne. "Immune Responses at the Maternal-Fetal Interface." *Science Immunology* 4 (2019) eaat6114.

Aplin, John D., Jenny E. Myers, Kate Timms, and Melissa Westwood. "Tracking Placental Development in Health and Disease." *Nature Reviews Endocrinology* 16 (2020) 479–94.

Arcaro, Michael J., Peter F. Schade, Justin L. Vincent et al. "Seeing Faces Is Necessary for Face-Domain Formation." *Nature Neuroscience* 20 (2017) 1404–12.

Ashby, Roland, Chris Mulherin, John Pilbrow, and Stephen Ames, eds. *A Reckless God?* Reservoir Victoria: ISCAST Nexus, 2018.

Attig, Jan, George R. Young, Louise Hosie, et al. "LTR Retroelement Expansion of the Human Cancer Transcriptome and Immunopeptidome Revealed by De Novo Transcript Assembly." *Genome Research* 29 (2019) 1578–90.

Atzil, Shir, Wei Gao, Isaac Fradkin, and Lisa F. Barrett "Growing a Social Brain." *Nature Human Behaviour* 2 (2018) 624–36.

Baker, Maggie, Stephen G. Lindell, Carlos A. Driscoll, et al. "Early Rearing History Influences Oxytocin Receptor Epigenetic Regulation in Rhesus Macaques." *Proceedings of the National Academy of Sciences of the USA* 114 (2017) 11769–74.

Bauckham R. *Bible and Ecology*. London: Darton, Longman and Todd, 2009.

Bergman, Kristin, Pampa Sarkar, Thomas G. O'Connor, et al. "Maternal Stress during Pregnancy Predicts Cognitive Ability and Fearfulness in Infancy." *Journal of the American Academy of Child and Adolescent Psychiatry* 46 (2007) 1454–63.

Bibliography

Bermudez-Mora, Filipe, Farhath Badsha, Sabina Kanton, et al. "Differences and Similarities between Human and Chimpanzee Neural Progenitors during Cerebral Cortex Development." *eLife* 5 (2016) e18683.

Bian, Shuhui, Yu Hou, Xin Zhou, et al., "Single Cell Multiomics Sequencing and Analyses of Human Colorectal Cancer." *Science* 362 (2018) 1060–63.

Bianco, Federica, and Serene Lecce. "Translating Child Development Research into Practice: Can Teachers Foster Children's Theory of Mind in Primary School?" *British Journal of Educational Psychology* 86 (2016) 592–605.

Bick, Johanna, Nathan Fox, Charles Zeanah, and Charles A. Nelson. "Early Deprivation, Atypical Brain Development, and Internalizing Symptoms in Late Childhood." *Neuroscience* 342 (2017) 140–53.

Bick, Johanna, and Charles A. Nelson. "Early Experience and Brain Development." *Wiley Interdisciplinary Reviews. Cognitive Science* 8 (2017), e1387.

Bick, Johanna, Tong Zhu, Catherine Stamoulis, et al. "Effect of Early Institutionalization and Foster Care on Long-Term White Matter Development." *JAMA Pediatrics* 169 (2015) 211–19.

Biernat, Monika M., Donata Urbaniak-Kujda, Jaroslaw Dybko, et al. "Fecal Microbiota Transplantation in the Treatment of Intestinal Steroid-Resistant Graft Versus-Host Disease: Two Case Reports and a Review of the Literature." *Journal of International Medical Research* 48 (2020) 300060520925693.

Bimson, John J. "Reconsidering a 'Cosmic Fall.'" *Science and Christian Belief* 18 (2006) 63–81.

Binder, Christian, Filip Cvetkovski, Felix Sellberg, et al. "CD2 Immunobiology." *Frontiers in Immunology* 11 (2020) 1090.

Bolze, Pierre-A., Marine Mommert, and Francois Mallet. "Contributions of Syncytin and other Endogenous Retroviral Envelopes to Human Placenta Pathologies." *Progress in Molecular Biology and Translational Science* 145 (2017) 111–62.

Bonnaud, Bertrand, Jean Beliaeff, Olivier Bouton, et al. "Natural History of the ERVWE1 Endogenous Retroviral Locus." *Retrovirology* 2 (2005) 57.

Booy, Evan P., Ewan K. McRae, Peyman Ezzati, et al. "Comprehensive Analysis of the BC200 Ribonucleoprotein Reveals a Reciprocal Regulatory Function with CSDE1/UNR." *Nucleic Acids Research* 46 (2018) 11575–91.

Brattas, Per L., Marie E. Jonsson, Liana Fasching, et al. "TRIM28 Controls a Gene Regulatory Network Based on Endogenous Retroviruses in Human Neural Progenitor Cells." *Cell Reports* 18 (2017) 1–11.

Breed, Elise R., Masashi Watanabe, and Kristin A. Hogquist. "Measuring Thymic Clonal Deletion at the Population Level." *Journal of Immunology* 202 (2019) 3226–33.

Briggs, Andrew, Hans Halvorson, and Andrew Steane. *It Keeps Me Seeking*. Oxford: Oxford University Press, 2018.

Briney, Bryan, Anne Inderbitzen, Collin Joyce, and Dennis R. Burton. "Commonality Despite Exceptional Diversity in the Baseline Human Antibody Repertoire." *Nature* 566 (2019) 393–97.

Buchrieser Julian, Severine A. Degrelle, Therese Couderc, et al. "IFITM Proteins Inhibit Placental Syncytiotrophoblast Formation and Promote Fetal Demise." *Science* 365 (2019) 176–80.

Burnett, Deborah L., Peter Schofield, David B. Langley, et al. "Conformational Diversity Facilitates Antibody Mutation Trajectories and Discrimination between Foreign

Bibliography

and Self-Antigens." *Proceedings of the National Academy of Sciences of the USA* 117 (2020) 22341–50.
Burns, Kathleen H. "Our Conflict with Transposable Elements and Its Implications for Human Disease." *Annual Review of Pathology: Mechanisms of Disease* 15 (2020) 51–70.
Bussey, Kimberly J., Luis H. Cisneros, Charles H. Lineweaver, and Paul C. W. Davies. "Ancestral Gene Regulatory Networks Drive Cancer." *Proceedings of the National Academy of Sciences of the USA* 114 (2017) 6160–62.
Butterfield, Herbert. *Christianity and History*. London: Fontana, 1957.
Cahill, Thomas. *The Gifts of the Jews*. New York: Random House, 1998.
Cai, Yu Qing, Hang Hu Zhang, Xiang Zhi Wang, et al. "A Novel RFXANK Mutation in a Chinese Child with MHC II Deficiency: Case Report and Literature Review." *Open Forum Infectious Diseases* 7 (2020) ofaa314.
Camargo, Chico. "Physics Makes the Rules, Evolution Rolls the Dice [book review]." *Science* 361 (2018) 236.
Capron, Lauren E., Paul G. Ramchandani, and Vivette Glover. "Maternal Prenatal Stress and Placental Gene Expression of *NR3C1* and *HSD11B2*: The Effects of Maternal Ethnicity." *Psychoneuroendocrinology* 87 (2018) 166–72.
Caruso, Roberta, Bernard C. Lo, and Gabriel Nunez. "Host-Microbiota Interactions in Inflammatory Bowel Disease." *Nature Reviews Immunology* 20 (2020) 411–26.
Carver, Rebecca B., Jeremy Castera, Niklas Gericke, et al. "Young Adults' Belief in Genetic Determinism, and Knowledge and Attitudes towards Modern Genetics and Genomics: The PUGGS Questionnaire." *PLoS ONE* 12 (2017) e0169808.
Casanova, Emily L., and Miriam K. Konkel. "The Developmental Gene Hypothesis for Punctuated Equilibrium: Combined Roles of Developmental Regulatory Genes and Transposable Elements." *BioEssays* 42 (2020) e1900173.
Casola, Claudio, and Esther Betran. "The Genomic Impact of Gene Retrocopies: What Have We Learned from Comparative Genomics, Population Genomics, and Transcriptomic Analyses?" *Genome Biology and Evolution* 9 (2017) 1351–73.
Chapman, Alan. *Slaying the Dragons: Destroying Myths in the History of Science and Faith*. Oxford: Lion, 2013.
Chavatte-Palmer, Pascale, and Anne Tarrade. "Placentation in Different Mammalian Species." *Annales d'Endocrinologie* 77 (2016) 67–74.
Cheetham, Seth W., Geoffrey J. Faulkner, and Marcel E. Dinger. "Overcoming Challenges and Dogmas to Understand the Functions of Pseudogenes." *Nature Reviews Genetics* 21 (2020) 191–201.
Chen, Haidi, Li Chen, Yune Wu, et al. "The Exonization and Functionalization of an Alu-J Element in the Protein Coding Region of Glycoprotein Hormone Alpha Gene Represent a Novel Mechanism to the Evolution of Hemochorial Placentation in Primates." *Molecular Biology and Evolution* 34 (2017) 3216–31.
Chen, Haiying, Manni Sun, Jing Liu, et al. "Silencing of Paternally Expressed Gene 10 Inhibits Trophoblast Proliferation and Invasion." *PLoS ONE* 10 (2015) e0144845.
Chen, Han, and Xionglei He. "The Convergent Cancer Evolution toward a Single Cellular Destination." *Molecular Biology and Evolution* 33 (2015) 4–12.
Chen, Huan, Yuxian Zhang, Adam Yongxin Ye, et al. "BCR Selection and Affinity Maturation in Peyer's Patch Germinal Centres." *Nature* 582 (2020) 421–25.

Bibliography

Chen, Huimin, Hongfen Li, and Zhanju Liu. "Interplay of Intestinal Microbiota and Mucosal Immunity in Inflammatory Bowel Disease: A Relationship of Frenemies." *Therapeutic Advances in Gastroenterology* 13 (2020) 1756284820935188.

Chen, Lei, Qiang Qiu, Yu Jiang, et al. "Large-Scale Ruminant Genome Sequencing Provides Insights into Their Evolution and Distinct Traits." *Science* 364 (2019) eaav6202.

Chien, Yi-Ling, Miao-Chun Chou, Wen-Jiun Chou, et al. "Prenatal and Perinatal Risk Factors and the Clinical Implications on Autism Spectrum Disorder." *Autism* 23 (2018) 783–91.

Chishima, Takafumi, Junichi Iwakiri, and Michiaki Hamada. "Identification of Transposable Elements Contributing to Tissue-Specific Expression of Long Non-Coding RNAs." *Genes* 9 (2018) 23.

Churakov, Gennady, Fengjun Zhang, Norbert Grundmann, et al. "The Multi-Comparative 2-n-Way Genome Suite." *Genome Research* 30 (2020) 1508–16.

Chuong, Edward B. "The Placenta Goes Viral: Retroviruses Control Gene Expression in Pregnancy." *PLoS Biology* 16 (2018) e3000028.

Chuong, Edward B., Nels C. Elde, and Cedric Feschotte. "Regulatory Evolution of Innate Immunity through Co-Option of Endogenous Retroviruses." *Science* 351 (2016) 1083–87.

Cohen, Carla J., Rita Rebollo, Sonja Babovic, et al. "Placenta-Specific Expression of the Interleukin-2 (IL-2) Receptor β Subunit from an Endogenous Retroviral Promoter." *Journal of Biological Chemistry* 286 (2011) 35543–52.

Colling, Richard G. *Random Designer*. Bourbonnais, IL: Browning, 2004.

Collins, Francis S. *The Language of God*. New York: Free, 2006.

Comfort, Nathaniel. "How Science Has Shifted Our Sense of Identity." *Nature* 574 (2019) 167–70.

Conway Morris, Simon, ed. *The Deep Structure of Biology*. West Conshohocken, PA: Templeton Foundation, 2008.

———. "Evolution: Like Any Other Science It Is Predictable." *Philosophical Transactions of the Royal Society Series B* 365 (2010) 133–45.

———. *Life's Solution: Inevitable Humans in a Lonely Universe*. Cambridge: Cambridge University Press, 2003.

———. "The Predictability of Evolution: Glimpses into a Post-Darwinian World." *Naturwissenschaften* 96 (2009) 1313–37.

Cooke, Susanna L., Adam Shlien, John Marshall, et al. "Processed Pseudogenes Acquired Somatically during Cancer Development." *Nature Communications* 5 (2014) 3644.

Cornelis, Guillaume, Matis Funk, Cecile Vernochet, et al. "An Endogenous Retroviral Envelope Syncytin and Its Cognate Receptor Identified in the Viviparous Placental *Mabuya* Lizard." *Proceedings of the National Academy of Sciences of the USA* 114 (2017) E10991–11000.

Coulson, Charles A. *Science and Christian Belief*. London: Fontana, 1958.

Creeth, Hugo D. J., Grainne I. McNamara, Simon J. Tunster, et al. "Maternal Care Boosted by Paternal Imprinting in Mammals." *PLoS Biology* 16 (2018) e2006599.

Crist, Eileen. "Reimagining the Human." *Science* 362 (2018) 1242.

Dahl, Audun. "How, Not Whether: Contributions of Others in the Development of Infant Helping." *Current Opinion in Psychology* 20 (2018) 72–76.

Dang, Ha X., Bradley A. Krasnick, Brian S. White, et al. "The Clonal Evolution of Metastatic Colorectal Cancer." *Science Advances* 6 (2020) eaay9691.

Bibliography

Dannehl, Katharina, Winfried Rief, and Frank Euteneuer. "Childhood Adversity and Cognitive Functioning in Patients with Major Depression." *Child Abuse and Neglect* 70 (2017) 247–54.

Davies, Paul, and Niels Henrik Gregersen, eds, *Information and the Nature of Reality: From Physics to Metaphysics*. Cambridge: Cambridge University Press, 2010.

De Groef, Bert, Stanislaw K. Wawrzyczek, Yugo Watanabe, et al. "Evolutionary Origin of the Type 2 Corticotropin-Releasing Hormone Receptor g Splice Variant." *Genes to Cells* 24 (2019) 318–23.

De Gruchy, John C. *Christianity and Democracy*. Cambridge: Cambridge University Press, 1995.

de la Hera, Belen, Jezabel Verade, Marta Garcia-Montojo, et al. "Human Endogenous Retrovirus HERV-Fc1 Association with Multiple Sclerosis Susceptibility: A Meta-Analysis." *PLoS ONE* 9 (2014) e90182.

Demetriou, Philippos, Enas Abu-Shah, Salvatore Valvo, et al. "A Dynamic CD2-Rich Compartment at the Outer Edge of the Immunological Synapse Boosts and Integrates Signals." *Nature Immunology* 21 (2020) 1232–43.

Denner, Joachim. "Expression and Function of Endogenous Retroviruses in the Placenta." *Acta Pathologica, Microbiologica, et Immunologica Scandinavica* 124 (2016) 31–43.

Dennis, Megan Y., Lana Harshman, Bradley J. Nelson, et al. "The Evolution and Population Diversity of Human-Specific Segmental Duplications." *Nature Ecology and Evolution* 1 (2017) 69.

Dobzhansky, Theodosius. "Nothing in Biology Makes Sense Except in the Light of Evolution." *American Biology Teacher* 35 (1973) 125–29.

Donnard, Elisa, Pranitha Vangala, Shaked Afik, et al. "Comparative Analysis of Immune Cells Reveals a Conserved Regulatory Lexicon." *Cell Systems* 6 (2018) 381–394.e7.

Doronina Liliya, Gennady Churakov, Andrej Kuritzin, et al. "Speciation Network in Laurasiatheria: Retrophylogenomic Signals." *Genome Research* 27 (2017) 997–1003.

Doronina Liliya, Andreas Matzke, Gennady Churakov, et al. "The Beaver's Phylogenetic Lineage Illuminated by Retroposon Reads." *Scientific Reports* 7 (2017) 43562.

Doronina, Liliya, Olga Reising, Hiram Clawson, et al. "True Homoplasy of Retrotransposon Insertions in Primates." *Systematic Biology* 68 (2019) 482–93.

Dowell, Jonathan, Benjamin A. Elser, Rachel E. Schroeder, and Hanna E. Stevens. "Cellular Stress Mechanisms of Prenatal Maternal Stress: Heat Shock Factors and Oxidative Stress." *Neuroscience Letters* 709 (2019) 134368.

Duarte, Dane G. G., Maila deC. L. Neves, Maicon R. Albuquerque, et al. "Gray Matter Brain Volumes in Childhood-Maltreated Patients with Bipolar Disorder Type I: A Voxel-Based Morphometric Study." *Journal of Affective Disorders* 197 (2016) 74–80.

Dunn-Fletcher, Caitlin E., Lisa M. Muglia, Mihaela Pavlicev, et al., "Anthropoid Primate-Specific Retroviral Element THE1B Controls Expression of *CRH* in Placenta and Alters Gestation Length." *PLoS Biology* 16 (2018) e2006337.

Einsiedel, Lloyd, Hai Pham, Mohammad Radwanur R. Talukder, et al. "Pulmonary Disease Is Associated with Human T-Cell Leukaemia Virus Type 1c Infection: A Cross-Sectional Survey in Remote Aboriginal Australian Communities." *Clinical Infectious Diseases* (2020) doi:10.1093/cid/ciaa1401.

Einsiedel, Lloyd, Hai Pham, Kim Wilson, et al. "Human T-Lymphotropic Virus Type 1c Subtype Proviral Loads, Chronic Lung Disease and Survival in a Prospective Cohort of Indigenous Australians." *PLoS Neglected Tropical Diseases* 12 (2018) e0006281.

Bibliography

Einsiedel, Lloyd, Richard J. Woodman, Maria Flynn, et al. "Human T-Lymphotropic Virus Type 1 Infection in an Indigenous Australian Population: Epidemiological Insights from a Hospital-Based Cohort Study." *BMC Public Health* 16 (2016) 787.

Engelman, Alan N., and Peter Cherepanov. "Retroviral Intasomes Arising." *Current Opinion in Structural Biology* 47 (2017) 23–29.

Etchegaray, Ema, Magali Naville, Jean-Nicolas Volff, and Zofia Haftek-Terreau. "Transposable Element-Derived Sequences in Vertebrate Development." *Mobile DNA* 12 (2021) 1.

Evans, Craig. *Fabricating Jesus*. Nottingham, UK: IVP, 2007.

Evans, John H. *What Is a Human?* New York: Oxford University Press, 2016.

Evener, Vincent. "Spirit and Truth: Reckoning with the Crises of Covid-19 for the Church." *Dialog* (2020) doi: 10.1111/dial.12594.

Ewart, Paul. "The Necessity of Chance: Randomness, Purpose and the Sovereignty of God." *Science and Christian Belief* 21 (2009) 111–31.

Fee, Gordon D. *Paul, the Spirit, and the People of God*. Peabody, MA: Hendrickson, 1996.

Ferrari, Gabriella A., Ylenia Nicolini, Elisa Demuru, et al. "Ultrasonographic Investigation of Human Fetus Responses to Maternal Communicative and Non-Communicative Stimuli." *Frontiers in Psychology* 7 (2016) 354.

Feusier, Julie, W. Scott Watkins, Jainy Thomas, et al. "Pedigree-Based Estimation of Human Mobile Element Retrotransposition Rates." *Genome Research* 29 (2019) 1567–77.

Figueiro-Filho, Ernesto A., B. Anne Croy, James N. Reynolds, et al. "Diffusion Tensor Imaging of White Matter in Children Born from Preeclamptic Gestations." *American Journal of Neuroradiology* 38 (2017) 801–6.

Figueiro-Filho, Ernesto A., Lauren E. Mak, James N. Reynolds, et al. "Neurological Function in Children Born to Preeclamptic and Hypertensive Mothers—a Systematic Review." *Pregnancy Hypertension* 10 (2017) 1–6.

Finik, Jackie, Jessica Buthmann, Wenyan Zhang, et al. "Placental Gene Expression and Offspring Temperament Trajectories: Predicting Negative Affect in Early Childhood." *Journal of Abnormal Child Psychology* 48 (2020) 783–95.

Finlay, Graeme J. "The Amazing Placenta: Evolution and Lifeline to Humanness." *Zygon: Journal of Religion and Science* 55 (2020) 306–26.

———. *The Gospel According to Dawkins*. London: Austin-Macauley, 2017.

———. *Human Evolution: Genes, Genealogies and Phylogenies*. Cambridge: Cambridge University Press, 2013.

———. "Interaction between Genes and the Relational Environment During Development of the Social Brain." *Science and Christian Belief* 30 (2018) 102–15.

Fitzgibbon, Gillian, and Kingston H. G. Mills. "The Microbiota and Immune-Mediated Diseases: Opportunities for Therapeutic Intervention." *European Journal of Immunology* 50 (2020) 326–37.

Forsdyke, Donald R. "Two-Signal Half-Century: From Negative Selection of Self-reactivity to Positive Selection of Near-Self-Reactivity." *Scandinavian Journal of Immunology* 89 (2019) e12746.

Freedman, Alexa A., Alison L. Cammack, Jeff R. Temple, et al. "Maternal Exposure to Childhood Maltreatment and Risk of Stillbirth." *Annals of Epidemiology* 27 (2017) 459–65.

Frodl, Thomas, Deborah Janowitz, Lianne Schmaal, et al. "Childhood Adversity Impacts on Brain Subcortical Structures Relevant to Depression." *Journal of Psychiatric Research* 86 (2017) 58–65.

Bibliography

Fujino, Hiroshi, Kunihiro Fukushima, and Akie Fujiyoshi. "Theory of Mind and Language Development in Japanese Children with Hearing Loss." *International Journal of Pediatric Otorhinolaryngology* 96 (2017) 77–83.
Funk, Mathis, Guillaume Cornelis, Cecile Vernochet, et al. "Capture of a Hyena-Specific Retroviral Envelope Gene with Placental Expression Associated in Evolution with the Unique Emergence among Carnivorans of Hemochorial Placentation in Hyaenidae." *Journal of Virology* 93 (2019) e01811–18.
Furman, David, Judith Campisi, Eric Verdin, et al. "Chronic Inflammation in the Etiology of Disease across the Life Span." *Nature Medicine* 25 (2019) 1822–32.
Gagne, Deanna L., and Marie Coppola. "Visible Social Interactions Do Not Support the Development of False Belief Understanding in the Absence of Linguistic Input: Evidence from Deaf Adult Homesigners." *Frontiers in Psychology* 8 (2017) 837.
Gee, Dylan G. "Sensitive Periods of Emotion Regulation: Influences of Parental Care on Frontoamygdala Circuitry and Plasticity." *New Directions for Child and Adolescent Development* 153 (2016) 87–110.
Gemmell, Patrick, Jotun Hein, and Aris Katzourakis. "The Exaptation of HERV-H: Evolutionary Analyses Reveal the Genomic Features of Highly Transcribed Elements." *Frontiers in Immunology* 10 (2019) 1339.
Gemmell, Patrick, Jotun Hein, and Aris Katzourakis. "Phylogenetic Analysis Reveals that ERVs 'Die Young' but HERV-H Is Unusually Conserved." *PLoS Computational Biology* 12 (2016) e1004964.
Gerstung, Moritz, Clemency Jolly, Ignaty Leshchiner, et al. "The Evolutionary History of 2,658 Cancers." *Nature* 578 (2020) 122–28.
Gianfrancesco, Olympia, Vivien J. Bubb, and John P. Quinn. "SVA Retrotransposons as Potential Modulators of Neuropeptide Gene Expression." *Neuropeptides* 64 (2017) 3.
Gibbons, Ann. "New Tools Offer Clues to How the Human Brain Takes Shape." *Science* 358 (2017) 705–6.
Giberson, Karl W. *Abraham's Dice*. New York: Oxford University Press, 2016.
Giberson, Karl W., and Francis S. Collins. *The Language of Science and Faith: Straight Answers to Genuine Questions*. Downers Grove, IL: IVP, 2011.
Gingerich, Owen. *God's Planet*. Cambridge: Harvard University Press, 2014.
———. *God's Universe*. Cambridge: Harvard University Press, 2006.
Glassman, Michael L., Nathan de Groot, and Abraham Hochberg. "Cancer, Evolution and Birth: Reliving our Ancestral Past." *Medical Hypotheses* 46 (1996) 13–16.
Glover, Viviette, and Lauren Capron. "Prenatal Parenting." *Current Opinion in Psychology* 15 (2017) 66–70.
Glover, Vivette, Kieran J. O'Donnell, Thomas G. O'Connor, and Jane Fisher. "Prenatal Maternal Stress, Fetal Programming, and Mechanisms Underlying Later Psychopathology—a Global Perspective." *Development and Psychology* 30 (2018) 843–54.
Gonzalez-Mariscal, Gabriela, and Angel I. Melo. "Bidirectional Effects of Mother-Young Contact on the Maternal and Neonatal Brains." *Advances in Experimental Medicine and Biology* 1015 (2017) 97–116.
Grandi, Nicole, Marta Cadeddu, Jonas Blomberg, and Enzo Tramontano. "Contribution of Type W Human Endogenous Retroviruses to the Human Genome: Characterization of HERV-W Proviral Insertions and Processed Pseudogenes." *Retrovirology* 13 (2016) 67.

Bibliography

Gruchot, Joel, David Kremer, and Patrick Kury. "Neural Cell Responses upon Exposure to Human Endogenous Retroviruses." *Frontiers in Genetics* 10 (2019) 655.

Guernsey, Michael W., Edward B. Chuong, Guillaume Cornelis, et al. "Molecular Conservation of Marsupial and Eutherian Placentation and Lactation." *eLife* 6 (2017) e27450.

Gunton, Colin E. *Christ and Creation*. Carlisle, UK: Paternoster, 1992.

Guo, Caiwei, Hyun-Hwan Jeong, Yi-Chen Hsieh, et al. "Tau Activates Transposable Elements in Alzheimer's Disease." *Cell Reports* 23 (2018) 2874–80.

Halpern, Mark. "How Children Learn their Mother Tongue: They Don't." *Journal of Psycholinguistic Research* 45 (2016) 1173–81.

Hancks Dustin C., and Haig H. Kazazian. "Roles for Retrotransposon Insertion in Human Disease." *Mobile DNA* 7 (2016) 9.

Hao, Yue, Hyuk Jin Lee, Michael Baraboo, et al. "Baby Genomics: Tracing the Evolutionary Changes that Gave Rise to Placentation." *Genome Biology and Evolution* 12 (2020) 35–47.

Harlow, Daniel C. "After Adam: Reading Genesis in an Age of Evolutionary Science." *Perspectives on Science and Christian Faith* 62 (2010) 179–95.

Harrison, Peter. *The Bible, Protestantism and the Rise of Natural Science*. Cambridge: Cambridge University Press, 1998.

Hart, David B. *Atheist Delusions: The Christian Revolution and Its Fashionable Enemies*. New Haven, CT: Yale University Press, 2009.

———. *The Experience of God*. New Haven, CT: Yale University Press, 2013.

Hauerwas, Stanley, and William H. Willimon. *Resident Aliens*. Nashville: Abingdon, 1989.

He, Yaoxi, Xin Luo, Bin Zhou, et al. "Long-Read Assembly of the Chinese Rhesus Macaque Genome and Identification of Ape-Specific Structural Variants." *Nature Communications* 10 (2019) 4233.

Hegyi, Hedi. "GABBR1 Has a HERV-W LTR in Its Regulatory Region—a Possible Implication for Schizophrenia." *Biology Direct* 8 (2013) 5.

Heijmans, Corrine M. C., Natasja G. de Groot, and Ronald E. Bontrop. "Comparative Genetics of the Major Histocompatibility Complex in Humans and Nonhuman Primates." *International Journal of Immunogenetics* 47 (2020) 243–60.

Hemberger, Myriam, Courtney W. Hanna, and Wendy Dean. "Mechanisms of Early Placental Development in Mouse and Humans." *Nature Reviews Genetics* 21 (2020) 27–43.

Henry, Carl F. H., ed. *Horizons of Science: Christian Scholars Speak Out*. New York: Harper and Row, 1978.

Hentze, Charlotte, Henrik Walter, Elisabeth Schramm, et al. "Functional Correlates of Childhood Maltreatment and Symptom Severity during Affective Theory of Mind Tasks in Chronic Depression." *Psychiatry Research Neuroimaging* 250 (2016) 1–11.

Heyes, Cecilia M., and Chris D. Frith. "The Cultural Evolution of Mind Reading." *Science* 344 (2014) 1243091–96.

Hirakawa, Mika, Hidenori Nishihara, Minoru Kanehisa, and Norihiro Okada. "Characterisation and Evolutionary Landscape of AmnSINE1 in Amniota Genomes." *Gene* 441 (2009) 100–110.

Hobson, Theo. *God Created Humanism: The Christian Basis of Secular Values*. London: SPCK, 2017.

Bibliography

Holdt, Lesca M., Steve Hoffman, Kristina Sass, et al. "Alu Elements in *ANRIL* Non-Coding RNA at Chromosome 9p21 Modulate Atherogenic Cell Functions through Trans-Regulation of Gene Networks." *PLoS Genetics* 9 (2013) e1003588.
Hotamisligil, Gokhan S. "Inflammation, Metaflammation and Immunometabolic Disorders." *Nature* 542 (2017) 177–85.
Hua, Ying, Jing Wang, Dong-Lan Yuan, et al. "A Tag SNP in Syncytin-2 3-UTR Significantly Correlates with the Risk of Severe Preeclampsia." *Clinica Chimica Acta* 483 (2018) 265–70.
Huang, Shengfeng, Xin Tao, Shaochun Yuan, et al. "Discovery of an Active RAG Transposon Illuminates the Origins of V(D)J Recombination." *Cell* 166 (2016) 102–14.
Huber-Lang, Markus, John D. Lambris, and Peter A. Ward. "Innate Immune Response to Trauma." *Nature Immunology* 19 (2018) 327–41.
Hurtado, Larry W. *Destroyer of the Gods: Early Christian Distinctiveness in the Roman World.* Waco, TX: Baylor University Press, 2016.
Hutchings, David, and Tom McLeish. *Let There Be Science.* Oxford: Lion Hudson, 2017.
Imakawa, Kazuhiko, and So Nakagawa. "The Phylogeny of Placental Evolution through Dynamic Integrations of Retrotransposons." *Progress in Molecular Biology and Translational Science* 145 (2017) 89–109.
Inanici, Sinem Y., Mehmet A. Inanici, and A. Tevfik Yoldemir. "The Relationship between Subjective Experience of Childhood Abuse and Neglect and Depressive Symptoms during Pregnancy." *Journal of Forensic and Legal Medicine* 49 (2017) 76–80.
Irie, Masahito, Akihiko Koga, Tomoko Kaneko-Ishino, and Fumitoshi Ishino. "An LTR Retrotransposon-Derived Gene Displays Lineage-Specific Structural and Putative Species-Specific Functional Variations in Eutherians." *Frontiers in Chemistry* 4 (2016) 26.
Jaki, Stanley L. *Science and Creation.* Edinburgh: Scottish Academic Press, 1986.
Jang, Hyo Sik, Nakul M. Shah, Alan Y. Du, et al. "Transposable Elements Drive Widespread Expression of Oncogenes in Human Cancers." *Nature Genetics* 51 (2019) 611–17.
Jang, Seonghui, Heegwon Shin, Jungmin Lee, et al. "Regulation of BC200 RNA-Mediated Translation Inhibition by hnRNP E1 and E2." *FEBS Letters* 591 (2017) 393–405.
Janney, Alina, Fiona Powrie, and Elizabeth H. Mann. "Host-Microbiota Maladaptation in Colorectal Cancer." *Nature* 585 (2020) 509–17.
Janssen, Anna B., Darlene A. Kertes, Grainne I. McNamara, et al. "A Role for the Placenta in Programming Maternal Mood and Childhood Behavioural Disorders." *Journal of Neuroendocrinology* 28 (2016) doi: 10.1111/jne.12373.
Jarvis, Erich D. "Evolution of Vocal Learning and Spoken Language." *Science* 366 (2019) 50–54.
Jeeves, Malcolm, ed. *Rethinking Human Nature: A Multidisciplinary Approach.* Grand Rapids: Eerdmans, 2011.
Jiang, Jiayue-Clare, and Kyle R. Upton. "Human Transposons Are an Abundant Supply of Transcription Factor Binding Sites and Promoter Activities in Breast Cancer Cell Lines." *Mobile DNA* 10 (2019) 16.
Jjingo, Daudi, Andrew B. Conley, Jianrong Wang, et al. "Mammalian-Wide Interspersed Repeat (MIR)-Derived Enhancers and the Regulation of Human Gene Expression." *Mobile DNA* 5 (2014) 14.
Johnson, Welkin E. "Origins and Evolutionary Consequences of Ancient Endogenous Retroviruses." *Nature Reviews Microbiology* 17 (2019) 355–70.

Bibliography

Johnston, Randal N., S. Balakrishna Pai, and Rekha B. Pai. "The Origin of the Cancer Cell: Oncogeny Reverses Phylogeny." *Biochemistry Cell Biology* 70 (1992) 831–34.

Joly-Lopez, Zoe, and Thomas E. Bureau. "Exaptation of Transposable Element Coding Sequences." *Current Opinion in Genetics and Development* 49 (2018) 34–42.

Jones, Peter A., Hitoshi Ohtani, Ankur Chakravarthy and Daniel D. De Carvalho. "Epigenetic Therapy in Immune-Oncology." *Nature Reviews Cancer* 19 (2019) 151–61.

Jonsson, Marie E., Per Ludvik Brattas, Charlotte Gustafsson, et al. "Activation of Neuronal Genes via LINE-1 Elements upon Global DNA Demethylation in Human Neural Progenitors." *Nature Communications* 10 (2019) 3182.

Ju, Yeong Seok, Jose M. C. Tubio, William Mifsud, et al. "Frequent Somatic Transfer of Mitochondrial DNA into the Nuclear Genome of Human Cancer Cells." *Genome Research* 25 (2015) 814–24.

Judge, Edwin. "The Religion of the Secularists." *Journal of Religious History* 38 (2014) 307–19.

Jue, Nathaniel K., Robert J. Foley, David N. Reznick, et al. "Tissue-Specific Transcriptome for *Poeciliopsis prolifica* Reveals Evidence for Genetic Adaptation Related to the Evolution of a Placental Fish." *G3: Genes, Genomes, Genetics* 8 (2018) 2181–92.

Jung, Hyunchul, Jung Kyoon Choi, and Eunjung A. Lee. "Immune Signatures Correlate with L1 Retrotransposition in Gastrointestinal Cancers." *Genome Research* 28 (2018) 1136–46.

Jung, Yi-Deun, Hee-Eun Lee, Ara Jo, et al. "Activity Analysis of LTR12C as an Effective Regulatory Element of the *RAE1* Gene." *Gene* 634 (2017) 22–28.

Kahyo, Tomoaki, Hidetaka Yamada, Hong Tao, et al. "Insertionally Polymorphic Sites of Human Endogenous Retrovirus-K (HML-2) with Long Target Site Duplications." *BMC Genomics* 18 (2017) 487.

Kaiser, Christopher B. *Creation and the History of Science*. London: Marshall-Pickering, 1991.

Kamal S., C. C. Kerndt, and S. L. Lappin. "Genetics, Histocompatibility Antigen." In *StatPearls*. Treasure Island: StatPearls, 2020. https://www.ncbi.nlm.nih.gov/books/NBK541023/

Kanton, Sabina, Michael J. Boyle, Zhisong He, et al. "Organoid Single-Cell Genomic Atlas Uncovers Human-Specific Features of Brain Development." *Nature* 574 (2019) 418–22.

Kapusta, Aurelie, Zev Kronenberg, Vincent J. Lynch, et al. "Transposable Elements Are Major Contributors to the Origin, Diversification, and Regulation of Vertebrate Long Noncoding RNAs" *PLoS Genetics* 9 (2013) e1003470.

Karamitros. Timocratis, Tara Hurst, Emanuele Marchi, et al. "Human Endogenous Retrovirus-K HML-2 Integration within *RASGRF2* Is Associated with Intravenous Drug Abuse and Modulates Transcription in a Cell-Line Model." *Proceedings of the National Academy of Sciences of the USA* 115 (2018) 10434–39.

Kavurma, Canem, Fatma V. Tas, Burcu S. Demirgoren, et al. "Do Serum BDNF Levels Vary in Self-Harm Behavior among Adolescents and Are They Correlated with Traumatic Experiences?" *Psychiatry Research* 258 (2017) 130–35.

Kazazian, Haig H., and John V. Moran. "Mobile DNA in Health and Disease." *New England Journal of Medicine* 377 (2017) 361–70.

Keener, Craig S. *The Historical Jesus of the Gospels*. Grand Rapids: Eerdmans, 2009.

Keillor, Steven J. *God's Judgements*. Downers Grove, IL: IVP, 2007.

Bibliography

Khuat, Lam T., Catherine T. Le, Chien-Chun Steven Pai, et al. "Obesity Induces Gut Microbiota Alterations and Augments Acute Graft-Versus-Host Disease after Allogeneic Stem Cell Transplantation." *Science Translational Medicine* 12 (2020) eaay7713.

Kingsbury, Mila, Murray Weeks, Nathalie MacKinnon, et al. "Stressful Life Events during Pregnancy and Offspring Depression: Evidence from a Prospective Cohort Study." *Journal of the American Academy of Child and Adolescent Psychiatry* 55 (2016) 709–16.

Kitano, Shohei, Hikaru Kurasawa, and Yasunori Aizawa. "Transposable Elements Shape the Human Proteome Landscape via Formation of Cis-Acting Upstream Open Reading Frames." *Genes to Cells* 23 (2018) 274–84.

Kitazawa, Moe, Masaru Tamura, Tomoko Kaneko-Ishino, and Fumitoshi Ishino. "Severe Damage to the Placental Fetal Capillary Network Causes Mid- to Late Fetal Lethality and Reduction in Placental Size in Peg11/Rtl1 KO Mice." *Genes to Cells* 22 (2017) 174–88.

Knight, George A. F. *I AM: This Is My Name*. Grand Rapids: Eerdmans, 1983.

Kojima, Kenji K. "Human Transposable Elements in Repbase: Genomic Footprints from Fish to Humans." *Mobile DNA* 9 (2018) 2.

Konig, Adrio. *The Eclipse of Christ in Eschatology*. Blackwood, Australia: New Creation, 1999.

———. *Here Am I: A Believer's Reflection on God*. Grand Rapids: Eerdmans, 1982.

———. *New and Greater Things: Re-Evaluating the Biblical Message on Creation*. Pretoria: UNISA, 1988.

Konig, Adrio, Erasmus van Niekerk, and D. F. Olivier. *Systematic Theology (Doctrine of Creation)*. Pretoria: UNISA, 1986.

Konig, Maximilian F. "The Microbiome in Autoimmune Rheumatic Disease." *Best Practice and Research Clinical Rheumatology* 34 (2020) 101473.

Korpela, Katri, Otto Helve, Kaija-Leena Kolho, et al. "Maternal Fecal Microbiota Transplantation in Cesarean-Born Infants Rapidly Restores Normal Gut Microbial Development: A Proof-of-Concept Study." *Cell* 183 (2020) 324–34.

Kratimenos, Panagiotis, and Anna A. Penn. "Placental Programming of Neuropsychiatric Disease." *Pediatric Research* 86 (2019) 157–64.

Kronenberg, Zev N., Ian T. Fiddes, David Gordon, et al. "High-Resolution Comparative Analysis of Great Ape Genomes." *Science* 360 (2018) eaar6343.

Kumsta, Robert, Sarah J. Marzi, Joana Viana, et al. "Severe Psychosocial Deprivation in Early Childhood Is Associated with Increased DNA Methylation across a Region Spanning the Transcription Start Site of CYP2E1." *Translational Psychiatry* 6 (2016) e830.

Labanski, Alexandra, Jost Langhorst, Harald Engler, and Sigrid Elsenbruch. "Stress and the Brain-Gut Axis in Functional and Chronic-Inflammatory Gastrointestinal Diseases: A Transdisciplinary Challenge." *Psychoneuroendocrinology* 111 (2020) 104501.

Lamoureux, Denis O. *I Love Jesus and I Accept Evolution*. Eugene OR: Wipf & Stock, 2009.

Lane, Tony, *The Lion Concise Book of Christian Thought*. Tring, UK: Lion, 1984.

Lapp, Hannah E., and Richard G. Hunter. "Early Life Exposures, Neurodevelopmental Disorders, and Transposable Elements." *Neurobiology of Stress* 11 (2019) 100174.

Leonard, Julia A., Yuna Lee, and Laura E. Schultz. "Infants Make More Attempts to Achieve a Goal When They See Adults Persist." *Science* 357 (2017) 1290–94.

Bibliography

Leung, Marco L., Alexander Davis, Ruli Gao, et al. "Single-Cell DNA Sequencing Reveals a Late-Dissemination Model in Metastatic Colorectal Cancer." *Genome Research* 27 (2017) 1287–99.

Levy, Orr, Binyamin A. Knisbacher, Erez Y. Levanon, and Shlomo Havlin. "Integrating Networks and Comparative Genomics Reveals Retroelement Proliferation Dynamics in Hominid Genomes." *Science Advances* 3 (2017) e1701256.

Lewis, C. S. *The Problem of Pain*. Glasgow: Fontana, 1957.

Lieber, Michael R. "Transposons to V(D)J Recombination: Evolution of the RAG Reaction." *Trends in Immunology* 40 (2019) 668–70.

Lin, Lan, Peng Jiang, Shihao Shen, et al. "Large-Scale Analysis of Exonised Mammalian-Wide Interspersed Repeats in Primate Genomes." *Human Molecular Genetics* 18 (2009) 2204–14.

Lippard, Elizabeth T. C., and Charles B. Nemeroff. "The Devastating Clinical Consequences of Child Abuse and Neglect: Increased Disease Vulnerability and Poor Treatment Response in Mood Disorders." *American Journal of Psychiatry* 177 (2020) 20–36.

Liu, Jianbo, Yumin Fang, Jingbo Gong, et al. "Associations between Suicidal Behaviour and Childhood Abuse and Neglect: A Meta-Analysis." *Journal of Affective Disorders* 220 (2017) 147–55.

Lodato, Michael A., Mollie B. Woodworth, Semin Lee, et al. "Somatic Mutation in Single Human Neurons Tracks Developmental and Transcriptional History." *Science* 350 (2015) 94–98.

Lokossou, Adjimon G., Caroline Toudic, Phuong Trang Nguyen, et al. "Endogenous Retrovirus-Encoded Syncytin-2 Contributes to Exosome-Mediated Immunosuppression of T Cells." *Biology of Reproduction* 102 (2020) 185–98.

Lu, Xiaoyin, Rui Wang, Cheng Zhu, et al. "Fine-Tuned and Cell-Cycle-Restricted Expression of Fusogenic Protein Syncytin-2 Maintains Functional Placental Syncytia." *Cell Reports* 21 (2017) 1150–59.

Lucas, Ernest C., Denis R. Alexander, Sam R. J. Berry, et al. "The Bible, Science and Human Origins." *Science and Christian Belief* 28 (2016) 74–99.

Lynch, Vincent J., Mauris C. Nnamani, Aurelie Kapusta, et al. "Ancient Transposable Elements Transformed the Uterine Regulatory Landscape and Transcriptome during the Evolution of Mammalian Pregnancy." *Cell Reports* 10 (2015) 551–61.

Macaulay, Erin C., Aniruddha Chatterjee, Xi Cheng, et al. "The Genes of Life and Death: A Potential Role for Placental-Specific Genes in Cancer." *BioEssays* 39 (2017) 1700091.

Macaulay, Erin C., Hester E. Roberts, Xi Cheng, et al. "Retrotransposon Hypomethylation in Melanoma and Expression of a Placenta-Specific Gene." *PLoS ONE* 9 2014 e95840.

Macaulay, Erin. C., Robert J. Weeks, Simon Andrews, and Ian M. Morison. "Hypomethylation of Functional Retrotransposon-Derived Genes in the Human Placenta." *Mammalian Genome* 22 (2011) 722–35.

MacKay, Donald M. *The Clockwork Image*. London: IVP, 1974.

Maraska, Federica, Erica Gasparotto, Benedetto Polimeni, et al. "The Sophisticated Transcriptional Response Governed by Transposable Elements in Human Health and Disease." *International Journal of Molecular Sciences* 21 (2020) 3201.

Masson, G. *Frederick II of Hohenstaufen*. London: Secker and Warburg, 1957.

McConville, J. Gordon, and Karl Moller, eds. *Reading the Law: Studies in Honour of Gordon J. Wenham*. London: T. & T. Clark, 2007.

McCreight, Jennifer C., Sean E. Schneider, Damien B. Wilburn, and Willie J. Swanson. "Evolution of MicroRNA in Primates." *PLoS ONE* 12 (2017) e0176596.

Bibliography

McKnight. S. *The King Jesus Gospel*. Grand Rapids: Zondervan, 2011.
McLaughlin, Katie A., Margaret A. Sheridan, and Charles A. Nelson. "Neglect as a Violation of Species-Expectant Experience: Neurodevelopmental Consequences." *Biological Psychiatry* 82 (2017) 462–71.
McLeish, Tom. "Evolution as an Unwrapping of the Gift of Freedom." *Scientia et Fides* 8 (2020) 43–64.
———. *Faith and Wisdom in Science*. Oxford: Oxford University Press, 2014.
Meadows, Jennifer R. S., and Kerstin Lindblad-Toh. "Dissecting Evolution and Disease Using Comparative Vertebrate Genomics." *Nature Reviews Genetics* 18 (2017) 624–36.
Messer, Neil. *Christian Ethics and Selfish Genes*. London: SCM, 2007.
Mitchell, Caitlyn, and Debra L. Silver. "Enhancing Our Brains: Genomic Mechanisms Underlying Cortical Evolution." *Seminars in Cell and Developmental Biology* 76 (2018) 23–32.
Mommert, Marine, Olivier Tabone, Audrey Guichard, et al. "Dynamic LTR Retrotransposon Transcriptome Landscape in Septic Shock Patients." *Critical Care* 24 (2020) 96.
Monk, Catherine, Claudia Lugo-Candelas, and Caroline Trumpff. "Prenatal Developmental Origins of Future Psychopathology: Mechanisms and Pathways." *Annual Review of Clinical Psychology* 15 (2019) 317–44.
Monteleone, Alessio M., Palmiero Monteleone, Fabrizio Esposito, et al. "The Effects of Childhood Maltreatment on Brain Structure in Adults with Eating Disorders." *World Journal of Biological Psychiatry* 20 (2019) 301–9.
Moog, Nora K., Christine M. Heim, Sonja Entringer, et al. "Childhood Maltreatment Is Associated with Increased Risk of Subclinical Hypothyroidism in Pregnancy." *Psychoneuroendocrinology* 84 (2017) 190–96.
Morrow, Anne S., and Miguel T. Villodas. "Direct and Indirect Pathways from Adverse Childhood Experiences to High School Dropout among High-Risk Adolescents." *Journal of Research on Adolescence* 28 (2018) 327–41.
Muller, Victor, Rob J. de Boer, Sebastian Bonhoeffer, and Eors Szathmary. "An Evolutionary Perspective on the Systems of Adaptive Immunity." *Biological Reviews* 93 (2018) 505–28.
Muraille, Eric. "Diversity Generator Mechanisms Are Essential Components of Biological Systems: The Two Queen Hypothesis." *Frontiers in Microbiology* 9 (2018) 223.
Nakagawa, Hidewaki, and Masashi Fujita. "Whole Genome Sequencing Analysis for Cancer Genomics and Precision Medicine." *Cancer Science* 109 (2018) 513–22.
Nakanishi, Akiko, Naoki Kobayashi, Asuka Suzuki-Hirano, et al. "A SINE-Derived Element Constitutes a Unique Modular Enhancer for Mammalian Diencephalic Fgf8." *PLoS ONE* 7 (2012) e43785.
Nataf, Serge, Juan Uriagereka, and Antonio Benitez-Burraco. "The Promoter Regions of Intellectual Disability-Associated Genes are Uniquely Enriched in LTR Sequences of the MER41 Primate-Specific Endogenous Retrovirus: An Evolutionary Connection between Immunity and Cognition." *Frontiers in Genetics* 10 (2019) 321.
Navarro, Fabio C. P., and Pedro A. F. Galante. "A Genome-Side Landscape of Retrocopies in Primate Genomes." *Genome Biology and Evolution* 7 (2015) 2265–75.
Nelson, Charles A., and Laurel J. Gabard-Durnam. "Early Adversity and Critical Periods: Neurodevelopmental Consequences of Violating the Expectable Environment." *Trends in Neurosciences* 43 (2020) 133–43.

Bibliography

Nemazee, David. "Mechanisms of Central Tolerance for B Cells." *Nature Reviews Immunology* 17 (2017) 281–84.

Nemeroff, Charles B. "Paradise Lost: The Neurobiological and Clinical Consequences of Child Abuse and Neglect." *Neuron* 89 (2016) 892–909.

Netten, Anouk P., Carolien Rieffe, Lizet Ketelaar, et al. "Terrible Twos or Early Signs of Psychopathology? Developmental Patterns in Early Identified Preschoolers with Cochlear Implants Compared with Hearing Controls." *Ear and Hearing* 39 (2018) 495–502.

Netten, Anouk P., Carolien Rieffe, Wim Soede, et al. "Can You Hear What I Think? Theory of Mind in Young Children with Moderate Hearing Loss." *Ear and Hearing* 38 (2017) 588–97.

Ng, Kevin W., Jan Attig, George R. Young, et al. "Soluble PD-L1 Generated by Endogenous Retroelement Exaptation is a Receptor Antagonist." *eLife* 8 (2019) e50256.

Nishihara, Hidenori. "Retrotransposons Spread Potential *Cis*-Regulatory Elements During Mammary Gland Evolution." *Nucleic Acids Research* 47 (2019) 11551–62.

———. "Transposable Elements as Genetic Accelerators of Evolution: Contribution to Genome Size, Gene Regulatory Network Rewiring and Morphological Innovation." *Genes and Genetic Systems* 94 (2020) 269–81.

Nishihara, Hidenori, Naoki Kobayashi, Chiharu Kimura-Yoshida, et al. "Coordinately Co-Opted Multiple Transposable Elements Constitute an Enhancer for Wnt5a Expression in the Mammalian Secondary Palate." *PLoS Genetics* 12 (2016) e1006380.

Noll, Angela, Norbert Grundmann, Gennady Churakov, et al. "PAC-Genome Presence/Absence Compiler: A Web Application to Comparatively Visualize Multiple Genome-Level Changes." *Molecular Biology and Evolution* 32 (2015) 257–86.

Noll, Angela, Carsten A. Raabe, Gennady Churakov, et al. "Ancient Traces of Tailless Retropseudogenes in Therian Genomes." *Genome Biology and Evolution* 7 (2015) 889–900.

Oh, Insoo, and Jiyeon Song. "Mediating Effect of Emotional/Behavioural Problems and Academic Competence between Parental Abuse/Neglect and School Adjustment." *Child Abuse and Neglect* 86 (2018) 393–402.

Ohtani, Hitoshi, Minmin Liu, Wanding Zhou, et al. "Switching Roles for DNA and Histone Methylation Depend on Evolutionary Ages of Human Endogenous Retroviruses." *Genome Research* 28 (2018) 1147–57.

Ohtani, Hitoshi, Andreas D. Ørskov, Alexandra S. Helbo, et al. "Activation of a Subset of Evolutionarily Young Transposable Elements and Innate Immunity Are Linked to Clinical Responses to 5-Azacytidine." *Cancer Research* 80 (2020) 2441–50.

Oksenhendler, Eric, Jocelyn Turpin, Raphael Lhote, et al. "Persistent Risk of Adult T-Cell Leukemia/Lymphoma after Neonatal HTLV-1 Infection through Exchange Transfusion." *International Journal of Hematology* 105 (2017) 859–62.

Okubo, Ryo, Takeshi Inoue, Naoki Hashimoto, et al. "The Mediator Effect of Personality Traits on the Relationship between Childhood Abuse and Depressive Symptoms in Schizophrenia." *Psychiatry Research* 257 (2017) 126–31.

Oord, Thomas J. *The Uncontrolling Love of God: An Open and Relational Account of Providence*. Downers Grove IL: IVP, 2016.

Otsuka, Ayano, Yoshikazu Takaesu, Mitsuhiko Sato, et al. "Interpersonal Sensitivity Mediates the Effects of Child Abuse and Affective Temperaments on Depressive Symptoms in the General Adult Population." *Neuropsychiatric Disease and Treatment* 13 (2017) 2559–68.

Bibliography

Packer, Michael S., and David R. Liu. "Methods for the Directed Evolution of Proteins." *Nature Reviews Genetics* 16 (2015) 379–94.

Park, Bo Y., Dawn P. Misra, John Moye, et al. "Placental Gross Shape Differences in a High Autism Risk Cohort and the General Population." *PLoS ONE* 13 (2018) e0191276.

Payer, Lindsay M., and Kathleen H. Burns. "Transposable Elements in Human Genetic Disease." *Nature Reviews Genetics* 20 (2019) 760–72.

Pehrsson, Erica C., Mayank N. K. Choudhary, Vasavi Sundaram, and Ting Wang. "The Epigenomic Landscape of Transposable Elements across Normal Human Development and Anatomy." *Nature Communications* 10 (2019) 5640.

Pennisi, Elizabeth. "Meet the Psychobiome." *Science* 368 (2020) 570–73.

Phillips, Tom J., Hannah Scott, David A. Menassa, et al. "Treating the Placenta to Prevent Adverse Effects of Gestational Hypoxia on Fetal Brain Development." *Scientific Reports* 7 (2017) 9079.

Pisano, Maria P., Nicole Grandi, Marta Cadeddu, et al. "Comprehensive Characterization of the Human Endogenous Retrovirus HERV-K(HML-6) Group: Overview of Their Structure, Phylogeny and Contribution to the Human Genome." *Journal of Virology* 93 (2019) e00110–19.

Plant, Dominic T., Fergal W. Jones, Carmine M. Pariante, and Susan Pawlby. "Association between Maternal Childhood Trauma and Offspring Childhood Psychopathology: Mediation Analysis from the ALSPAC Cohort." *British Journal of Psychiatry* 211 (2017) 144–50.

Platt, Jeffrey L., Mayara G. de Mattos Barbosa, and Marilia Cascalho. "The Five Dimensions of B Cell Tolerance." *Immunological Reviews* 292 (2019) 180–93.

Platt II, Roy N., Michael W. Vandewege and David A. Ray. "Mammalian Transposable Elements and Their Impacts on Genome Evolution." *Chromosome Research* 26 (2018) 25–43.

Polkinghorne, John. *One World*. London: SPCK, 1986.

———. *Quarks, Chaos and Christianity*. London; Triangle SPCK, 1994.

———. *Reason and Reality*. London: SPCK, 1991.

———. *Science and Christian Belief*. London: SPCK, 1994.

———. *Science and Creation*. London: SPCK, 1988.

———. *Science and Providence*. London: SPCK, 1989.

———. *The Way the World Is*. London: Triangle SPCK, 1983.

Pontis, Julien, Evarist Planet, Sandra Offner, et al. "Hominoid-Specific Transposable Elements and KZFPs Facilitate Human Embryonic Genome Activation and Control Transcription in Naive Human ESCs." *Cell Stem Cell* 24 (2019) 724–35.

Preston, Stephanie D. "The Rewarding Nature of Social Contact." *Science* 357 (2017) 1353–54.

Proctor, Laura J., Terri Lewis, Scott Roesch, et al. "Child Maltreatment and Age of Alcohol and Marijuana Initiation in High-Risk Youth." *Addictive Behaviors* 75 (2017) 64–69.

Prudhomme, Sarah, Guy Oriol, and Francois Mallet. "A Retroviral Promoter and a Cellular Enhancer Define a Bipartite Element Which Controls *env* ERVWE1 Placental Expression." *Journal of Virology* 78 (2004) 12157–68.

Pulendran, Bali, and Mark M. Davis. "The Science and Medicine of Human Immunology." *Science* 369 (2020) eaay4014.

Qiu, Yichun, and Claudia Kohler. "Mobility Connects: Transposable Elements Wire New Transcriptional Networks by Transferring Transcription Factor Binding Motifs." *Biochemical Society Transactions* 48 (2020) 1005–17.

Bibliography

Quide, Yann, Xin H. Ong, Sebastian Mohnke, et al. "Childhood Trauma-Related Alterations in Brain Function During a Theory-of-Mind Task in Schizophrenia." *Schizophrenia Research* 189 (2017) 162–68.

Raghavan, Ramkripa, Blandine B. Helfrich, Sandra R. Cerda, et al. "Preterm Birth Subtypes, Placental Pathology Findings, and Risk of Neurodevelopmental Disabilities during Childhood." *Placenta* 83 (2019) 17–25.

Ratsep, Matthew T., Angelina Paolozza, Andrew F. Hickman, et al. "Brain Structural and Vascular Anatomy Is Altered in Offspring of Pre-Eclamptic Pregnancies: A Pilot Study." *American Journal of Neuroradiology* 37 (2016) 939–45.

Renz, Harald, and Chrysanthi Skivaki. "Early Life Microbial Exposures and Allergy Risks: Opportunities for Prevention." *Nature Reviews Immunology* 21 (2020) 177–91.

Rilling, James K., and Larry J. Young. "The Biology of Mammalian Parenting and Its Effect on Offspring Social Development." *Science* 345 (2014) 771–76.

Rodic, Nemanja, Jared P. Steranka, Alvin Makohon-Moore, et al. "Retrotransposon Insertions in the Clonal Evolution of Pancreatic Ductal Adenocarcinoma." *Nature Medicine* 21 (2015) 1060–64.

Rodriguez-Martin, Bernardo, Eva G. Alvarez, Adrian Baez-Ortega, et al. "Pan-Cancer Analysis of Whole Genomes Identifies Driver Rearrangements Promoted by LINE-1 Retrotransposition." *Nature Genetics* 52 (2020) 306–18.

Roerink, Sophie F., Nobuo Sasaki, Henry Lee-Six, et al. "Intra-Tumour Diversification in Colorectal Cancer at the Single Cell Level." *Nature* 556 (2018) 457–62.

Rohozinski, Jan. "Lineage-Independent Retrotransposition of UTP14 Associated with Male Fertility Has Occurred Multiple Times Throughout Mammalian Evolution." *Royal Society Open Science* 4 (2017) 171049.

Rolston III, Holmes. *Genes, Genesis and God: Values and Their Origins in Natural and Human History*. Cambridge: Cambridge University Press, 1999.

Roslund, Marja I., Riikka Puhakka, Mira Gronroos, et al. "Biodiversity Intervention Enhances Immune Regulation and Health-Associated Commensal Microbiota among Daycare Children." *Scientific Advances* 6 (2020) eaba2578.

Rudwick, Martin J. S. *Earth's Deep History*. Chicago: University of Chicago Press, 2014.

Sanna, Serena, Natalie R. van Zuydam, Anubha Mahajan, et al. "Causal Relationships among the Gut Microbiome, Short-Chain Fatty Acids and Metabolic Diseases." *Nature Genetics* 51 (2019) 600–605.

Sasaki, Takeshi, Hidenori Nishihara, Mika Hirakawa, et al. "Possible Involvement of SINEs in Mammalian-Specific Brain Formation." *Proceedings of the National Academy of Sciences of the USA* 105 (2008) 4220–25.

Savage, Abigail L., Vivien J. Bubb, Gerome Breen, and John P. Quinn. "Characterisation of the Potential Function of SVA Retrotransposons to Modulate Gene Expression Patterns." *BMC Evolutionary Biology* 13 (2013) 101.

Savage, Abigail L., Thomas P. Wilm, Kejhal Khursheed, et al. "An Evaluation of a SVA Retrotransposon in the FUS Promoter as a Transcriptional Regulator and Its Association to ALS." *PLoS ONE* 9 (2014) e90833.

Scheidell, Joy D., Kelly Quinn, Susan P. McGorray, et al. "Childhood Traumatic Experiences and the Association with Marijuana and Cocaine Use in Adolescence through Adulthood." *Addiction* 113 (2018) 44–56.

Schluter, Jonas, Jonathan U. Peled, Bradford P. Taylor, et al. "The Gut Microbiota Is Associated with Immune Cell Dynamics in Humans." *Nature* 588 (2020) 303–7.

Bibliography

Schrader, Lukas, and Jurgen Schmitz. "The Impact of Transposable Elements in Adaptive Evolution." *Molecular Ecology* 28 (2019) 1537–49.

Scott, Elizabeth A., Elizabeth Bruning, Raymond W. Nims, et al. "A 21st Century View of Infection Control in Everyday Settings: Moving from the Germ Theory of Disease to the Microbial Theory of Health." *American Journal of Infection Control* 48 (2020) 1387–92.

Scott, Emma C., Eugene J. Gardner, Ashiq Masood, et al. "A Hot L1 Retrotransposon Evades Somatic Repression and Initiates Human Colorectal Cancer." *Genome Research* 26 (2016) 745–55.

Shallie, Philemon D., and Thajasvarie Naicker. "The Placenta as a Window to the Brain: A Review on the Role of Placental Markers in Prenatal Programming of Neurodevelopment." *International Journal of Developmental Neuroscience* 73 (2019) 41–49.

Shields, Grant S., Chandler M. Spahr, and George M. Slavich. "Psychosocial Interventions and Immune System Function: A Systematic Review and Meta-Analysis of Randomised Clinical Trials." *Journal of the American Medical Association Psychiatry* 77 (2020) 1031–43.

Short, Annabel K., and Tallie Z Baram. "Early-Life Adversity and Neurological Disease: Age-Old Questions and Novel Answers." *Nature Reviews Neurology* 15 (2019) 657–69.

Skamaki, Kalliopi, Stephane Emond, Matthieu Chodorge, et al. "In Vitro Evolution of Antibody Affinity via Insertional Scanning Mutagenesis of an Entire Antibody Variable Region." *Proceedings of the National Academy of Sciences of the USA* 117 (2010) 27307–18.

Snyder-Mackler, Noah, Joseph R. Burger, Lauren Gaydosh, et al. "Social Determinants of Health and Survival in Humans and Other Animals." *Science* 368 (2020) eaax9553

Soares, Michael J., Kaela M. Varberg, and Khursheed Iqbal. "Hemochorial Placentation: Development, Function, and Adaptations." *Biology of Reproduction* 99 (2018) 196–211.

Sonnenburg, Justin L., and Erica D. Sonnenburg. "Vulnerability of the Industrialized Microbiota." *Science* 366 (2019) eaaw9225.

Sonuga-Barke, Edmund J. S., Mark Kennedy, Robert Kumsta, et al. "Child-to-Adult Neurodevelopmental and Mental Health Trajectories after Early Life Deprivation: The Young Adult Follow-Up of the Longitudinal English and Romanian Adoptees Study." *Lancet* 389 (2017) 1539–48.

Sousa, Andre M. M., Kyle A. Meyer, Gabriele Santpere, et al. "Evolution of the Human Nervous System Function, Structure and Development." *Cell* 170 (2017) 226–47.

Southgate C., C. Deane-Drummond, P. D. Murray, et al. *God, Humanity and the Cosmos.* Harrisburg, PA: Trinity, 1999.

Spanner, Douglas. *Biblical Creation and the Theory of Evolution.* Exeter, UK: Paternoster, 1987.

Spencer, Nick. *The Evolution of the West.* Louisville, KY: Westminster John Knox, 2018.

Stachler, Matthew D., Amaro Taylor-Weiner, Shouyong Peng, et al. "Paired Exome Analysis of Barrett's Esophagus and Adenocarcinoma." *Nature Genetics* 47 (2015) 1047–55.

Steane, Andrew. *Faithful to Science.* Oxford: Oxford University Press, 2014.

Stebegg, Marisa, Saumya D. Kumar, Alyssa Silva-Cayetano, et al. "Regulation of the Germinal Center Response." *Frontiers in Immunology* 9 (2018) 2469.

Bibliography

Steenberg, M. C. *Irenaeus on Creation.* Leiden: Brill, 2008.
Stokholm Jakob, Jonathan Thorsen, Martin J. Blaser, et al. "Delivery Mode and Gut Microbial Changes Correlate with an Increased Risk of Childhood Asthma." *Science Translational Medicine* 12 (2020) eaax9929.
Stott, John R. W. *God's New Society.* Leicester, UK: IVP, 1979.
Straughen, Jennifer K., Dawn P. Misra, George Divine, et al. "The Association between Placental Histopathology and Autism Spectrum Disorder." *Placenta* 57 (2017) 183–88.
Sugimoto, Jun, Danny J. Schust, Tadatsugu Kinjo, et al. "Suppressyn Localization and Dynamic Expression Patterns in Primary Human Tissues Support a Physiologic Role in Human Placentation." *Scientific Reports* 9 (2019) 19502.
Sugimoto, Jun, Makiko Sugimoto, Helene Bernstein, et al. "A Novel Human Endogenous Retroviral Protein Inhibits Cell-Cell Fusion." *Scientific Reports* 3 (2013) 1462.
Suryawanshi, Hemant, Pavel Morozov, Alexander Straus, et al. "A Single-Cell Survey of the Human First-Trimester Placenta and Decidua." *Science Advances* 4 (2018) eaau4788.
Tang, Alva, Nathan A. Fox, Charles A. Nelson, et al. "Externalizing Trajectories Predict Elevated Inflammation among Adolescents Exposed to Early Institutional Rearing: A Randomized Clinical Trial." *Psychoneuroendocrinology* 109 (2019) 104408.
Tang, Wanxianfu, Seyoung Mun, Aditya Joshi, et al. "Mobile Elements Contribute to the Uniqueness of Human Genome with 15,000 Human-Specific Insertions and 14 Mbp Sequence Increase." *DNA Research* 25 (2018) 521–33.
Tashiro, Kensuke, Anne Teissier, Naoki Kobayashi, et al. "A Mammalian Conserved Element Derived from SINE Displays Enhancer Properties Recapitulating Satb2 Expression in Early-Born Callosal Projection Neurons." *PLoS ONE* 6 (2011) e28497.
Teratani, Toshiaki, Yohei Mikami, Nobuhiro Nakamoto, et al. "The Liver–Brain–Gut Neural Arc Maintains the Treg Cell Niche in the Gut." *Nature* 585 (2020) 591–96.
Thurner, Lorenz, Sylvia Hartmann, Frank Neumann, et al. "Role of Specific B-Cell receptor Antigens in Lymphomagenesis." *Frontiers in Oncology* 10 (2020) 604865.
Tibu, Florin, Margaret A. Sheridan, Katie A. McLaughlin, et al. "Reduced Working Memory Mediates the Link between Early Institutional Rearing and Symptoms of ADHD at 12 Years." *Frontiers in Psychology* 7 (2016) 1850.
Timmermans, Sarah, Regine P. Steegers-Theunissen, Marijana Vujkovic, et al. "The Mediterranean Diet and Fetal Size Parameters: The Generation R Study." *British Journal of Nutrition* 108 (2012) 1399–1409.
Tokuyama, Maria, Yong Kong, Eric Song, et al. "ERVmap Analysis Reveals Genome-Wide Transcription of Human Endogenous Retroviruses." *Proceedings of the National Academy of Sciences of the USA* 115 (2018) 12565–72.
Tong, Jiaqi, Senthil K. Satyanarayanan, and Huanxing Su. "Nutraceuticals and Probiotics in the Management of Psychiatric and Neurological Disorders: A Focus on Microbiota-Gut-Brain-Immune Axis." *Brain, Behavior and Immunity* 90 (2020) 403–19.
Trigg, Roger. *Beyond Matter: Why Science Needs Metaphysics.* West Conshohocken, PA: Templeton, 2015.
Turco, Margherita Y., Lucy Gardner, Richard G. Kay, et al. "Trophoblast Organoids as a Model for Maternal-Fetal Interactions during Human Placentation." *Nature* 564 (2018) 263–67.
Turelli, Priscilla, Christopher Playfoot, Dephine Grun, et al. "Primate-Restricted KRAB Zinc Finger Proteins and Target Retrotransposons Control Gene Expression in Human Neurons." *Science Advances* 6 (2020) eaba3200.

Bibliography

Turner, Harold. *The Roots of Science*. Auckland: Deepsight Trust, 1998.

Turner, Jackson S., Julian Q. Zhou, Julianna Han, et al. "Human Germinal Centres Engage Memory and Naive B Cells after Influenza Vaccination." *Nature* 586 (2020) 127–32.

Underwood, Emily. "Screen for Childhood Trauma Triggers Debate." *Science* 367 (2020) 498.

Ursini, Jianluca, Giovanna Punzi, Qiang Chen, et al. "Convergence of Placenta Biology and Genetic Risk for Schizophrenia." *Nature Medicine* 24 (2018) 792–801.

Valk, Sofie L., Boris C. Bernhardt, Fynn-Mathis Trautwein, et al. "Structural Plasticity of the Social Brain: Differential Change after Social-Affective and Cognitive Mental Training." *Science Advances* 3 (2017) e1700489.

VanderWeele, Tyler J. "On the Promotion of Human Flourishing." *Proceedings of the National Academy of Sciences of the USA* 114 (2017) 8148–56.

van Lier, Yannouck F., Mark Davids, Nienke J. E. Haverkate, et al. "Donor Fecal Microbiota Transplantation Ameliorates Intestinal Graft-Versus-Host Disease in Allogeneic Hematopoietic Cell Transplant Recipients." *Science Translational Medicine* 12 (2020) eaaz8926.

Vasieva, Olga, Sultan Cetiner, Abigail Savage, et al. "Primate Specific Retrotransposons, SVAs, in the Evolution of Networks that Alter Brain Function." (2016) https://arxiv.org/pdf/1602.07642.

Vento-Tormo, Roser, Mirjana Efremova, Rachel A. Botting, et al. "Single Cell Reconstruction of the Early Maternal-Fetal Interface in Humans." *Nature* 563 (2018) 347–53.

Villa-Vicencio, Charles, and John De Gruchy. *Doing Ethics in Context*. Maryknoll, NY: Orbis, 1994.

Vissers, Constance, and Sophieke Koolen. "Theory of Mind Deficits and Social Emotional Functioning in Preschoolers with Specific Language Impairment." *Frontiers in Psychology* 7 (2016) 1734.

Vrljicak, Pavle, Emma S. Lucas, Lauren Lansdowne, et al. "Analysis of Chromatin Accessibility in Decidualizing Human Endometrial Stromal Cells." *FASEB Journal* 32 (2018) 2467–77.

Wade, Mark, Nathan A. Fox, Charles H. Zeanah, and Charles A. Nelson. "Long-Term Effects of Institutional Rearing, Foster Care, and Brain Activity on Memory and Executive Function." *Proceedings of the National Academy of Sciences of the USA* 116 (2019) 1808–13.

Wade, Mark, Nathan A. Fox, Charles H. Zeanah, et al. "Telomere Length and Psychopathology: Specificity and Direction of Effects within the Bucharest Early Intervention Project." *Journal of the American Academy of Child and Adolescent Psychiatry* 59 (2020) 140–48.

Wade, Mark, Charles H. Zeanah, Nathan A. Fox, et al. "Stress Sensitization among Severely Neglected Children and Protection by Social Enrichment." *Nature Communications* 10 (2019) 5771.

Wade, Mark, Charles H. Zeanah, Nathan A. Fox, and Charles A. Nelson. "Global Deficits in Executive Functioning Are Transdiagnostic Mediators between Severe Childhood Neglect and Psychopathology in Adolescence." *Psychological Medicine* 50 (2020) 1687–94.

Wagner, Roger, and Andrew Briggs. *The Penultimate Curiosity: How Science Swims in the Slipstream of Ultimate Questions*. Oxford: Oxford University Press, 2016.

Bibliography

Waltke, Bruce K., and Cathi J. Fredericks. *Genesis: A Commentary*. Grand Rapids: Zondervan, 2001.

Walton, John H. *The Lost World of Genesis One*. Downers Grove, IL: InterVarsity, 2009.

Wang, Ying, Jun Liu, Peter D. Burrows, and Ji-Yang Wang. "B-cell Development and Maturation." *Advances in Experimental Medicine and Biology* 1254 (2020) 1–22.

Wang, Jianrong, Cristina Vicente-Garcia, Davide Serrugia, et al. "MIR Retrotransposon Sequences Provide Insulators to the Human Genome." *Proceedings of the National Academy of Sciences of the USA* 112 (2015) E4428–37.

Ward, Michelle C., Simin Zhao, Kaixuan Luo, et al. "Silencing of Transposable Elements May Not Be a Major Driver of Regulatory Evolution in Primate iPSCs." *Elife* 7 (2018) e33084.

Wargo, Jennifer A. "Modulating Gut Microbes." *Science* 369 (2020) 1302–3.

Warren, Ian A., Magali Naville, Domitille Chalopin, et al. "Evolutionary Impact of Transposable Elements on Genomic Diversity and Lineage-Specific Innovation in Vertebrates." *Chromosome Research* 23 (2015) 505–31.

Welsh, Marilyn C., Eric Peterson, and Molly M. Jameson. "History of Childhood Maltreatment and College Academic Outcomes: Indirect Effects of Hot Execution Function." *Frontiers in Psychology* 8 (2017) 1091.

Wenham, David. *Paul: Follower of Jesus or Founder of Christianity?* Grand Rapids: Eerdmans, 1995.

Wenham, Gordon J. *Exploring the Old Testament Volume 1: The Pentateuch*. London: SPCK, 2003.

———. *Genesis 1–15*. Word Bible Commentary. Nashville: Thomas Nelson, 1987.

West, Rachel C., Hao Ming, Dierdre M. Logsdon, et al. "Dynamics of Trophoblast Differentiation in Periimplantation–Stage Human Embryos." *Proceedings of the National Academy of Sciences of the USA* 116 (2019) 22635–42.

Willyard, Cassandra. "How Gut Bacteria Alter the Brain." *Nature* 590 (2021) 22–25.

Witt, Andreas, Rebecca C. Brown, Paul L. Plener, et al. "Child Maltreatment in Germany: Prevalence Rates in the General Population." *Child and Adolescent Psychiatry and Mental Health* 11 (2017) 47.

Worthing, Mark. *Unlikely Allies: Monotheism and the Rise of Science*. Eugene, OR: Wipf & Stock, 2019.

Wright, Dorianne B., Heidemarie K. Laurent, and Jennifer C. Ablow. "Mothers Who Were Neglected in Childhood Show Differences in Neural Response to Their Infant's Cry." *Child Maltreatment* 22 (2017) 158–66.

Wright, N. T. *How God Became King*. London: SPCK, 2012.

———. *Jesus and the Victory of God*. London: SPCK, 1996.

———. *The New Testament and the People of God*. Minneapolis: Fortress, 1992.

———. *Paul and the Faithfulness of God*. London: SPCK, 2013.

———. *The Resurrection of the Son of God*. London: SPCK, 2003.

———. *Scripture and the Authority of God*. London: SPCK, 2005.

———. *Surprised by Hope*. New York: HarperCollins, 2008.

———. *Surprised by Scripture*. London: SPCK, 2014.

Wright, N. T., and Michael F. Bird. *The New Testament in Its World*. London: SPCK, 2019.

Xia, Zhouchunyang, Dawn R. Cochrane, Michael S. Anglesio, et al. "LINE-1 Retrotransposon-Mediated DNA Transductions in Endometriosis Associated Ovarian Cancers." *Gynecologic Oncology* 147 (2017) 642–47.

Bibliography

Xue, Bei, Tiansheng Zeng, Lisha Jia, et al. "Identification of the Distribution of Human Endogenous Retroviruses K (HML-2) by PCR-Based Target Enrichment Sequencing." *Retrovirology* 17 (2020) 10.

Yang, Lei, Michael Emerman, Harmit S. Malik, and Richard N. McLaughlin Jnr. "Retrocopying Expands the Functional Repertoire of APOBEC3 Antiviral Proteins in Primates." *eLife* 9 (2020) e58436.

Ye, Mengliang, Christel Goudot, Thomas Hoyler, et al. "Specific Subfamilies of Transposable Elements Contribute to Different Domains of T Lymphocyte Enhancers." *Proceedings of the National Academy of Sciences of the USA* 117 (2020) 7905–16.

Zani, Ashley, Lizhi Zhang, Temet M. McMichael, et al. "Interferon-Induced Transmembrane Proteins Inhibit Cell Fusion Mediated by Trophoblast Syncytins." *Journal of Biological Chemistry* 294 (2019) 19844–51.

Zapatka, Marc, Ivan Borozan, Daniel S. Brewer, et al. "The Landscape of Viral Associations in Human Cancers." *Nature Genetics* 52 (2020) 320–30.

Zhang, Xiao-Ou, Thomas R. Gingeras, and Zhiping Weng. "Genome-Wide Analysis of Polymerase III-Transcribed Alu Elements Suggests Cell-Type–Specific Enhancer Function." *Genome Research* 29 (2019) 1402–14.

Zhang, Yanxiao, Ting Li, Sebastian Preissl, et al. "Transcriptionally Active HERV-H Retrotransposons Demarcate Topologically Associating Domains in Human Pluripotent Stem Cells." *Nature Genetics* 51 (2019) 1380–88.

Zhang, Yuhang, Tat Cheung Cheng, Guangrui Huang, et al. "Transposon Molecular Domestication and the Evolution of the RAG Recombinase." *Nature* 569 (2019) 79–84.

Zhu, Yihui, Charles E. Mordaunt, Dag H. Yasui, et al. "Placental DNA Methylation Levels at *CYP2E1* and *IRS2* Are Associated with Child Outcome in a Prospective Autism Study." *Human Molecular Genetics* 28 (2019) 2659–74.

Zoonomia Consortium. "A Comparative Genomics Multitool for Scientific Discovery and Conservation." *Nature* 587 (2020) 240–45.

Zundler, Sebastian, Verena Tauschek, and Markus F. Neurath. "Immune Cell Circuits in Mucosal Wound Healing: Clinical Implications." *Visceral Medicine* 36 (2020) 129–36.

Index

Adam, 55, 138-40, 155
affinity maturation, 100, 101
African great ape, 14, 17, 64-66, 118, 120, 123, 141
allergy, 92, 104, 113, 114
'already but not yet', 44, 45
amino acids, xi, 96, 98
amphioxus, 97, 98
amplification, xv
amygdala, 74-76
Ancient Near East, 19, 20, 138
ancient repetitive element (ARE); *see* repetitive element
antibody, 91, 96-102, 103n37, 159; heavy chain, 96; light chain, 96
antigen(s), 96, 100, 101, 104, 107, 159, 162
anxiety, 55, 56, 67, 68, 73, 74, 78, 106
ape(s), xvi, 1, 14, 15, 17, 18, 27-29, 33, 35, 37, 56, 63-65, 68, 84, 95, 120-24, 126, 159, 161
Aristotle, 26, 59
Assyria, 19
atheism, 24, 25
attention deficit hyperactivity disorder (ADHD), 54, 56, 77, 82
Atzil, Shir, 87
Augustine, 89, 141
autoantibody redemption, 102
autoimmunity, 102, 104, 106, 113, 163
autism spectrum disorder (ASD), 54, 65, 73, 77

Babylon, 19, 46
Bacon, Francis, 26
bara, 42
Barrett's esophagus, xiv
Bible, 18-19, 25, 29, 42, 52, 89, 134, 139, 140, 151, 153
Bimson, John, 139
Biologos, xv
BLAST search engine, xvi, 13, 16, 17, 67, 68, 120, 123, 126, 166-68
body of Christ, 84, 91, 92, 107-15
bonobo, 12, 18
brain(s), xiii, xiv, xvi, 31, 32, 41, 53, 54, 61-66, 68-71, 73-83, 88-90, 106, 108; social, 32, 62, 73, 83, 85, 89, 90, 104
Briggs, Andrew, 25, 26, 144
Butterfield Herbert, 51, 144, 150

Cahill, Thomas, 142
Caiaphas, 48
cancer(s), xiv, xv, xvii, 4, 5n4, 78, 88n113, 116-18, 121-24, 128-29, 131, 132, 135, 137, 142, 143, 152, 166; colorectal, 113; esophageal, xiv, xv; leukemia, 7, 105n46, 108, 129, 131; liver, 121; lung, 130, 131; osteosarcoma, 137; pancreatic, 130, 131; trophoblastic, 53; therapy, 92, 95, 96, 105, 121
cardiovascular disease, 78, 88n113, 113

Index

cell(s), xi, xiii–xv, 2–9, 33–38, 40, 62, 92, 105n46, 107, 108, 111, 112, 114, 117, 128, 133, 136, 144, 159–63, 167; B lymphocyte, 47, 91, 96, 97, 99–103, 112, 159; cancer or tumor, xiv, 4, 5, 95, 121, 128, 132; decidual, 39; dendritic, 94; germline, 5, 8, 11, 12, 15, 16, 69, 162; neural or neuronal, 61, 65, 71, 75–78; somatic, 2, 7, 131, 163; syncytiotrophoblast, 33–35, 37, 38, 163; T lymphocyte, 47, 96–99, 102, 103, 112; cytotrophoblast, 33–35, 36, 38, 57, 163
cerebral cortex, 77, 78, 89; prefrontal (PFC), 74, 75
cesarian section, 105, 113
chance, 31, 41, 47, 49–51, 147–49; and necessity, 99, 116, 148–50
chaos, 46, 47, 145, 148
Chapman, Allan, 24
chimpanzee, x, 12–14, 17, 18, 28, 62, 63, 70, 120
Chinese tree shrew, 15, 16
chromatin, 2
chromosome(s), x, xi, xiv, 3, 4, 6, 8, 33, 35, 78, 124, 159, 161
Clarke, Jonathan, 133, 153n138
clone(s), xiii, xiv, 5, 100, 101, 131, 160
cognition, 53, 56, 57, 64, 71–73, 75, 77, 78, 80, 87–89, 106
Colling, Richard, 47, 102
Collins, Francis, xv
colugo, 15, 16
Comfort, Nathaniel, 27, 114
common ancestry, xvi, xvii, 5, 8, 9, 11, 17, 63, 161
contingency, 31, 51, 54, 116, 136, 144, 147, 151
convergence, 49, 149, 150
Conway Morris, Simon, 149
cosmogony, 19, 138
cosmos, 21, 23, 42, 116, 140, 156, 158
Coulson, C.A., 134, 146

covenant, 21, 29, 48, 114, 134, 137, 139, 154, 156
creatio continua, 42
creatio ex nihilo, 43
creatio ex vetere, 43–45
creation, xvii, 1, 2, 21–24, 27, 29, 30, 41–45, 104, 116, 117, 133–37, 139, 140, 143, 145–49, 153–58; as ontological origin, 23; perfection of, 52, 157, 158
creation stories, 1, 19–21, 138
cross, of Jesus, xvii, 46, 135, 137, 153, 155, 157, 158
culture, of cells, 34, 62, 162; of humanity, 26, 52, 72, 85, 88, 115, 151, 152
cytokine(s), 57, 106, 160

Darwin, Charles, 19, 25, 29, 44
Dawkins, Richard, 24–25
day-care centers, 105
deafness, 71, 72
death, 103, 112, 115, 142, 156; of cells, 102, 112; of Jesus, xvii, 49, 136, 137, 141, 154, 155, 157, 158; of organisms or people, 34, 44, 45, 117, 121, 139, 140
deletion(s), xiv, 3, 63, 64, 120, 160, 162
depression, 56, 57, 67, 73–75, 78, 106
Descartes, Rene, 84
determinism, 70, 79, 91, 92, 104, 135, 137
development, 9, 40, 108, 141, 144, 146, 152; of neural system and brain, xiii, xiv, 31, 32, 53, 57, 58, 61–63, 69, 71, 74–76, 78, 89, 90, 103, 104; of cancer, xiv, 117, 121–23, 128, 131, 136; of the community of Christ, 112 ; immune, 47, 96, 99, 104, 106, 111, 112; of mammary gland, 39; of organisms, 2, 4, 32, 36, 39, 53, 55, 56, 59, 62, 86, 107, 154; phylogenetic, 12, 17, 43, 63,

Index

116, 117, 131, 154; placental, 31, 35, 37–39, 42, 47–49; of ToM, 71–73, 81, 82, 88
Dfam database, 13, 37, 67, 120, 167
diabetes, 53, 78, 88n113, 113, 122
disease(s), 7, 8, 45, 53, 64–66, 74, 78, 88n113, 92, 102, 104–6, 113, 116, 121–23, 129, 132, 133, 135–37, 142, 152, 153, 155, 162, 163
DNA, xi, xii, xvi, 1–3, 5–11, 13, 15-17, 28, 30, 31, 35, 37–39, 42, 43, 45, 52, 54, 63, 64, 77, 92, 93, 96–99, 117, 126, 128, 129, 131, 132, 137, 151, 159–65; sequencing, 2, 4, 117, 128, 160, 167
DNA bases, xi, 2, 3, 12, 160
Dobzhansky, Theodosius, 158
domestication, of genes, 33, 35, 40, 45, 50, 54, 98, 110, 160
dysbiosis, 104, 105
dysplasia, xiv

embryo, xiii, 37, 39, 49
emotion(s), 56, 57, 71, 73–78, 82, 83
endogenous retrovirus(es) (ERVs), xv, 2, 8, 9, 11, 12–14, 33, 35, 37, 39–41, 45, 47, 50, 62, 64, 65, 92–96, 98, 118, 120–22, 132, 160, 161, 164, 166, 167; ERV9, 126, 127; ERV-Fc1, 64; ERVFRD1, 36, 37; ERV-K, 12–14, 120, 121; ERV-W, 64; ERV-WE1, 33, 34n5, 35; LTR12c, 118, 120; MER41, 64, 65, 93, 94; MER50, 37; MER57E1, 37
endonuclease, 6, 9–11
enhancer, xi, xii, 63, 69, 94, 160, 163, 164, 166
Enlightenment, 27, 83, 84
environment, xvi, xvii, 2n1, 28, 36, 50, 54–56, 58, 62n1, 91, 92, 105–7, 109, 113, 121, 123, 149; social, 57, 59, 62, 69, 70, 73, 75, 80, 81, 83, 88, 89, 107

epigenetic(s), 2n1, 54, 65, 74, 77, 123, 160
epitope, 96, 99, 103
'eschatogeny', 155
eschatology, 30, 115n121, 117, 137, 142, 153–55, 158
eschaton, 42, 116, 142
Eschatos, 52, 154
essential kenosis, 145
eternal life, 86, 87, 89, 158
Eve, 138, 139
evil(s), 104, 111, 115, 133, 142–44, 153–55, 157
evolution, biological, ix, x, xiii, xv-xvii, 1, 2, 4, 17, 22–33, 37, 39–44, 46, 50–52, 61–65, 73, 79, 83, 92, 98, 99–101, 107, 116–18, 124, 126, 131–35, 137, 138, 141, 147–52, 157, 158, 160; of cancer, xiv, 4, 5n4, 124, 128, 129, 131, 132, 135–38, 141; directed, 103; of values, 142
Ewart, Paul, 50, 147
exaptation, of genes, 39, 40, 50, 160
executive function, 73, 75, 77, 78
externalizing, 73, 74, 82

Fabre, Jean-Henri, 134
fall, 116, 138–42
Fee, Gordon, 109
feral children, 85
fetus, 32, 35, 36, 38, 56, 57, 59, 75
forbidden experiment, 70, 73, 77, 84
Frederick II of Hohenstaufen, 70, 84
freedom, ontological, 116, 136, 144, 135, 147
Frith, Chris, 72, 73

Galton, Francis, 29
gene(s), xi, xii, 2, 10, 11, 31, 33, 34, 38–40, 45, 47, 50, 54, 62–71, 78, 79, 81, 83, 89, 91, 93–95, 98–102, 105–7, 124, 126–28, 130, 131, 136, 151, 159–61, 163–65; *AIM2*, 93, 94; *AKT2*, xv; *ANRIL*, 122, 123;

Index

gene(s) (*continued*),
   APOBEC3G, 124; *APOBEC3I*,
   124, 125; *BC200*, 68; *BMP4*,
   40; *CCNE1*, xv; *CDKN2A*,
   xiv; *CRH*, 37; *envelope* (*env*),
   33, 35–37; *FGF8*, 69; *FOPNL*,
   129; *FUS*, 66, 67; *GABBR1*,
   64; *GABBR2*, 67; *GATA6*,
   xv; *HSD11B1*, 57; *HSD11B2*,
   57; *IGH*, 96, 97; *INSL4*, 37;
   KCNH5, 38; *KCNJ6*, 67; *MET*,
   xiv; MHC, 110; *MIR320B1*,
   63; *NEDD9*, 64; *NR3C1*, 57;
   PARK7, 66, 67; *PEG10*, 38,
   50; *PEG11*, 38, 50; *PHLDA2*,
   57, 58; *RAE1*, 118; *RAG1*,
   97, 98; *RAG2*, 97, 98; *RPS13*,
   16; *SATB2*, 69; *SIRH11*, 69;
   suppressyn, 35, 37; *syncytin-1*,
   34, 35, 37; *syncytin-2*, 34, 53;
   SYT1, 123, 124; *TP53*, xiv;
   TP63, 121; *UTP14A*, 124;
   UTP14C, 124, 125; *WNT5a*,
   40; *ZNF689*, 121
generation of diversity (GoD), 96, 103
gene regulation, 31, 33, 35, 37, 39, 40, 57, 64, 65, 69, 118, 123, 160, 166; networks, 35, 37–39, 49, 61, 64, 65, 165
Genesis, book of, 1, 2, 18–22, 30, 46, 80, 138–41, 143
genetic algorithms, 103
Genie, 85
genome(s), x, xii, xvi, 1, 2, 4–17, 31, 33, 35–40, 45, 50, 62, 63, 65, 69, 70, 83, 92, 95, 96, 98; 117, 118, 120, 121, 123, 124, 126, 128, 129, 144, 161, 162, 164–68; sequencing, 2, 4, 117, 128
genomics, comparative, 2, 4, 17, 31, 33, 41, 61, 63, 116
genre, 19, 138
gibbon, 13, 123
Gingerich, Owen, 21, 24, 26, 146
God, ix, x, xvi, xvii, 5, 18, 20–30, 32, 41–44, 46–50, 51n80, 52, 55, 61–62, 85–90, 103, 104, 107, 108, 111, 112, 114–16, 118, 133–48, 151–57; of creation, xvi, 21–24, 42–44, 46, 80, 86, 151, 155, 157; of grace, 27–29, 56, 107; of love, 26, 43, 63, 87, 135–37, 142, 143, 145, 147, 149, 153; of redemption, 21, 45, 86, 142, 151; as Sustainer of history, 23, 43, 44; as triune, 23, 88, 89, 140
gods, 19, 21, 22, 29
Gordon, Robert, 21
gorilla, x, 12, 14, 18, 39, 120
graft-versus-host (GvH) disease, 105, 110
gray matter, 75, 76, 78, 161
great ape, 12–14, 65, 120, 127, 167n2
Greek (thought), philosophers, 24, 25, 59, 60, 80
Gunton, Colin, 23, 84, 86, 88, 140, 143, 153, 155

Halvorson, Hans, 25, 26, 144
Harlow, Daniel, 20
Harrison, Peter, 44, 141
Hart, David Bentley, 23, 29, 84
Hauerwas, Stanley, 111, 151
Haught, John, 148, 151
healing, 111, 115, 143; as function of immune system, 92; as Jesus' work to inaugurate the Kingdom of God, 136, 139, 146, 154
hermeneutic key, 51, 52, 154
Heyes, Cecilia, 72, 73
historical sciences, x, 42, 44, 52, 150
history, xvii, 1, 2, 18, 21, 23–25, 27, 30, 42–46, 48, 49, 51, 52, 117, 135, 136, 140, 142, 144, 145, 147–49, 152, 155–57; of cancers, xiv, xv, 4, 128; of the church, 108, 143, 150; developmental, xiv, 32, 47, 51–53, 99; of DNA, 1, 11; evolutionary or phylogenetic, x, xvi, xvii, 5, 11, 12, 14–17,

Index

21, 23, 26, 30, 33, 37, 40–45, 49, 52, 54, 55, 61, 63, 65, 69, 103, 116, 124, 127, 132, 134, 135, 143, 144, 148, 152, 154, 155; human, 5, 17, 41, 44, 49, 51, 115, 139, 141–44, 147, 150, 153–55, 158; of Israel, xvii, 18, 41, 43, 48, 49, 51, 52, 116, 137, 139, 143, 151–56; of Jesus, 154, 155
history, ambiguity of, 45, 48, 49, 51n80, 116, 132, 136, 142, 143, 152–54
homoplasy, 9, 161
hormone, 32, 56, 57; corticotropin-releasing hormone (CRH), 37, 67; cortisol, 56, 57, 160; glycoprotein hormone-alpha (GPHα), 38; oxytocin, 63; progesterone, 39; thyroid, 75; thyroid-stimulating hormone, 75
Human Genome Project, xv, 8
humanity, 2, 20, 27–31, 42, 43, 45, 62, 79, 82, 89, 106, 107, 116, 135, 137, 140, 143, 145, 154–58
Hutchings, 47, 89

image of God, 22, 28–30, 32, 52, 53, 107, 108, 112, 132
imago Dei; *see* image of God
immune system, xvi, 8, 36, 47, 91, 92, 99, 105–10, 112–15, 121, 162, 163; adaptive, xvii, 47, 91, 92, 96, 98, 99, 104, 107, 110, 111, 114; innate, 91–96, 98, 107
immunological tolerance, 36, 39, 104
immunometabolic disease, 113
incarnation, 56, 137, 140, 147, 154, 155, 158
inflammasome, 93, 95
inflammation, xiv, 54, 57, 64, 73, 78, 93–95
insertion, 3, 5, 8, 9, 11–13, 15–17, 33, 35–38, 49, 51, 63, 67, 68, 93–95, 103n37, 118, 120, 121–29, 131, 148, 161, 162, 165, 167

insulator, 164, 166
integrase; *see* endonuclease
Intelligent Design Theory, 26
interferons, 34, 36, 93–95, 160
internalizing, 73, 74, 76, 78
interpretation, 30, 61, 89, 135, 136; of biological history, xvii, 17, 26, 44, 51, 116, 151; of history, 1, 51, 52; of intentions, 71, 74; of natural selection, 103, 104; of scripture, 2, 19, 20, 22, 138, 139, 141; of story, 151
Irenaeus, 141, 154, 155
Israel, 18, 20–22, 41–45, 48, 49, 51, 52, 114, 116, 137–140, 142, 143, 151–57

Jeeves, Malcolm, 30
Jesus, ix, xvi, xvii, 23, 27, 28, 30, 43, 45, 46, 48, 49, 52, 55, 79, 86, 87, 90, 104, 116, 134, 136, 137, 140, 141, 147, 153–58
Jews, xvii, 41, 45, 108, 142
Job, book of, 46, 139
jumping gene; *see* transposable element

Kingdom of God, 136, 137, 139, 140, 146, 154
Knight, George, 46, 52n82, 134n38
knowing, interpersonal, xvii, 22, 61, 62, 84–90
Konig, Adrio, ix, 135, 136n48, 145, 148, 153, 154
ktizo, 42

language, 62, 70–73, 78, 83, 85
Lewis, C.S., 84, 88, 133
love, x, 43, 55, 56, 58–60, 63, 71, 79, 81–84, 87, 88, 109, 112, 135–37, 143, 145, 147, 152, 153, 155

MacKay, Donald, ixn1, 80
magnetic resonance imaging (MRI), functional, 74, 75; structural, 75, 77, 78, 89

Index

major histocompatibility complex (MHC), 109, 110
mammal, x, xvii, 4, 9, 11, 14, 32, 33, 37–40, 45, 49, 50, 63, 69, 94; eutherian or placental, 38, 39, 45, 58, 59, 62, 69, 98, 160; metatherian or marsupial, 38, 40, 69, 160
mammary gland, 32, 39–41, 47, 62
Maori, 55
McLeish, Tom, 46, 47, 89
mentalization; *see* theory of mind (ToM)
Mesopotamia, 19, 29; epics of, 19
Messer, Neil, 86
metaflammation, 113
microbiota, 105, 106
microbiota hypothesis, 104
milk, 39, 40, 105
mind, 41, 52n82, 53–55, 62, 71–74, 79–82, 86, 87n108, 89, 90, 106
mind reading; *see* theory of mind (ToM)
monoclonal, monoclonality, xv, 5, 117, 128, 129, 161
monophyletic, monophylicity, 5, 13, 14, 117, 162, 165
monotheism, 21, 24
mutagen, xii, 102, 144
mutation, x, xiii–xvii, 2–6, 8, 9, 11–13, 31, 32, 41, 45, 62, 65, 92, 96, 99–101, 110, 116–18, 120, 124, 126, 128, 129, 131, 137, 142, 145, 149, 160–62, 167, 168

natural selection; *see* selection
NCBI (National Center for Biotechnology Information), xvi, 13, 16, 17, 37, 67, 68, 120, 123, 126, 166
neglect, childhood, 62, 71, 73–78, 82, 104
neuroplasticity, 74, 162
new creation, 29, 42–45, 80n77, 90, 113, 140, 141, 146, 156

New World monkeys, 13, 17, 33, 122, 123
nurture, 55, 62, 71, 73, 74, 81–83

Old World monkeys, 13, 14, 17, 33, 35, 37, 63, 120, 121, 122, 127
Old World primates (Old World monkeys and apes), 16, 67, 141
oncogeny, 117, 131
Oord, Thomas J., 136, 143, 145, 148
orang-utan, x, 12–14, 120, 123
organoids, 62, 162
orphanages, Romanian, 77, 78
orthologous, 17, 165–67

palate, 40
pathobiont, 104, 162
pathology, pathologies, 35, 53, 54, 59, 64, 92, 113
parents, parenthood, 32, 58, 59, 63, 71, 74, 82, 87, 141
Paul, Saint, xi, 23, 55, 79, 80, 87, 107–9, 111–13, 140n68, 153
person(s), 26–28, 45, 48, 52, 56, 59, 61–63, 69, 71, 79–81, 83–88, 90, 104, 106, 107, 114, 133, 139, 140, 142, 144, 145, 147, 152, 154, 157, 158
phagocytosis, 92
phylogeny, 117, 131, 154, 155
Pilate, Pontius, 48
placenta, xvi, 31–35, 37–38, 41, 47–60, 62, 128, 136, 142, 160, 163
Plato, 80
Plutarch, 59
Polkinghorne, John, 24, 28, 43n47, 44, 49n72, 133, 141, 143, 144, 146, 147, 149, 156n159,
polytheism, 20–22, 44
preeclampsia, 53
prenatal parenting, 32, 56
primate, 4, 9, 14–17, 30, 33–35, 37, 39, 52, 66, 69, 88n113, 93, 94, 98, 122, 126, 127, 141, 142, 156, 157; anthropoid or simian, 15–17, 36–38, 63, 65,

Index

68, 93, 122, 124, 141, 159; hominoid or ape, 17, 39, 55, 161; prosimian, 15, 16, 27, 36, 123, 126
promoter, xi, xii, 163
protein, xi, xii, 2, 3, 10, 15, 33, 35, 36, 47, 50, 68, 96, 109, 159–61, 163, 166; AIM2, 93; IL-2 receptor β, 37; INSL4 protein, 37; interferon-induced transmembrane proteins, 34; PD-L1, 98; PEG10, 38; PEG11, 38; protoRAG, 98; RAG1 and 2, 97–99, 110; suppressyn, 35; syncytin-1 and -2, 33, 35, 36, 53; TP53, 3; zinc finger, 65
providence, xvii, 32, 41, 117, 145, 146, 153; eschatological doctrine of, 153
psychopathology, 53, 74, 76–78, 82, 104
Ptolemy, 26
punctuated equilibrium, 40
purpose, xvii, 1, 2, 21, 24–28, 30–32, 41, 44, 48–50, 52, 89n120, 103, 110, 132, 134, 135, 137, 141, 145–47, 150–52, 154

randomness, 10, 11, 31, 32, 35, 41, 45–50, 103, 145, 148
recapitulation, 154, 155
receptor editing, 102
redemption, xvii, 21, 45, 141, 143, 156
relationship, interpersonal, 32, 61, 69, 87, 89, 90, 104, 106, 112, 134, 145, 157
repetitive element, xi, xii, xv, xvi, 8, 9, 40, 91, 162
resurrection, xvii, 29, 43, 80, 87, 106, 136, 141, 154, 156–58
retrocopy, 10, 15, 16, 124, 125, 129, 166
retrogene, 10
retrovirus, retroviral, 2, 6–9, 31, 33, 35, 36, 45, 49, 53, 64, 117, 118, 120, 124, 126–29, 131 141, 142, 144, 145, 148, 160, 162
reverse transcriptase, 6, 11, 162
ribosome, 15, 161–63
RNA, xi, xii, 2, 6–8, 10, 11, 15, 16, 34, 63, 64, 70, 96, 97, 118, 121, 124, 159–63, 165, 167; double-stranded, 7, 95; messenger, 2, 3, 10, 16, 17, 124, 126, 161; nonprotein-coding, xi, 10, 38, 68, 160, 164, 166; ribosomal, 10, 15, 16, 162, 167; transfer, 10, 167
Rolston, Holmes, 48, 134, 148, 151

Salimbene, friar, 70
schizophrenia, 54, 64, 65, 74
science, ix, x, xv, 1, 17, 19, 21, 22, 24–30, 42, 62, 79, 81, 103, 134, 138, 146, 167n2
scientism, 27
selection, xvi, xvii, 47, 83, 91, 92, 98–104, 107, 124, 134
septic shock, 95
shalom, 115, 137
sign language, 72
sin, sinners, 21, 45, 137, 139, 140, 143, 155
social Darwinism, 29
society, sociality, 29, 59, 60, 69, 73, 79, 82, 83–85, 88, 90, 108, 133, 152
socialization, 73, 81, 85
somatic hypermutation, 100, 101
species-expectant experience, 62, 89, 90
spirit, as property of persons, 80, 81, 142; of God, 28, 79, 86, 89, 108–10, 115, 153, 158
Steane, Andrew, 25, 26, 50, 81, 86, 144, 145
Steenberg, M. C., 141
stochastic process; *see* randomness
story, 20, 27, 30, 39, 51, 134, 135, 138–42, 147, 151–57

Index

stress, xiv, 56, 57, 67, 73, 74, 76, 113, 160
subclone, xiii, xiv, 5n4, 128
suffering(s), 28, 44–46, 87, 104, 117, 132, 135, 137, 142, 145, 153
symbiont(s), 104, 106, 114, 163
synapse, 71, 78, 82, 163;
    immunological, 111
Sumer, 19

target site, 6, 7, 11–13, 33, 38, 94, 125, 167; target site duplication, 6, 7, 9, 10, 12, 13, 15, 17, 68, 94, 118, 120, 123, 125, 126, 128, 141, 164, 165, 167
tehom, 46
tetraploidy, xiv
teleology; *see* purpose
theogony, 19, 138
theology, xv, 1, 46, 52, 132, 135, 138, 141n74, 154, 155
thymus, 96, 102, 112
tolerance, immunological, 36, 39, 104
transcription, 64, 95, 159, 163
transcription factor(s), xi, xii, 65, 93, 94, 159, 163
transposable element(s), xv, 2, 7–11, 13–16, 28, 31, 37–40, 45, 47, 49, 50, 61, 62, 65, 67, 68, 92, 94, 97, 98, 103n37, 117, 118, 121–24, 126–33, 140–42, 144, 146, 148, 160, 161, 164–67; Alu, 38, 39, 121–23, 127, 164, 166; AmnSINE1, 69, 164, 166; FLAM, 68; LINE-1, 65, 164, 166; LINE2, 98; L1PA2, 38, 123, 124; MIR, 40, 94, 98, 164, 166; *sushi-ichi*, 38, 68; SVA, 65–67, 164, 166
transposases, 97
tumors; *see* cancers
Turner, Harold, ix

UCSC (University of California Santa Cruz) Genome Browser, xvi, 37, 67, 123, 126, 166
universe; *see* cosmos

virus, 34, 152, 163; herpes simplex, 34; human immunodeficiency virus (HIV), 8; human T cell leukemia virus type 1 (HTLV1), 7, 128, 129, 131; influenza, 101; rubella, 34; SARS-CoV-2; xiii, 163; Zika, 34

Walton, John, 134
Wenham, David, 109
Wenham, Gordon, 18, 20, 21
whenua, 55
White, Bob, 133
white matter, 53, 76–78, 83, 163
Willimon, William, 111, 151
Worthing, Mark, 146
Wright, N. T., 29, 108, 110, 139, 143, 150, 156

Xenophon, 59

Zizioulas, John, 88
zoe aionios; *see* eternal life

www.ingramcontent.com/pod-product-compliance
Lightning Source LLC
Chambersburg PA
CBHW031359230426
43670CB00006B/595